FOCUS on Community College Success

SECOND EDITION

Constance Staley
University of Colorado, Colorado Springs

Prepared by

John Cowles

Ric Underhile

WADSWORTH
CENGAGE Learning™

Australia • Brazil • Japan • Korea • Mexico • Singapore • Spain • United Kingdom • United States

TABLE OF CONTENTS

TEST BANK by Ric Underhile and John Cowles

ADDITIONAL RESOURCES by Constance Staley

Introducing...

Teaching with F🖰CUSPoints

FOCUS on Community College Success comes with an array of ancillary materials for the classroom, which can be accessed via the Power Lecture CD.

The most innovative of these tools is "**FOCUS**Points: An interactive Teaching Tool" that allows you to select from varied, multimedia options in class—all located in one spot. You decide where to focus during class, point, and click. Each chapter of *FOCUS* has an accompanying PowerPoint slideshow that will help you and your students navigate the chapter in class. Using this interactive tool with links inserted, you can do activities in the text, show *FOCUS* TV episodes, listen to chapter iAudio summaries, add YouTube videos, other Internet content, or your own materials—easily and conveniently—all with this one, flexible tool. This set of instructions will help you use and customize this tool. (Instructions are provided for PowerPoint 2003.)

FOCUSPoints [FP] will allow you as an instructor to:

1. Encourage students to read ahead **and** bring their textbooks to class for hands-on use. Students are more likely to read if they know the material will be used in class.

2. Choose what to focus on by pointing and clicking in class. Review the chapter's **FP** slides in advance, so that you know what you might want to select. Jot down a list of "must do" activities and bring it with you to class. However, **FP** also allows you make on-the-spot decisions as you teach, based on time constraints and students' interest. If you have time, delve into an activity. If not, skip it. Choosing which points to focus on will be your option.

3. Work through exercises as a class and generate opportunities for rich, applied, personalized instruction and discussion. You may even wish to allow your students to vote on one activity, beyond those you've already selected, to complete in class.

4. Provide online materials that match the text itself in content and appearance. Each chapter of *FOCUS* begins with a page of solid color, and this color palette has been used to create the slides (but you may change them if you wish).

5. Tailor in-class materials to particular groups or sections of the course.

6. Vary how you teach the course from term to term to keep yourself engaged as an instructor.

7. For your benefit as an instructor (and for the benefit of your students), the slides follow the text closely. Maximum information has been provided on the slides. If you are new to the text, you may find this to be a helpful feature. However, as you become more familiar

with the material, you may wish to omit some bullets or sub-bullets. Or if you wish, you may animate the bullets, so that they disappear after discussion or change to a lighter color. This will put the main visual emphasis on the current point you're discussing in class and simplify the slide.

*(**Important Note**: FP will only work automatically if you actually "point and click." You must click on a button—or wherever you see the hand cursor icon. If you proceed through the slideshow by simply hitting the space bar or using the down arrow key, you will not be able to jump back and forth between slides automatically. Each chapter's **FP** has built-in hyperlinks to make navigation easy.)*

FP Buttons on the Opening Menu Slide:

- *Lecture.* If you click this top button, you will be guided through chapter lecture material. However, note that **FP**s are designed not only as lecture prompts, but also as discussion prompts. A slide may consist of a single image you can use to get your students engaged in a discussion about a main topic in the chapter.

- *Chapter Exercise.* If you click on this button, you will be taken to a menu slide that lists all the activities in the chapter. From there you can select an activity you'd like to do in class. Or decide which activity or activities you'd like to cover, and then allow your students to select another one they're interested in. Page numbers are always provided so that your students may turn to the activity in the book and work together in pairs or small groups, or the entire class can jump in.

- *FOCUS TV*: If you click on this button, you will be taken to menu slide that leads you to a humorous, yet content-driven, short television-like episode that coordinates with the individual chapter. (Note: Most, but not all, chapters have a TV episode available). The *FOCUS* TV slide will allow you to decide whether to show the episode first, preview the episode's discussion questions first, etc. (*Note: TV shows last from five to ten minutes. Larger files may take some time to load.*)

- *iAudio Chapter Summary*: If you click on this button, you will be taken to a short podcast to preview or review the chapter's highlights.

- *Other*: This link is provided so that you can insert your own material, play a YouTube or news clip, connect to a slideshow you have created yourself, etc. If you use the activity called "Group Ad" in chapter 6 in which students work in small groups to create a TV ad for each chapter using PowerPoint, you may use your "Other" button to link to these files. (Ask students to submit their ad before class and hyperlink it to the FOCUSPoints slideshow for the chapter.) See **Point 3** below for further information.

Please read the seven points below for further clarification.

Point 1

Click directly on one of the five colored buttons to start class. Each color represents a particular option. This introductory menu slide will always show the chapter's case study character and chapter title. The palette of colors used in the book are also used in the slideshows to tie what's on screen to what appears in the text. (Note: Chapters without a TV show do not include a *FOCUS* TV button.)

Point 2

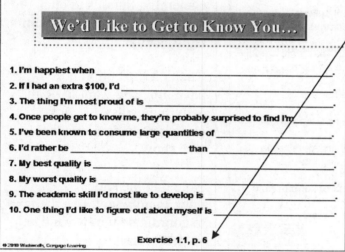

Once you go to a chapter exercise, its page number(s) is always provided so that students may turn to the appropriate page in their textbooks and participate.

If an activity is long, only the first portion may show on the slide. When you have finished with the activity, click *anywhere* on the activity slide (wherever you see the hand cursor) to return to the slide you were viewing previously.

Point 3

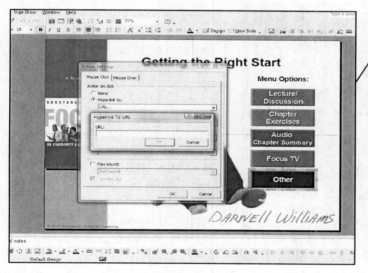

If you decide to use the black "Other" button provided to link to a YouTube, for example, *right click* on the "Other" button, choose "hyperlink to URL," and then type in the URL address. (*Linking will only work, however, if you are on your campus Internet system or in a wireless environment with the Internet available.*) You may also *left click* on the "Other" button itself and rename it. "Other" will allow you to link to many different types of files. Or you may choose to ignore this button and use only the material provided in the slideshow.

Point 4

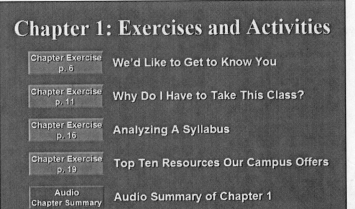

If your students are highly kinesthetic learners, you may wish to use exercises and activities in class only. If so, begin the slideshow approximately halfway through with this gray slide (in every chapter's **FP**).

Choose the activities you'd like to focus on with your students and click on the appropriate buttons. Or let your students help you decide.

Point 5

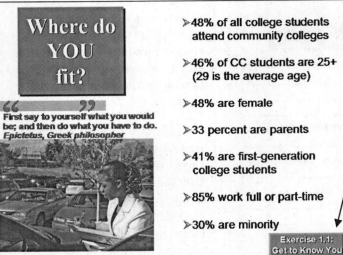

Generally, buttons to click on always appear in the **bottom right corner** of slides.

Click on the button if you have time and want to do the activity in class, or click elsewhere to continue the slideshow.

Note that the slides intentionally look like the text to coordinate the two and help students learn.

Point 6

When you click on "*FOCUS TV*" on the opening menu slide, you will be taken to a slide like this one that allows you several options: 1) click to play the episode, 2) click to go to discussion questions about the episode, 3) click to go back to the opening menu slide, or 4) click to go to the gray "Exercises and Activities" slide described in **Point 4**. After you have played the TV episode, simply close the viewing box, and you will be back on this **FP** slide.

Point 7

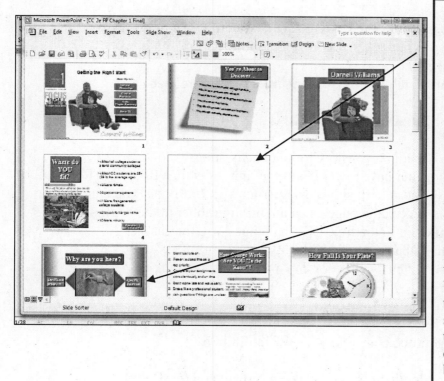

You may create new slides to insert your own material (or delete some slides from a slideshow). All slides are titled to make this process work automatically.

PowerPoint recognizes titles, not slide numbers. In the example here, an instructor has added two new slides (#5 and #6). When the instructor gets to slide 7, the first slide with a hyperlink, the button will still work (even though the slide numbers have now changed) because PP will go searching for the <u>title</u> of the linked slide. (Note: You may not always be able to see the titles. Sometimes, to give the slideshow variety and add interest, the slides are formatted somewhat differently and titles are hidden behind other objects.)

You may access **FP** slides via the Power Lecture CD that comes with *FOCUS*.

Important Note: One of PowerPoint's idiosyncrasies is that it will only play files you've linked to if they are **saved in the same folder**. If you move a chapter's **FP** to your faculty storage account or a flash drive, for example, to add or rearrange files, then you must also move other linked files (from outside the slideshow) there as well. (If you link to a student group's "TV Ad," an activity in chapter 6, the music file must be located in the came folder as their PowerPoint.) The best way to do this may be to copy all the FOCUSPoints on the CD in their entirety into a folder on your computer or onto a flash drive you bring with you to class, and put any other files you've linked out to there as well.

"Other" Button Suggestions
Compiled by Jessica Smith, Student, University of Colorado, Colorado Springs

You may wish to begin class from time to time by using your **FP** "Other" button to link to a YouTube video or other item you find on the Internet that relates to chapter material—or to a presentation of your own. Right click the "Other" button on the menu slide of the chapter's "FOCUSPoints," and type in the URL. Here are some suggestions for all of the chapters in *FOCUS*:

CHAPTER 1: GETTING THE RIGHT START

1. Elements of Greatness: http://www.youtube.com/watch?v=q5kn4OBRxro
Tie this YouTube to Jason Gaulden's poem, "Passion in Action," on p. xxv.
2. Increasing Your Confidence:
http://www.youtube.com/watch?v=__Gs02ZmUmE&feature=related

CHAPTER 2: BUILDING DREAMS, SETTING GOALS

1. "Gloria": http://en.wikipedia.org/wiki/Gloria_(Them_song)
If your students are young and have never heard the famous sixties Rock and Roll Hall of
Fame song written by Northern Irish singer/songwriter Van Morrison, you can play a
sound clip of it from this Wikipedia page as an attention-grabber at the beginning of
class. This song is mentioned in the FOCUS Challenge Case for chapter 2.
2. "Yes We Can – Barack Obama Music Video":
http://www.youtube.com/watch?v=jjXyqcx-mYY&feature=related.

CHAPTER 3: LEARNING ABOUT LEARNING

1. MBTI: http://www.youtube.com/watch?v=WF1sqE8lb0o
2. MI Interactivity Test:
http://www.thirteen.org/edonline/concept2class/mi/w1_interactive1.html

CHAPTER 4: MANAGING YOUR TIME AND ENERGY

1. Time Management for Non-Traditional First Year Students
http://www.youtube.com/watch?v=jHZxlW9xftk&feature=related
2. Tales of Mere Existence "Procrastination"
http://www.youtube.com/watch?v=4P785j15Tzk
3. Barry Schwartz on the *Paradox of Choice*, the "Cultivate Your Curiosity" in this
chapter 4, p. 86). (This is a long video from a TED conference; you may want to play a
selected portion.)
http://www.ted.com/index.php/talks/barry_schwartz_on_the_paradox_of_choice.html

CHAPTER 5: THINKING CRITICALLY AND CREATIVELY

1. "Monty Python Argument Clinic": http://www.youtube.com/watch?v=teMlv3ripSM
This sketch is referenced in the chapter on p. 105.

CHAPTER 6: DEVELOPING TECHNOLOGY, RESEARCH, AND INFORMATION LITERACY SKILLS

1. "Stalking Sarah" Australian
http://www.youtube.com/watch?v=E_Ws7K_Nudg&feature=related
2. "Facebook Cyberstalking" UK News
http://www.youtube.com/watch?v=JMAPeYwcvaQ

3. Facebook and Internet Addiction on CBS News "Are You Hooked on Facebook?"
http://www.cbsnews.com/video/watch/?id=4205062n%3fsource=search_video
4. "Cyber Bullying - NJN News"
http://www.youtube.com/watch?v=D9rppzQiHaA&feature=related
5. "Miss Teen USA 2007 – South Carolina Answers A Question":
http://www.youtube.com/watch?v=lj3iNxZ8Dww.

CHAPTER 7: ENGAGING, LISTENING, AND NOTE-TAKING IN CLASS

1. Randy Pausch's Last Lecture: http://www.youtube.com/watch?v=ji5_MqicxSo
Show this lecture in class, after dividing your students into the four groups representing the four different note-taking strategies described in this chapter. After the lecture, have them literally "compare notes."
2. Tony Buzan on Mindmapping:
http://www.youtube.com/watch?v=MlabrWv25qQ&feature=related

CHAPTER 8: DEVELOPING YOUR MEMORY

1. "Rain Man – Casino Scene": Rainman's astounding memory is put to use in Las Vegas: http://www.youtube.com/watch?v=RW1qHA5Hqwc&feature=related

CHAPTER 9: READING AND STUDYING

1. Reading Decline in Kids:
http://www.cbsnews.com/video/watch/?id=3519104n%3fsource=search_video
2. "Studying at Oxford University": (a model of excellence)
http://www.youtube.com/watch?v=vxAU88LxLis&feature=PlayList&p=A9438BDC681A1AFC&index=0&playnext=1

CHAPTER 10: TAKING TESTS

1. Test Anxiety: http://www.youtube.com/watch?v=n2DgB3X2Afg
2. Test Stress Reduction: The Navy SEALS Way:
http://www.youtube.com/watch?v=0S9YsqERT34

CHAPTER 11: BUILDING RELATIONSHIPS

1. A fun musical example of how diversity enriches our lives (click on each animal and a new "voice" enters to combine with the others)
http://svt.se/hogafflahage/hogafflaHage_site/Kor/hestekor.swf

CHAPTER 12: CHOOSING A COLLEGE MAJOR AND CAREER

1. Daniel Pink: Choosing a Major
http://www.youtube.com/watch?v=S2qc2DcdUL4&feature=related
2. "How To Find A Job After College"
http://www.videojug.com/film/how-to-find-a-job-after-college-2

CHAPTER 13: CREATING YOUR FUTURE

1. "Keith Ferrazzi: What is Networking?"
http://www.youtube.com/watch?v=cTU2FkVyoUw&feature=PlayList&p=EF1846ADBB
4CE20C&playnext=1&index=51
2. "Keith Ferrazzi: How Do I Start Networking?"
http://www.youtube.com/watch?v=aVwYWt_BfF8&feature=PlayList&p=EF1846ADBB
4CE20C&index=52&playnext=2&playnext_from=PL
3. "Protect Your Dreams": A scene from The Pursuit of Happiness.
http://www.youtube.com/watch?v=MEGSiX0JA-s&feature=related

INTRODUCTION

by Constance Staley

> "Teaching is the greatest act of optimism." ~*Colleen Wilcox*

So you're going to teach a first-year seminar? Great! What an opportunity to get to know your students in a small class format, refine your teaching skills, and enhance your own learning! Many instructors say teaching a first-year seminar has changed the way they teach *all* their classes and that, perhaps for the first time, they truly understand a fundamental truth of best practice: high expectations *and* high support. Perhaps you're new to the course, or you may be a seasoned instructor using *FOCUS on Community College Success* for the first time. You may be working with "traditional" first-year students or non-traditional adult students. Regardless, teaching this multi-disciplinary skills course can reinforce something you already know: that teaching is about relationship-building. Unlike large lecture classes, in a first-year seminar you have the luxury of doing just that. Some say that building relationships with students today is more essential than ever. Countless books and articles have been written about today's college students. What does the literature say about them?

> "Millennials [born between roughly 1980 and 1994] have grown up with more choices and more selectivity in the products and services they use, which is why they do not have, for example, a generational music…. They rarely read newspapers—or, for that matter, books. They are impatient and goal oriented. They hate busywork, learn by doing, and are used to instant feedback. They want it *now*. They think it's cool to be smart. They have friends from different ethnic backgrounds. They want flexibility—in the classroom and in their lives. 'To get this generation involved, you have to figure out a way to engage them and make their learning faster at the end of the day. Is it possible to do that? I think the answer is yes, but the jury is out.'"[1]

While this description may or may not fit your experience, many of us with decades of teaching experience know that things have changed. It's become more challenging, many instructors believe, to "compete" with television, the Internet, movies, music, and all the distractions available in our culture (hence the title of this textbook, *FOCUS*). Engaging students requires increased effort and creativity, and students want more from us, like ready access and quick results. That's why I believe teaching is more challenging than ever; however, along with the challenges comes greater potential for fulfillment. That's why I wrote *FOCUS on Community College Success*: to help you in your search to "figure out a way to engage them and make their learning faster at the end of the day." *FOCUS* is rich with options for you and filled a variety of built-in features for your

---

[1] (2007, January 5). How the new generation of well-wired multitaskers is changing campus culture. *Chronicle of Higher Education.* Available at http://chronicle.com/weekly/v53/i18/18b01001.htm

students, whether they are millennial students or otherwise. Just as students learn differently, instructors teach differently. We each have our own styles and methods, but we also eagerly pursue ways to do it better. A first-year seminar course is "all about them" (meant in the best sense of the phrase) and how much they can learn and *apply*, not only in your course, but in all their classes and their careers beyond college.

One of my graduate students asked me recently, "Why do you care so much about teaching? Why have you devoted your career to becoming the best teacher you can be?" I thought about it for a moment and replied, "My motives are selfish. I care so much about teaching because that is how I learn." She nodded in recognition and smiled.

As I thought about writing the introduction for John Cowles's Instructor's Resource Manual for *FOCUS on Community College Success*, one of my favorite stories of all time came to mind:

> The huge printing presses of a major Chicago newspaper began malfunctioning on the Saturday before Christmas, putting all the revenue for advertising that was to appear in the Sunday paper in jeopardy. None of the technicians could track down the problem. Finally, a frantic call was made to the retired printer who had worked with these presses for over forty years. "We'll pay anything; just come in and fix them," he was told.
>
> When he arrived, he walked around for a few minutes, surveying the presses; then he approached one of the control panels and opened it. He removed a dime from his pocket, turned a screw ¼ of a turn, and said, "The presses will now work correctly." After being profusely thanked, he was told to submit a bill for his work.
>
> The bill arrived a few days later, for $10,000.00! Not wanting to pay such a huge amount for so little work, the printer was told to please itemize his charges, with the hope that he would reduce the amount once he had to identify his services. The revised bill arrived: $1.00 for turning the screw; $9,999.00 for knowing which screw to turn.
>
> ~Anonymous

Teaching *is* the greatest act of optimism, as the Colleen Wilcox quotation asserts at the beginning of this introduction, not because today's students are so challenging to teach, but because we believe in the power of students to learn. We know that we can help them discover "which screw to turn" as learners. Underneath it all, we have confidence in our students, who will build a future for us, our children, and our society. We have faith in the power of higher education to transform lives. And finally, we believe in ourselves as *we* learn to become better teachers from *them*.

What is this course about?

> "The great end of education is to discipline rather than to furnish the mind; to train it to the use of its own powers rather than to fill it with the accumulation of others." ~*Tryon Edwards*

A first-year seminar course is about many things: helping students understand themselves and teaching them how to successfully navigate the first year of college. They will learn about how they learn and what motivates them. They will identify campus resources and understand that using these opportunities effectively will help them to succeed. They will comprehend the benefits of managing time and money, and the consequences of not doing so. They will develop specific academic skills such as thinking critically and creatively, reading, writing, and speaking, as well as enhance specific study skills such as memory techniques, note-taking, studying, and taking tests effectively. They will learn about choosing majors and careers, and ways to develop life-long skills in managing relationships, valuing diversity, and working toward wellness.

Bloom asserted many years ago that teachers have three types of goals: *affective*, *behavioral*, and *cognitive*. As opposed to upper-level discipline-based courses, for example, which emphasize the cognitive domain primarily, in first-year seminars, affective, behavioral, and cognitive goals are more equally weighted. Instructors work to cultivate attitudes and beliefs in first-year students, to foster behaviors that will lead to academic success, and to help them learn about learning from a variety of vantage points and in a variety of ways. Many faculty are most comfortable working in the cognitive domain because, after all, we are subject matter experts: psychologists, mathematicians, or historians, for example. An upper division philosophy course will operate heavily in the cognitive domain. However, research dictates that we must operate in all three domains, despite the specific course content being taught, and in a first-year seminar, instructors must be comfortable with all three types of teaching and learning goals.

Ultimately, first-year seminars are about *metacognition*: "Metacognition is about having an 'awareness of [your] own cognitive machinery and how the machinery works.' It's about knowing the limits of your own learning and memory capabilities, knowing how much you can accomplish within a certain amount of time, and knowing what learning strategies work for you."[2]

Interestingly, you may have students who will assert that "they know all this stuff" because it is "common sense." However, in the words of French philosopher Voltaire, "Common sense is not so common." Show them that while they may *recognize* that the book's suggestions about college success *make sense*, they could not generate or *recall* them on their own because they really don't "know this stuff." And of course, *knowing* the information and *applying* it are two different things altogether.

Why is the course important?

> "The task of the excellent teacher is to stimulate 'apparently ordinary' people to unusual effort. The tough problem is not in identifying winners: it is in making winners out of ordinary people." ~*K. Patricia Cross*

---

[2] [Staley, C. (2009). *FOCUS on College Success*. Belmont, CA: Wadsworth; Meichenbaum, D., Burland, S., Gruson, L., & Cameron, R. (1985). Metacognitive assessment. In S. Yussen (Ed.), *The growth of reflection in children*. Orlando, FL: Academic Press.]

Some academicians undervalue skills courses of any kind. Theory always trumps skills in their minds. And as a multidisciplinary skills course, a first-year seminar is even more suspect. However, the first year of college is the foundational year. If students are successful in the first year, their chances of graduating are greatly enhanced. Often, students' grades in their first-year seminar courses are predictive of their overall first-term success. As Pascarella and Terenzini assert, "In short, the weight of evidence indicates that FYS [first-year seminar] participation has statistically significant and substantial, positive effects on a student's successful transition to college….And on a considerable array of other college experiences known to be related directly and indirectly to bachelor's degree completion."[3]

First-year seminar instructors (and motivated students) understand the value of connecting with other students and an instructor who is invested in their success, of honing academic skills, and of applying what they learn across all their courses. First-year seminar courses are about making "winners" out of *all* students who will internalize and apply what they learn.

How is a first-year seminar different from other academic courses? How is the course organized?

> "In teaching it is the method and not the content that is the message...the drawing out, not the pumping in." *~Ashley Montagu*

First-year seminar courses come in all shapes and sizes. According to the 2006 national survey conducted by the National Resource Center on the First-Year Experience and Students in Transition:

Models

- 60% of reporting institutions offer extended orientation seminars
- 28% offer academic seminars with generally uniform content across sections
- 26% offer academic seminars on various topics
- 15% offer pre-professional or discipline-linked seminars
- 22% offer basic study skills seminars
- 20% offer a hybrid
- 4% offer some "other" type of first-year seminar

(Note: Percentages are rounded off; some schools offer more than one type of seminar.)

Course Objectives (regardless of the model)

1. Develop academic skills
2. Provide an orientation to campus resources and services
3. Self-exploration/personal development

---

[3] [Pascarella, E. T., & Terenzini, P. T. (2005). *How college affects students: A third decade of research.* San Francisco: Jossey-Bass, p. 403.]

Course Topics

1. Study skills
2. Critical thinking
3. Campus resources
4. Academic Planning/Advising
5. Time management

[For further information, see http://www.sc.edu/fye/research/surveyfindings/surveys/survey06.html]

You'll notice that *FOCUS* covers 13 different, multifaceted topics that are known to contribute to student success, including those identified as the most common components of first-year seminars nationally. Each chapter is grounded in research (documented in endnotes so that citations are not intrusive), and the learning system and features, which are part of the book's infrastructure, are carried throughout the text. Students may not even realize the extent to which they are being motivated, challenged, and supported as they develop as learners.

There is no one right way to teach a first-year seminar although themes contributing to success may be found across institutions and programs. What then makes a first-year seminar successful? According to Randy Swing, Senior Fellow for the Policy Center on the First Year of College, the answer to that question is *engaging pedagogy*: "If your seminar intends to produce learning outcomes in critical thinking, writing, reading, and oral presentation skills; connections with faculty; or time management skills, then a critical first step is to ensure that seminars are delivered with a high level of engaging pedagogy ... a variety of teaching methods; meaningful discussion and homework; challenging assignments; productive use of class time; and encouragement for students to speak in class and work together."[4]

First-year seminars must include many different ways to get students engaged in course material. Because so many students are multimodal and kinesthetic learners today, we must be creative in designing ways to engage them. Engagement is a primary underlying goal of the *FOCUS* experience—"drawing out, not pumping in"—as is building a community of learners who understand the value of this unique course to their current and future success.

Instead of simply discussing the chapter each week, change the format from time to time: set up a debate; actually do the alcohol poisoning case study in chapter 5; divide the class into smaller groups, and let each class group teach part of a chapter; or VARK a chapter and let groups teach portions based on their common learning style preferences; employ a community-based service-learning project; bring in a panel of professionals representing

---

[4] [Swing, R. (2002). http://209.85.173.104/search?q=cache:q8hFMHQ-354J:www.csuchico.edu/vpaa/FYEpdf/First_Year_Initiative_Benchmark_Study.pdf+Randy+Swing+%22engaging+pedagogies%22&hl=en&ct=clnk&cd=2&gl=us; http://209.85.173.104/search?q=cache:q8hFMHQ-354J:www.csuchico.edu/vpaa/FYEpdf/First_Year_Initiative_Benchmark_Study.pdf+%22first-year+seminar%22+%22engaging+pedagogies%22&hl=en&ct=clnk&cd=2&gl=us]

different careers; follow some of John's activity suggestions, or try one of the new activities I've developed for inclusion later in this manual. As I've often said, a steak dinner may taste good, but would you want the same meal every evening for a month? Vary how you spend your class time, so that students are curious about what to expect and come to class ready to be engaged. If you're using FOCUSPoints in class, you will be able to navigate each chapter easily and do hands-on activities (with page numbers) right in class.

Am I qualified to teach the course?

> "Effective teaching may be the hardest job there is." ~*William Glasser*

Institutions have different rules about qualifications, but if you have been invited to teach a college success course, you are undoubtedly qualified. Someone has recognized your teaching expertise and your ability to build relationships with learners. No one has an advanced degree in college success, but as a faculty member, student affairs professional, or adjunct instructor, you yourself have been academically successful. If you are a faculty member, remember that regardless of whether you teach chemistry, sociology, or geography, for example, most college professors have not received instruction on the practice of teaching even though they are well versed in their disciplines. If you are a counselor or advisor, you bring a helpful skill set to this course, and if are teaching as an adjunct, you have real-world experience to bring to the classroom.

Teaching, as the quotation above notes, is difficult. Good teaching is at times downright exhausting. But noting the outcomes, accepting the gratitude of thankful students, and observing their future success is more than worth the effort. Attend the first-year seminar faculty training sessions provided by your institution. Use your first-year seminar colleagues for support, exchange reflections about the *FOCUS* features and activities that have worked well, and share new ideas. Work together as a group to develop a mission statement, rubrics, and a set of desired, intentional learning outcomes. And as you're advised later in John Cowles's chapter-by-chapter guide, make notes to yourself about what you've learned in teaching each topic, and record what you may want to do differently next time. Record these observations while you're teaching the course, so that when you teach it again, you won't have forgotten.

How should I communicate with my students?

> "The most important knowledge teachers need to do good work is a knowledge of how students are experiencing learning and perceiving their teacher's actions." ~*Steven Brookfield*

The quality and quantity of communication with your students are essential to your students' success and your satisfaction with your teaching experience. Consider these suggestions:

- **Set guidelines**. Will you accept text messages? Will you give students your home or cell phone numbers? Will you communicate via Facebook, MySpace, or neither? Will you hold virtual office hours? Will you require students to communicate via your institution's e-mail system, as opposed to all the other options available (yahoo, gmail, etc.) Will you expect a certain level of grammatical correctness, even in informal messages? Will you require a tone of mutual support and "professionalism"? Will you encourage your students to check their e-mail accounts daily (at a minimum)? Think beforehand about the best ways to develop relationships with your students, and let them know how you'd like to communicate with them.

- **Praise, when it's warranted**. You've experienced it: you open an e-mail message from a student that says, "I really enjoyed class today. I'd never thought about many of the things we discussed. Thanks for being such a great teacher." Do the same for your students, either face-to-face or electronically. It only takes a few seconds to write a student a message like this: "Wow! The presentation you gave in class today was brilliant. I could tell how much time you invested in researching the topic and creating your PowerPoint slides. Thanks for all your hard work!" Positive reinforcement goes a long way.

- **Respond right away**. If at all possible, take quick action when it comes to your students' success. Recently I received an e-mail from a student that read, "Professor Staley, I've been traumatized by something that happened recently in my home town. I can't continue. Today I'm going to drop all my classes, forfeit my scholarship, and leave school." When I got that e-mail, I placed a few phone calls and wrote back, "Dear _____, This is a very important decision. Let's talk about it before you do anything. My Assistant Director and the Dean will meet you in your financial aid advisor's office in an hour." The group rallied around her, and today she's in school and doing well. That one moment in time was critical. Of course, it's not always possible to respond quickly. Had I been busy in meetings or otherwise away from my computer, this student's future might have been very different. But sometimes timing is critical in getting students over a hump.

- **Be persistent**. If a student is missing in your small class, give him a call on your cell phone, and pass the phone around so that all his classmates also invite him to class. Look up his schedule and wait for him outside another class to ask him what's up. I once staged an "intervention" when I heard that one of my students didn't have his assigned presentation done, so he was playing hacky sack with his friends outside the building instead of coming to class. The entire group went outside and "captured" him and brought him to class. When he turned around and saw 16 people approaching him, he said, "But I don't have my assignment done" to which the group replied, "Come to class, anyway!" He was deeply touched by this gesture of support, came to class, and never missed again. You may not go to such extraordinary measures with more mature students, but in this case, our wayward first-year student learned his lesson. Experiences like this one have contributed to my philosophy in this course: Remember that first-year students are "under construction," so go the extra mile.

- **Pay attention.** If you begin to notice that one week a student is hyperactive and the following week, this same student seems deeply depressed, take note. If this up and down behavior becomes a pattern, see if you can find out why. Behavior like this could be a sign of problems at home, drug use, or a mood disorder. Intervention may be required. If need be, ask the student if she'd like you to walk her over to the Counseling Center. You may feel that you are being intrusive or that it's inappropriate for teachers to "go there." However, my personal philosophy after many years of teaching is that we must pay attention to what gets in the way of learning, and if students need help, it's our job to help them get it. You may not be a trained counselor, and it's not appropriate to solve students' problems for them. But as an administrator I met recently likes to say, "There's a difference between *caring* and *carrying*." Of course, not all students will accept your help, but you will know that you have tried.

- **Provide meaningful, specific, frequent, and timely feedback.** One of students' biggest pet peeves is instructors who take forever to return assignments, appear not to have read students' papers, or provide minimal feedback: "B" with no explanation or rationale, for example. It's a two-way street, they believe, and if they're expected to invest in their coursework and turn in assignments promptly, they expect the same from us. Instead of simply marking a paper with a "B," provide rubrics in advance for why assignments deserve particular grades and provide specific critiques: "This paper does a good job of addressing the major goal of the assignment, which is to choose a position on a controversial topic and support your position. But the assignment asks for specific types of evidence from a minimum of three books, four journal articles, and five websites…, etc." Students need regular, detailed feedback from you in order to know how to improve their work and grow academically.

What do I need to know if I'm teaching this course for the first time?

> "Teaching can be compared to selling commodities. No one can sell unless someone buys… [Yet] there are teachers who think they have done a good day's teaching irrespective of what pupils have learned." ~*John Dewey*

It is my personal belief that college success happens when three sets of goals intersect: *academic* goals, (students') *personal* goals, and (class and campus) *community* goals. In my mind, it looks like this:

(Note the activity on page 226 related to this point.) This belief is at the core of first-year seminars, and in my view, instructors must adopt it and base their teaching and interaction with students on it.

As you prepare to teach a first-year seminar for the first time, read, study, and learn as much as you can about effective teaching and about today's learners. Check out the online resources listed in the Additional Resources at the back of this manual, for example, The Boyer Commissions' "Reinventing Undergraduate Education," or the American Association of Colleges and University's report, "Greater Expectations," or their publication, *Liberal Education*, or the Jossey-Bass magazine/journal called *About Campus*. When you begin to look, you'll see that illuminating resources are everywhere. Use this manual and the online CourseMate. Get to know your colleagues, and your students, individually and collectively. Watch out for non-cognitive variables that get in the way of learning. And above all, make sure learning is taking place. Do "One-Minute" papers (or index cards) at the end of class to find out what students valued most and what's still confusing. If you're insecure, ask for volunteers from your class to act as the course "Board of Directors." Meet with these representatives, get feedback from them about how things are going, or if your institution uses peer mentors, solicit that input from him or her. Consult the Teaching and Learning Center on your campus. It's possible that experts there can come to class to observe your teaching, invite you to faculty workshops on best practices in teaching, or provide you with materials to read. Generally speaking, help is only a phone call, an e-mail, or a jaunt across campus away.

How can I rejuvenate the course if I've been teaching it for years?

> "One new feature or fresh take can change everything." ~*Neil Young*

After teaching any course for a number of years, many instructors find themselves searching for new ways to do things, whether the course they want to update is a discipline-based course such as math or literature or a first-year seminar course. Among other goals we have in this quest is our own need to keep ourselves fresh, engaged, and up-to-date. Refresh your memory about things you already know, like Chickering and Gamson's now 20-year-old "Seven Principles of Best Practice." Good practice:

1. encourages student-faculty contact.
2. encourages cooperation among students.
3. encourages active learning.
4. gives prompt feedback.
5. emphasizes time on task (as opposed to multitasking, perhaps?).
6. communicates high expectations.
7. respects diverse talents and ways of knowing.[5]

Because of the comprehensive coverage of topics, the built-in activities, and its integrated learning system, *FOCUS* will most definitely play a role in reinvigorating your course. It may help you see topics you've taught before differently. As writer Thomas Higginson notes, "Originality is simply a pair of fresh eyes." One of the intentional strategies used in the *FOCUS* learning experience is helping students not only discover *what* to do, but *how* to do it, *why* doing it is important—and then actually doing it! With new resources at your fingertips, you will undoubtedly find yourself considering new approaches to teaching your first-year seminar. The preface of your Annotated Instructor's Edition of *FOCUS* outlines each new feature, point by point, and the role each one plays in first-year seminar big challenges: retention, motivation, varied learning styles, time management, and.engagement.

Beyond the natural innovations that come with using a new text, you may reinvigorate your course by deliberately deciding to infuse it with a specific innovation, either in your own section of the course or across the entire program. Here are three examples to consider.

- **Service-Learning:** *FOCUS* discusses service-learning in several different places (including a featured box in chapter 11 of *FOCUS*). If your students could benefit from real-world writing experiences, for example, pair each one with a senior citizen in the community to co-author the elder's "memoirs." If you have a preponderance of students with text anxiety, have them teach chapter 10 on test-taking to middle school children through a newly launched community-based program. Allow students to select a *FOCUS* chapter and design a service-learning experience of their own within parameters you set. Somehow linking the requirement to the text or particular features of your campus or community will communicate the value and relevance of service-learning, so that students see the integral role it plays (as opposed to seeming like busywork). Or consider using a term-long activity such as "Reflecting on Service: 5 C's Journals" in *50 Ways to Leave Your Lectern* (p. 92) to connect the classroom and the community-based service-learning project through journals. Many schools have added service-learning to their programs with excellent results. While you must think through grading this type of activity and deciding how much of the course it should be worth,

---

[5] [Chickering, A. W., & Gamson, Z. F. (1987). Seven principles for good practice in undergraduate education. *The Wingspread Journal, 9*(2). See also AAHE Bulletin, March, 1987.]

service-learning is as excellent way to encourage students to bond with one another, particularly if they work in groups, and come to value the application of what they are learning in your class.

- **Peer Mentors:** If your program does not yet employ the assistance of peer mentors, this is another possible innovation with potentially broad-based positive results. Former first-year seminar students with strong academic and leadership skills can be nominated by their first-year seminar faculty, apply competitively for, and be selected to work with each section of the course. These students should be trained, ideally through a class on teaching and learning in which the specifics of your program and the issues that relate to your current first-year students can be discussed. Often first-year students connect with these role models, and they can serve in a liaison capacity, becoming a valuable aid to retention.

- **Faculty Development:** Although this theme has run through many of the suggestions in this introduction, faculty training cannot be overemphasized. First-year seminar instructors typically come from a variety of academic and professional backgrounds. Training helps them move beyond the "borders" of their disciplines and focus on students. Over time faculty can become increasingly specialized in the intricacies of their research. However, coming together with faculty and staff from across the campus to focus specifically on teaching and learning can change the way they teach *all* their courses. Strong faculty training programs are almost always behind strong first-year seminar programs, and most institutions, I'm convinced, could benefit in many ways by doing more.

How does this course relate to my discipline?

> "Systems thinking is a discipline for seeing wholes. It is a framework for seeing interrelationships rather than things, for seeing patterns of change rather than static 'snapshots.'" ~*Peter Senge*

If you teach courses in another discipline, and you're teaching a first-year seminar for the first time, you may be wondering how the two intersect. Although they may seem miles apart to you, there may actually be more commonalities than you think. And of course, the best practices of teaching apply to both. As you'll read in *FOCUS*, knowledge is interconnected, and a variety of disciplines are included in the textbook. If you are a math teacher, you will resonate with the section in chapter 10 on test-taking and math anxiety. If you teach psychology, you'll notice that chapter 2 of *FOCUS* includes the work of Stanford psychologist Carol Dweck. If you are a student affairs professional, you will see elements of student development theories underlying everything in the book.

No matter which other discipline you teach, underneath or alongside the content is "advice" you give your students about how to master course material. Use your knowledge of this "hidden curriculum" and draw upon it in your first-year seminar course. Further, while a first-year seminar course is unique, don't be reluctant to touch on your disciplinary expertise. Students will be curious about other aspects of your job, the interrelationships between its various components, and why you wanted to teach a first-year seminar in addition to everything else you do.

Throughout *FOCUS*, the "static snapshot" of each chapter is woven together into an integrated "system" for better learning. And you will be interested, as Peter Senge notes in his quotation above, in the "patterns of change" in your students.

How will the course be different if I teach non-traditional versus traditional students?

"The learner should be actively involved in the learning process." ~*Malcolm Knowles*

Malcolm Knowles coined the term "andragogy," meaning the study of adult learning, as an equivalent to pedagogy. According to Knowles, these five issues are critical:

1. **The need to know**—adult learners need to know why they need to learn something before they will learn it.
2. **Learner self-concept**—adults are self-directed learners.
3. **Role of learners' experience**—adult learners have a variety of life experiences in which to ground their learning.
4. **Readiness to learn**—adults are motivated learners because they recognize the value of learning in dealing effectively with life situations.
5. **Orientation to learning**—adults prefer to see the practical value of applying learning to their everyday lives.[6]

You will note that *FOCUS* is designed to reach learners of all ages. Several of the *FOCUS* Challenge Cases involve adult learners, learners of different ethnicities, and learners with varied backgrounds. My goal was for every student reader to see him or herself reflected somewhere in the book.

Perhaps the greatest difference in using *FOCUS* to teach adult learners will be where you place emphases in the course, which examples you use, and how you design basic assignments and activities, using *problem-based learning*. For example, if you allow students to choose topics for their papers, traditional students may choose to research binge drinking or Greek issues on campus. Nontraditional learners may choose to research a current *problem* or challenge for which they're seeking a solution: buying a first home or finding day-care options in your town. Adult learners may be more motivated and focused, as faculty sometimes note, but they must still deal with myriad complexities in their busy lives. They may also have less confidence in their academic or technology skills. Regardless, they will want to share their backgrounds with class members and take practical applications that relate to their own lives from your course.

---

[6] [Knowles' Andragogy. Available at http://www.learningandteaching.info/learning/knowlesa.htm]

How can I get involved with my students if I'm a part-time instructor?

"Communication works for those who work at it." ~John Powell

If you are teaching a first-year seminar as an adjunct professor, particularly if you don't have an office on campus, you will need to capitalize on class time and rely on technology to connect with your students. But you can also be creative: hold your office hours in the school's cafeteria or library. Meet your class as a group for pizza, or if you're comfortable, invite them to your home to pick apples from the tree in your yard and bake a pie, for example. Just as you stay in touch with "long-distance" friends and relatives you care about, vow to do the same with your students. It's entirely possible to bond in ways other than those involving face-to-face contact.

How should I evaluate students? Isn't the point of a college success course to help students succeed?

"Success on any major scale requires you to accept responsibility...in the final analysis, the one quality that all successful people have...is the ability to take on responsibility."
~Michael Korda

This is an important question, one with which first-year seminar instructors often struggle. How should I grade a student who doesn't come to class or turn in assignments, despite my attempts to contact him or her? How much leeway should I give students in turning assignments in late? How do I balance *challenge* and *support*? These are common questions, and the assumptions behind these questions are the reason that some non first-year seminar faculty assume that first-year seminars are simply "hand-holding" classes in which all students receive "A's," regardless of their performance, when instead, first-year seminars are well-thought through, structured learning experiences in which expectations for college success are made clear and overt.

The answer to your own personal questions about balance will likely come with experience teaching the course. But what are we teaching students about their futures when we excuse them from responsibilities or when we give them amnesty from assignments that are documented in the syllabus from the beginning of the term? Emergencies notwithstanding, what lessons will they learn? Are their bosses likely to say, "That's OK, Wilson, I understand you've been busy. Why don't you take another week on the Jones project even though we were supposed to close the deal tomorrow?" Probably not.

It is clear that first-year seminar instructors walk a tightrope. My advice to instructors is to "clamp down supportively." As one expert in the field notes, "If we have minimal expectations for what beginning students can and will do, we set in motion a self-fulfilling prophecy." If we dumb down first-year seminar courses, students will "live down" to our expectations. I believe it's important, instead, to "challenge up."

Again, this is where your colleagues should work together to achieve consistency across sections of the course and resolve sticky issues. Engage in discussions. Develop standards across sections. Generate rubrics for grading: what *is* an A paper, a B paper, and so forth? Hold "norming" sessions in which all first-year seminar faculty grade the same set of papers and discuss their rationales. You may find that a chemistry professor, a sociology professor, and a history professor grade the same papers very differently, which will generate further discussion about practices and priorities.

Finally, a word that is often associated with evaluation is assessment; however, the words are not synonymous. Assessment is a concept that has generated countless books and articles with multiples theories and practices behind it. As a first-year seminar instructor, your focus is to evaluate your students' work with the ultimate goal of helping them succeed.

Whatever the model used, what are the desired learning outcomes of a college success course?

> "The classroom is a microcosm of the world; it is the chance we have to practice whatever ideals we cherish. The kind of classroom situation one creates is the acid test of what it is one really stands for." ~*Jane Tompkins*

As you have read here, some first-year seminar courses are extended orientation courses, some are discipline-based, some are interdisciplinary, some are gateway to general education courses. Regardless of which model is used, the goals are often similar, and it's best if you and your colleagues articulate these exact goals together. It has been my great fortune (and ultimate learning experience) to work with faculty at many, many institutions over the years, to have many questions put to me, and to learn a great deal from many other first-year seminar instructors. Whatever the specific goals are for your institution, the goals for *FOCUS* as a multifaceted learning experience for your students have been identified here, throughout the Annotated Instructor's Edition's preface, and in all the support materials available to you. My final suggestion in this Introduction to John Cowles's Instructor's Resource Manual is that you remember this last quotation by Jane Tompkins above, mount it in your office, and observe the way you live it every day.

USING *FOCUS*'S ADDITIONAL SPECIAL FEATURES

By Constance Staley

FOCUS on Community College Success has many unique features available via the text book, as well as the text's online CourseMate and the Power Lecture CD, to enrich the learning environment in your classroom. These features not only "VARK" the *FOCUS* experience to engage all types of learners, but they provide you as an instructor with options. You will undoubtedly prefer some features over others, based on your teaching style and the particular characteristics of your students. After you teach with *FOCUS* once, you will very likely find your favorite features to use. But the following year, you may have a very different group of first-year students and will need to select different features that will appeal to them. While many of these features are described elsewhere, such as the preface of the Annotated Instructor's Edition, they are listed here for your consideration, too.

 **FOCUS Challenge Case Studies**

- **Why should I use this feature?** The *FOCUS* Challenge Cases are, according to one reviewer, "the most realistic case studies I have come across." Students often respond: "How does this book know so much about me?" or "This story sounds just like my friend..." Why do they evoke such responses? Each *FOCUS* Challenge Case is based on an actual student or a composite of students I have worked with directly over the years. The stories are based on these students' experiences. After many years of teaching, instructors learn how to "get into first-year student's heads." And if we can't figure out a particular student, we ask, "What's going on?" Most first-year students struggle with something, even if they are gifted academically. Occasionally, a student may ask why the case studies are negative or primarily about problems. Research shows that negative role models help people learn. When things are going swimmingly, there is less cause for self-examination and discussion. Using real students in the book, in CourseMate, and as guests on the mock television shows (described below) provides a highly kinesthetic, real-life learning experience for your students. These 13 students (my own previous students at UCCS and one of my daughters and grandtwins!) are the *FOCUS* cast, and readers will see them in photos throughout the book. Readers should feel as if they know these people; and in my experience, readers often call them by name as they refer to parts of the book as if they were friends or acquaintances. If your students are experiencing similar problems as those described in the *FOCUS* Challenge Cases, they will learn that they are not alone. And the safety of discussing someone else's issues always helps students learn more about themselves.

- **How can I use this feature?** Case studies are excellent discussion generators. Generally, students are interested in other students. Ask your students to come to class ready to discuss Gloria or Derek or Anthony by jotting down answers to the

"What Do *YOU* Think?" questions immediately after the case, or put students in pairs or groups to discuss these questions. Consider using the Direct It! option by assigning a case study director and one or more actors. At the end of each chapter, students are asked to revisit the case, based on what they have learned by working through the chapter, by responding to a section called "*NOW* What Do You Think." Their opinions may have changed, based on new information they have learned. Something that seemed like a simple fix may be seen more realistically now, and students will have an opportunity to apply what they have just learned by summarizing their own "ending" to the case and then by asking themselves which information from the chapter they will apply to themselves and how, which provides reinforcement.

Entrance and Exit Interviews

- **Why should I use this feature?** Many institutions (perhaps even yours) spend thousands of dollars each year on commercial instruments to collect data about their students. Other institutions cannot afford such expenditures, have never found an instrument that suits their needs, or have never initiated this practice. For these reasons, *FOCUS* comes with its own built-in pre- and post-instruments to measure students' *expectations* of college at the outset, and their *experience* of college at the end of the course. The instruments appear in the text in the front and back matter for pencil and paper administration, on the text's Resource Center website for online administration, and via clicker technology with JoinIn on TurningPoint. Some of the questions are general in nature (How many hours per week do you expect to study for your classes?) and some are specific to *FOCUS* content, asking students which chapter topics they're most interested in and which they expect to be most difficult to apply. Not only will you learn about your students and their individual and collective characteristics, but you will be alerted to students who may need additional support or intervention. Students will learn about themselves, and your institution may wish to collect these data broadly about entering students each year. Some experts say that students decide whether to stay in school during the first few weeks of the term—or perhaps in the first few days! It's important to use the Entrance Interview immediately and meet with your students one-on-one, if possible, to discuss the results.

- **How can I use this feature?** Ask your students to fill out the Entrance Interview at the beginning of the course, either via technology or on paper. Alternatively, send it out before the course begins, along with summer reading materials or a welcome letter from your institution. Or if your first-year seminar program uses peer mentors, ask them to conduct actual one-on-one interviews, using the instrument and write down interviewees' responses. Do the same thing with the Exit Interview at the end of the course. The annotated versions of the Entrance and Exit Interviews in the Annotated Instructors' Edition give the rationale for each question and comparison guidelines for the two instruments so that you can note changes in individual students over the term.

FOCUS TV Mock Television Shows

- **Why should I use this feature?** According to Neilsen Media Research, the average college student watches 3 hours and 41 minutes of television per day. The VARK Learning Style Questionnaire categorizes television as kinesthetic, the preferred learning style of many of today's college students. *FOCUS* has devised an alternative way to deliver content by creating short, mock television shows. Some episodes are based on Bravo's 13 time Emmy-Award nominated program, "Inside the Actors Studio." [See http://www.bravotv.com/inside-the-actors-studio] James Lipton's (Dean Emeritus of Actors Studio's MFA drama program) insightful interviews of actors from stage to screen are "replicated" with Constance Staley as host and *FOCUS* cast members as guests. Episodes appear, along with discussion questions, in "YouTube" style on the text's Resource Center website for chapter 2 (Gloria Gonzales, "Building Dreams, Setting Goals"), chapter 8 (Kevin Baxter, "Developing Your Memory"), chapter 11 (Kia Washington, "Building Relationships"), and chapter 12 (Ethan Cole, "Choosing a College Major and a Career"). Scripts were written by New York comedy writer Matthew McClain, and a short comedy segment appears as part of each episode amidst content coverage for these chapters. The episodes were co-produced by Matthew McClain and Constance Staley in the television studios at the University of Colorado, Colorado Springs. Other episodes, simply called *FOCUS* TV, are available on the topics of test- taking, time management, critical thinking, reading, and procrastination.

- **How can I use this feature?** The television shows are excellent ways to introduce the chapters or to review them, since each episode generally covers the "You're About to Discover" bullets at the start of that chapter. You may show episodes in class, or ask students to view them at home and answer the questions on their own to discuss later in class, or they may e-mail you their responses.

MP3 Format iAudio Chapter Summaries

- **Why should I use this feature?** Today's students are wired for sound. Whenever you see them walking across campus, they're either on their cell phones or have their earplugs inserted. Some of their instructors podcast lectures as a way of re-viewing or pre-viewing (or in this case, listening rather than viewing) course content. Again, written by Matthew McClain, these approximately four-minute summaries (the length of a song, roughly) reinforce *FOCUS* content. Traveling home on the subway or pumping gas at the station, students can listen to them to get each chapter's "big ideas" by downloading these segments from CourseMate.

- **How can I use this feature?** You may use this feature however you wish: by asking students to listen to the podcasts during class via FOCUSPoints, immediately after class, for example, while ideas are fresh, as they prepare for quizzes, or before reading the chapter so they know what to watch for. The options are limitless. While aural learners may be most benefited by this feature, all students can use them to reinforce their learning since they are chapter content summaries.

Challenge Yourself Online Quizzes

- **Why should I use this feature?** Simply put, preparing for quizzes enhances learning and helps assure that students are doing assigned reading. However, Challenge Yourself Quizzes are different from most. Within each chapter quiz, questions are graduated according to cognitive complexity, generally following Bloom's Taxonomy.

- **How can I use this feature?** You may use this feature as you see fit, depending on the academic skills of your students. Indicate that the point of Challenge Yourself Quizzes is just that—to challenge yourself. Eventually, they should move beyond their comfort zones and try more challenging questions. Quizzes can easily be incorporated into online or classroom-based courses and the CourseMate allows students to automatically submit their scores to you or your peer mentor.

Team Career Exercises

- **Why should I use this feature?** Employers are unanimous about the fact that many of today's college students complete their degrees with technical expertise in their disciplines, but they are less adept at using "soft skills," like communication, collaboration, and teamwork. Available on CourseMate, *FOCUS* Team Career Exercises are creative applications of chapter material that are to be done in small groups or pairs, typically outside of class. The side benefit of the actual content learned about the workplace and careers, of course, is that students will need to work together to accomplish them. In each chapter, Team Career Exercises are referenced immediately after the "Create a Career Outlook" box.

- **How can I use this feature?** Assign these activities as homework and debrief in class or have students choose, for example, three Team Career Exercises to do with an ongoing group over the term and keep a learning log about their experiences.

When Moms and Dads Go to School (book for non-traditional students' children)

- **Why should I use this feature?** As a working woman who went back to school for both a master's degree and Ph.D. with two young children at home, I am particularly sensitive to the needs of non-traditional students. The challenges of raising a family while juggling academic courses and a job are overwhelming at times. *When Moms and Dads Go to School* is a picture book for children that explains the ups and downs of life as an adult student and parent. I have tested it with five-year olds, and they grasped the concepts very well.

- **How can I use this feature?** Students who are interested may access the book on CourseMate.

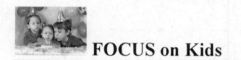

FOCUS on Kids

- **Why should I use this feature?** Sometimes primary-school aged children may not understand why Mom or Dad is so busy with college classes and homework. These worksheets for children give parents a way to connect with their children and explain the elements of *FOCUS* chapter content in children's terms. Each worksheet pulls out a main point of the chapter. For example, for chapter 2 (Building Dreams, Setting Goals), the worksheet is about making a birthday wish. But the worksheet points out that sometimes wishing is not enough; you must work to help make your wish come true. These worksheets can be used to generate dialogue, to give children a task to accomplish while Mom or Dad does homework, or even to help a parent start teaching college success skills to children at a very young age! They ask children to fill in basic responses, complete a puzzle, or draw a picture and then talk with Mom or Dad about it.

- **How can I use this feature?** Suggest to student parents that these are excellent worksheets to download from CourseMate and use with their children. The worksheets have been tested with six-year-olds, and they were found to generate much interest and lively conversations.

Orientation Materials

- **Why should I use this feature?** Many institutions struggle with organizing orientation programs for incoming first-year students and their families. How do we make sure our institution is well represented? How can we make certain students are engaged? Is too much information being presented, or too little, or the *right* information? What should be done about overly assertive parents? One suggestion is to conduct student and parent orientation sessions by grouping them by particular topic choices and using color PDFs of *FOCUS* Challenge Cases to generate discussion (students and money management, chapter 13; students and time management, chapter 4, etc.).

- **How can I use this feature?** When families sign up for orientation dates, ask them to register for particular mini-courses of interest (based on *FOCUS* chapters). You may wish to divide student and parent groups so that discussions can be directed more easily and train faculty and staff to facilitate these discussions.

 Common Reading Accompaniment or Chapter 1 of *FOCUS* as Stand-Alone Summer Reading

- **Why should I use this feature?** Many schools send a book or reader to incoming first-year students over the summer to serve as an initial common academic exercise. If a book is selected, the author of the book is sometimes invited to speak at an opening convocation ceremony. Although there are many ways to conduct a summer reading program, and even if your institution doesn't have one, consider sending a color PDF of the first chapter of *FOCUS* to each incoming student, along with a welcome letter or book before school starts. (Contact your Cengage/Wadsworth sales representative for details.) You may also wish to include a copy of the *FOCUS* Entrance Interview to collect data about students' initial expectations of college. Ask students to fill in these materials, mark up chapter 1 with questions and comments, and bring them as completed assignments to their first class. Many institutions report that students complete initial reading assignments—their first college homework ever—with vigor and arrive at school ready to go.

- **How can I use this feature?** Encourage students to mark up the chapter, fill in the exercises and activities on the color PDF, and come to class prepared to discuss Darnell Williams and the chapter's content. Doing so is an excellent way to launch the *FOCUS* experience and assure that students are engaged from day one.

DESIGNING A SYLLABUS WITH *FOCUS*

By Constance Staley

"The syllabus—what students eagerly await on the first day; a record of the class; one of the only artifacts to remain after the students move on. Your syllabus represents both an end and a beginning—a final product of your course planning and a valuable way to introduce yourself and the course to your students… Research indicates that outstanding instruction and a detailed syllabus are directly related."[1]

What should a syllabus include?

Here's a checklist to consider:

Basic Information
__ course title/number/section, days and times taught, location of class
__ semester and year course is being taught
__ your name and office number, office location, e-mail, phone number
__ office hours
__ website address or group e-mail addresses

Course or Section Description
__ goals/objectives/value of the course

Course or Section Texts/Materials
__ text: title, author, edition
__ where texts can be bought
__ other necessary equipment or materials (e.g., sticky notes or dots)

Course Schedule/Weekly Calendar
__ dates of all assignments and exams
__ dates when readings are due
__ holidays and special events (e.g., field trips, guest speakers)

Course or Section Policies
__ attendance/tardiness
__ class participation (if you choose to assign points)
__ late/missing assignments
__ academic dishonesty
__ explicit grading criteria
__ expectations/grading standards
__ accommodation for missed quizzes, etc.

---

[1] [Sinor and Kaplan, Center for Research on Learning and Teaching. Available at http://www.crlt.umich.edu/gsis/P2_1.html]

Other Handouts or Information Relevant to Your First-Year Seminar Course
__ availability of outside help (e.g., tutoring services, language labs, Writing Center)
__ unique class policies
__ a short bio about you
__ a written introduction or worksheet for the icebreaker
__ questions to answer so that you can announce the class profile the following week: "In this section, we have three athletes, one biology major, four musicians…"
__ color, art, symbols, a version of the syllabus cut up as a puzzle—be creative!
__ Entrance Interview from *FOCUS* for students to return to you

Credit Hour Variations and *FOCUS*

If your first-year seminar course is a three-hour course, you can capitalize on many of the *FOCUS* features. Because each chapter is rich, decide what has the most value for your students, and you'll be able to maximize all *FOCUS* has to offer and tailor the learning experience to your particular class. If your course is a one or two-hour course, consider these options:

- Use a custom edition of the book, eliminating chapters you have not covered traditionally

- Use the entire book, but selectively, in this manner: determine six essential chapters, and then allow your students to vote as a group on two more chapters to cover as course material. Giving students a voice can be important. (Or take a look at the results of question 16 on your students' Entrance Interviews, which asks them about their interest in each chapter of the text.) Students who wish to read more may elect to. (For example, when I have tried this in a one-credit course, some students have said things like this: "I'd like to read the relationships chapter on my own, even though the class has not selected it, because I'm having trouble with a relationship right now. Is that OK?")

- Divide the class up into six groups based on *FOCUS* features, for example:
    a) Challenge and Reaction steps
    b) Insight and Action steps
    c) C Factor: "Cultivate Your Curiosity"
    d) C Factor: "Create a Career Outlook"
    e) C Factor: "Control Your Learning"
    f) "To Your Health" and "How Full Is Your Plate?"

  Make these "permanent" groups throughout the course, if you wish, with several groups reporting each week on these features.

- Divide the class by VARK learning style preference groups, and since the largest proportion of students, statistically, is likely to be multimodal, group them by their highest VARK score, even if it is only slightly higher. Get students involved in "VARKing" the course by presenting material in their group's learning modality.

- Omit several chapters, formally, but ask student groups to present highlights of these chapters in class. For example, if you omit chapters 3, 7, and 10, divide the class into three groups, and designate one week on the syllabus for group presentations on these chapters. You may be amazed by what students come up with!

- Put selected portions of the course online. *FOCUS* materials are available for use with Blackboard or other Cengage courseware options.

- Bypass a few features, based on the characteristics of your group and your own preferences. For example, if you have used the VARK in the past and consider yourself well versed in it, have your students do the VARK assessment and cover all the VARK activities, and as a trade-off, elect not to cover something else. Few instructors cover every single option exactly as presented in every single textbook they use. Instead they tailor course materials to their own strengths and interests. That is always an instructor's prerogative, and I encourage you to adapt *FOCUS* materials to your needs and those of your students. FOCUSPoints will give you the option of making an on-the-spot decision about whether to click on an activity and do it in class or not.

A sample syllabus for a 16 week semester follows. For a trimester or quarter-based course, a course with fewer contact hours, or a course for at-risk, developmental, or probationary students, for example, omit some assignments or consider the suggestions above.

Sample Syllabus (16 week semester)

Course: College Success 101

1   **Getting the Right Start**
    Assignments:

2   **Building Dreams, Setting Goals**
    Assignments:

3   **Learning to Learn**
    Assignments:

4   **Managing Your Time, Energy and Money**
    Assignments:

5   **Thinking Critically and Creatively**
    Assignments:

6   **Developing Technology, Research, and Information Literacy**
    Skills Assignments:

7   **Engaging, Listening, and Note-Taking in Class**
    Assignments:

8   **Developing Your Memory**
    Assignments:

9   **Reading and Studying**
    Assignments:

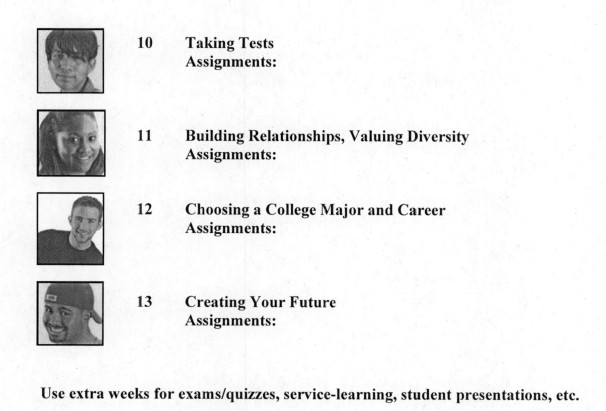

10   **Taking Tests**
          Assignments:

11   **Building Relationships, Valuing Diversity**
          Assignments:

12   **Choosing a College Major and Career**
          Assignments:

13   **Creating Your Future**
          Assignments:

Use extra weeks for exams/quizzes, service-learning, student presentations, etc.

(Add items from syllabus checklist.)

_____

FOCUS on Community College Success

Chapter Resources

By Catherine Andersen, John Cowles and Constance Staley
Revised and Updated by John Cowles and Ric Underhile

CHAPTER 1: GETTING THE RIGHT START

1. Why is this chapter important?

This chapter is geared to getting students started with the necessary foundation for college (and life) success. It will help demystify college and allow all learners to start on a level playing field, regardless of their age and life experience. College is a new world for most of the students in this course—and it comes with its own language! This chapter facilitates the acquisition of this new language and sets the foundation for success.

According to the American Association of Community Colleges, 43% of the undergraduate students in public colleges and universities in the United States are enrolled in community colleges [Source: American Association of Community Colleges (2010) Fast Facts. Retrieved July 29, 2010, from American Association of Community Colleges website: http://www.aacc.nche.edu]. If your students are similar to the ones surveyed, they have varied and multiple educational goals. Many students want to transfer to a four-year college or university while also earning an associate's degree. Others may wish to earn a career-oriented certificate—taking less time to earn while allowing them to "test the waters" of higher education. This chapter introduces students to the importance of educational planning. It includes an introduction to certificates and degrees, the development of a degree plan, and the importance of academic advising.

The chapter also introduces the concept of developmental education and the value of remediation to students. In a 2003 study on remedial enrollments, the National Center for Education Statistics (NCES) found that 42% of community college students enrolled in at least one remedial course. Other studies have estimated these rates to be even higher, approaching 63% (*Hispanic Outlook in Higher Education*, March 22, 2010). This chapter allows you the opportunity to set the stage for helping students understand the value of remediation and removing the stigma that can be attached to developmental coursework.

Finally, this first chapter of *FOCUS* launches a series of self-assessments and reflection tools, all aimed at helping students better understand themselves. They will learn that ***insight*** is not enough, but that they have to take ***action*** to achieve positive change. For some students, even the eventual realization that their dream may not be realistic can be a positive learning outcome in the long run. Without first understanding the "self," students cannot move on. Thus, this chapter is critical for establishing the framework for the rest of the course/text.

2. What are this chapter's learning objectives?

  ➢ Who goes to community colleges and the reasons for this choice
  ➢ What it takes to be a professional student
  ➢ What different types of degrees are available
  ➢ How to make the most of a syllabus

> ➤ Why developmental courses are important
> ➤ Why this college success course works

3. How should I launch this chapter?

One effective way to start the semester is to mail a copy of the Entrance Interview and a color PDF of chapter 1 from *FOCUS on Community College Success* with your welcome letter to students or your institution's common reading selection over the summer. (Color PDFs can be ordered from Cengage. See your Cengage sales representative for details.) Students can mark up the chapter, familiarize themselves with the book's format, and arrive at your first class ready to go! And you will get their true initial responses about what they expect college to be like on the Entrance Interview—before they've even started classes. (The Entrance Interview is also a great tool to generate an initial discussion during a one-on-one office visit with your individual students.)

Regardless of whether or not you send out chapter one before the term starts, it's important to think about what you'll do on the first day of class. Most instructors are somewhat nervous—as are students! Perhaps it's your first time teaching this course, or you may be a seasoned instructor determined to challenge yourself to do something a little different this year. Your students may be unusually quiet since they don't know you or the other students. Like Darnell Williams in the chapter 1 *FOCUS* Challenge Case, they may not have an identified major and may not be prepared for the rigor of college. If so, you clearly face a challenge, but there is plenty of evidence that suggests that student success courses like yours make a positive difference in students' persistence toward attaining a degree and in their overall success in college.

FOCUS on Community College Success was designed as a multifaceted, multimodal learning experience that strives to engage *all* students through podcasts, mock television shows, exercises, self-assessments, discussion prompts, reflective tools, and, of course, the written word.

Here are some pointers about how to get you and your class prepared, comfortable, engaged, and connected. In this first chapter, as in all chapters, you will focus on helping students understand the chapter's content, and more importantly, to apply it, not only in this course, but in all of their classes. By completing the exercises, reflecting on their responses, and sharing with others, students will gain insight into themselves. Once *insight* is gained, the challenge will be to help students take *action*. Action can be in the form of a verbal or written commitment to do something to change their behavior for the good—and then to do it and report back on the results.

Here are some tips to begin with:

- **Do consider sending a "welcome" letter as stated above**. This low-tech approach goes a long way in setting the tone for the rest of the term. The welcome letter should introduce you as the instructor, remind them of the time, location and start date for the class and also inform them about the textbook and any other required readings. (If you plan to use the text's online tools such as quizzes and

"FOCUS on Kids" worksheets or "CourseMate," make sure students acquire a book that comes with an Access Code to get online. Many online book vendors do not provide a version of the text that includes this code.) Additionally, it is a good idea to stress the importance of being present for the first day of class and ready to learn. The 2008 release of the Community College Survey of Student Engagement found that **67% of full-time students stated they spent 10 or fewer hours preparing for classes** in an average week. Furthermore, only **24% of community college students report that they always come to class prepared**. Help your students understand the importance of preparing for class, even the first one!

- **Don't allow students to skip the Readiness Check at the beginning of each chapter**. This activity will help students focus on whether they are ready to read and learn. Students using trial versions of *FOCUS* reported that Readiness Checks become a habit, one that they also perform, not just before they begin to read, but also mentally before class begins. This habit also extends to their other courses, which is one of the activity's intentional goals. The chapters end with a Reality Check that compares students' expectations at the beginning of the chapter with the actual experience of reading and responding to the material. The potential contrast helps students develop a more realistic approach to learning.

- **Ask students to complete the *FOCUS* Sneak Peek Challenge inside the front cover.** Either individually or in small groups, this is a great way to introduce students to the content in *FOCUS* and helps them learn the value of previewing texts. If done with a partner or in small groups, this can be a great first-day activity that will get students talking to each other.

- **Before diving into *FOCUS*, review the Meet the Cast section of the textbook.** This will provide some background for you and your students on the Challenge Case cast members used in this text. Students will appreciate knowing the cast and learning where they are from, each cast member's major, and their toughest first-year class.

- **Make sure students are comfortable with you and with each other** by using Exercise 1.1 **"We'd Like to Get to Know You"** or some similar activity.

- **Make an e-mail distribution list for the class,** including your e-mail, so that students have ways of contacting you and each other. Let students know how and when they can see or contact you. To help students learn your e-mail address, you might require them to send you an e-mail describing the most interesting thing they learned about someone or something in the first class session. You can begin the next class with a summary of what students sent you. If you are using a course management system such as Blackboard®, set up a discussion board with the topic "Introduce yourself!" and have students post an introduction. Remember to do one first so students will know what you are looking for. Consider holding your normal office hours in places other than your office: the student cafeteria, campus coffee shop, or library, for example. If you're willing to interact via social networking like Facebook, Twitter, or MySpace, or if you are open to accepting instant messages, text messages, or engage in online chats, let them know that as well.

- **Create a Facebook page for your class.** If you elect to send a welcome letter, include information on the Facebook page before class starts. Students can post on the class page wall and don't need to "friend request" you or provide you with their details unless they want to. This is a great way for students to introduce themselves and reduces first-day anxiety. This can also serve as a powerful teaching tool throughout the semester.

- **Engage in the activities yourself.** If you elect to do Exercise 1.1 **"We'd Like to Get to Know You,"** join in. It is important to create a climate for intellectual curiosity; when students see you participating, they become more motivated to participate themselves and see you as a student-centered teacher.

- **Help students find peer support.** For example, in Exercise 1.1 **"We'd Like to Get to Know You,"** in addition to having students simply introduce themselves or a classmate based on information they learn about each other, you can ask them to find someone who has the exact or similar answer to one of their questions. This "mate" can become the person they introduce to the class (if they introduce each other, rather than introducing themselves). A discussion could follow about commonalities (and differences) among class members. Creating conditions for social connectivity helps students knowing that they're "not alone," which is very reassuring to new students.

- **Have students take one of the self-assessments from the chapter, take the self-assessment yourself and tell the students your scores.** As much as they want to know about themselves, they also want to know about you. Discuss your scores as a group, and how all these scores will affect your work together throughout the course. Making abstract ideas more personal gets students more involved.

- **Consider how you'd like to work with developmental students and returning adult learners.** Developmental learners face many challenges, both in terms of academics and often, life situations in general. Your class may contain several students in developmental courses, or you may have an entire class of developmental learners. The material in *FOCUS on Community College Success* can be meaningful for a variety of learners. Developmental learners can benefit from the *FOCUS* Challenge Case about Darnell Williams. One modification for the Reaction section could be to provide the students with some time to jot down thoughts after you have read the questions aloud and then have the students join in the discussion. Asking questions such as "Does it sound like Darnell is ready for college English?" and "What courses are you in right now that Darnell could benefit from?" can assist in engaging developmental learners.

The *Developmental Students* annotations can be very helpful for bringing meaning to developmental learners. For example, a discussion of who goes to a community college (p. 6) can be helpful in illustrating the benefits and diversity found in a community college setting. Developmental learners may need more in-class practice with the concepts. For example, prior to discussing the How Full Is Your Plate? section, it may be helpful to provide students with a seven-day worksheet to help them see how they spend their weekly allotment of 168 hours.

Peer learning can be a powerful tool in teaching the developmental learner. One way to incorporate this technique is learning about campus resources. Developmental students often do not take the initiative to seek out help. Pair developmental learners with stronger students and send out "Resource Scavenger Teams" for Exercise 1.3 (p. 19). This is an opportunity to expose developmental learners to the services they may need.

Returning adult learners often have more than their share of anxiety about college. Fear of failure, or of not being perfect, and guilt from leaving loved ones at home while taking classes are common issues for returning adult learners. For some, it is the fear of being surrounded by young adults whom they see as having nothing in common with them.

There are several instructional strategies that can help reduce these fears and thoughts. For these students (much like developmental learners) it is important to learn who goes to a community college (p. 6). A variation of this discussion is to ask students in class the following types of questions:

How many students attend this college?
What do you think the average age is of students at this college?
How many students at this college work?
What percentage are students of color? Single parents? Working full-time?

Before doing this activity, obtain as many answers for your institution as possible. Offices like Institutional Research and Admissions and Records often have these facts available for your use. After students have made some guesses, provide them with the actual numbers from your school. They may be surprised!

Another way of decreasing anxiety and building rapport for returning adult learners is a journal assignment asking students to tell their life story. Sharing facts about their family, children, career—past, present and future—can be helpful. This can be done in conjunction with Reason 2: Going Back to School after a Break (p. 5). For students with small children at home, FOCUS on Kids worksheets are available on the online *FOCUS on Community College Success* website or CourseMate. Each worksheet is matched to the chapter's content and helps to open up conversations with students' young children about the importance of learning. Furthermore, these activities can help teach children the value of focusing!

4. How should I use the *FOCUS* Challenge Case?

Each chapter begins with a *FOCUS* Challenge Case about a real student (or a composite of several students) that depicts a challenging situation college students often face. The *FOCUS* Challenge Case is an integral part of the chapter and an excellent way to begin discussing the chapter's content. Typically, students can pinpoint another student's mistakes, and from there begin to consider and compare their own experiences. Case studies are a non-threatening way to trigger interest and apply each chapter's content. In addition, each case study contains visuals created specifically for the case. The visuals are designed to increase student curiosity in the case and provide clues about the featured student.

In chapter 1, we meet Darnell Williams, an undecided and underprepared community college student. Darnell did not find high school academically challenging, but by playing football he was able to maintain minimal interest and graduate. After sitting out for a year, Darnell has decided to enroll in his hometown community college. After two weeks Darnell has lost interest in his classes and realizes he is not in the best academic shape. As Darnell reflects on his experience he begins to blame his high school teachers for his academic struggles and comes to the realization that "this college thing is going to be more challenging that I thought."

You can use this *FOCUS* Challenge Case to discuss some of the issues Darnell faces. Undoubtedly, there may be several students in your class who share some of Darnell's issues. Case studies provide safe ways that students can detach and discuss, listen to other student's views of the issues, and identify with parts of the story.

Use the Darnell Williams story to get students to begin opening up and refer back to Darnell whenever you can. Ask students which of Darnell's qualities they see in themselves. Have them answer the "What Do YOU Think?" questions and pair up to discuss their responses, or ask students to work through the questions in small groups. Encourage students to debate their opinions within the group.

Return to Darnell's story in the Insight section on page 23. This is part of the Challenge → Reaction → Insight → Action steps briefly discussed below and introduced to students in chapter 2. Begin to brainstorm on how Darnell's English class could turn out. List the outcomes on the board and then link the problem-oriented outcomes with campus resources that could help a student in Darnell's situation. If students have a difficult time coming up with possible outcomes for Darnell, assign students to write or role-play the following possible outcomes:

- **Direct It!** Assign a "scene director" for the Challenge Case. Assign a student to role-play Darnell and another student to role-play his advisor and another student to play Professor Monroe. The director can stop the scene at any point and redirect the "actors" as well as get input from the "critics"—the other students in class!

- o Scene 1: Darnell works with Professor Monroe to improve his writing and uses a writing lab and a tutor for assistance.
- o Scene 2: Darnell meets with an advisor and after reviewing his high school grades and placement test results, decides he will withdraw from this course and take a developmental English course next semester.
- o Scene 3: Darnell meets with Professor Monroe, and she tells him his essay was one of the best in the class and he should consider a major in English or journalism—and write about sports.

5. What important features does this chapter include?

Readiness and Reality Checks

At the beginning of each chapter, students complete a Readiness Check and at the end, they complete a Reality Check. It is important to help students compare their expectations with their actual experience. Often students succumb to an "optimistic bias" and hope that something won't take as much time and effort as it actually will. "Reality Testing" is a critical aspect of Emotional Intelligence. A writing assignment or class discussion can be used to share students' pre and post chapter results.

Challenge → Reaction → Insight → Action steps

Throughout the book, students will be reminded about the learning system used in every *FOCUS* chapter: The Challenge → Reaction → Insight → Action (CRIA) system. Exposure to this four-step learning system begins in chapter 1, however the actual introduction to the system is found in chapter 2. Keep reminding students about this learning "chain reaction." Students need to understand that learning is different for each individual because it is based on what students already know about a subject.

Discuss the Challenge → Reaction "prompts" at the beginning of each chapter to help students assess what they already know; if they don't know much about the topic of the chapter coming up, that's understandable. That's why students are in college! If they know a great deal about what's coming, they're in a good position to learn even more.

Use Insight → Action prompts at the end of each chapter as you think best: as discussion generators, as threaded discussion questions for the entire class, or as written or e-mailed journal assignments. Require students to complete the CRIA steps in each chapter, based on the reading/writing level skills of your group and your course objectives. These four steps are repeated throughout the text in every chapter. Whenever appropriate connect students' discussion to this model.

How full is your plate?

All students can be *life-challenged,* running from class to class to job to home and more. Community college students often have additional hurdles to overcome. *How full is your plate?* is designed to help students think about life management and how to make corrections when needed. Consider having your students try the experiment in this chapter as they examine their peak energy times and how they coincide (or clash) with their typical study times. Another excellent way of helping students gain awareness to time management is to show the FOCUS TV segment on Procrastination, available on the *FOCUS* CourseMate or via the FOCUSPoints slideshow for this chapter.

6. Which in-text exercises should I use?

Four exercises are built into this chapter. Here are descriptions of why the exercises have been included, how much time each one will probably take, and how you might debrief them.

EXERCISE 1.1 WE'D LIKE TO GET TO KNOW YOU

Why do this activity?
This activity helps to create a classroom climate where students know each other, feel comfortable and included, and become willing to get involved.

What are the challenges and what can you expect?
This is a relatively easy activity and students enjoy getting out of their seats and interacting. Students should fill out the exercise, and then it can become the basis for classroom introductions.

How much time will it take?
It should take between 20-25 minutes, and the only materials needed are the students' textbooks.

How should I debrief?
It's a good idea to ask students the following question when they are done: Did they learn anything that surprised them? For example, someone might say that they were surprised to learn that "X" was working full time. Or that "Y" was a returning student, or that "Z" was commuting from a distance. If no one volunteers, be sure that you include something that surprised you. Conclude by talking about why it's important to build a community of learners at the start of the term.

EXERCISE 1.2 WHY DO I HAVE TO TAKE THIS CLASS?

Why do this activity?
This activity helps students identify the importance of working with an academic advisor to create an academic roadmap for their future. One reason given for not persisting in higher education is the absence of an academic plan. This activity helps students see how everything fits together and provides a visual reminder of what's next.

What are the challenges and what can you expect?
It's important that this first "homework" assignment be turned in, showing students that you expect them to do assignments and that you will hold them accountable. Students quickly pick up on the classroom climate, and if they are assigned an activity that does not have an accountability component; they may conclude that some assignments in the course can be written off as "busywork." If your college does not have degree plan worksheets available, you may need to create or modify one from another institution. Here are two you might use:
www3.austincc.edu/catalog/fy2008/deggens01.rtf
http://web.grcc.edu/counseling/2010/AA-MACRAOfall2010.pdf

How much time will it take?
This will vary depending on the advising resources at your college and how many students are in your class. The completion of this assignment can have long-term value for the student. You may want the student to meet with an advisor to assist in completion. An alternative would be to have students use the college catalog to assist in completing the academic plan. Consult with your advising center about lead time required for students to meet with an advisor or the possibility of inviting an advisor in class to assist students with this activity.

How should I debrief?
Ask individual students to share their plans when complete. Encourage students (like Darnell) who are undecided to concentrate on general education courses while also examining other courses that may serve as introductory courses to majors of which they have interest. This can be a good place for discussing the importance of prerequisites and taking developmental courses. Also, remind students that their plans may change if they change their major (or choose a major) and that it is normal to make adjustments to this plan.

EXERCISE 1.3 TOP 10 RESOURCES YOUR CAMPUS OFFERS

Why do this activity?
This activity is designed to help students to get know their campus and the resources available to them.

What are the challenges and what can I expect?
This activity can be done in several ways and has different challenges depending on the approach used. One way of doing this activity is to have students bring in college catalogs or handbooks that list the services available and work in groups or individually. Another approach is to treat it as a campus scavenger hunt. Send students out in teams to identify the service, its location and other relevant information. Make sure that the potential departments students will visit are given a heads-up that students will be coming in with questions!

How much time will it take?
This exercise can be done in as little as 20 minutes or extend to one hour depending on the method used, the size of the class and the size of your campus.

7. Which additional exercises might enrich students' learning?

Getting to Know You
Class activity
Materials needed: flip-chart paper, markers, masking tape
Time: 30-50 minutes
Goal: To help students to get to know each other and create a comfortable classroom environment
Students circulate around the room and write on sheets of posted flip chart paper with the same headings as in Exercise 1.1. For example, one sheet of paper would have the heading "I'm happiest when…" and students would add their responses to that paper. Then you may post individual students beside each list and read the lists to the entire class after everyone has had a chance to post all their responses.

Finding FOCUS
Class activity
Materials needed: index cards
Time: 10-15 minutes
Goal: To help students discover ways of overcoming common student problems
Hand students cards that state something that might cause a student to lose focus in school. Cards may include items such as these: your car broke down, your grandmother is ill, your expenses exceed what you expected, your babysitter's last day is Friday, and so forth. Depending on the size and composition of the class, make as many cards as you need. Ask students to hold up cards that cause students to lose focus, but situations they can change and refocus. Ask them how the hypothetical student can re-focus. Sometimes students will say that they couldn't change a situation, but with foresight and planning, they actually could.

Think/Pair/Share
Class activity
Materials needed: none
Time: 10-20 minutes
Goal: To get students discussing, involved, and engaged with the course material
Sometimes it's difficult to get a discussion going in class. This think/pair/share activity provides a mechanism for all students to get involved and can be used for any topic.

- **Think** individually about why the information is important, how it connects to student success, and why it was included in the text. You may wish to have them jot down their ideas. (3-5 minutes)

- **Pair** up with the student next to them and discuss their responses. The pair will then decide on one or two issues to bring up to the group (3-5 minutes).
- **Share** with the class their responses, and as a group the class will discuss some common themes. (5-10 minutes).

"Trading Places"

Created by Staley, C. (2003) originally based on "Trading Places" in Silberman, M. (1995).
Class activity
Materials needed: pad of sticky notes
Time: 10-20 minutes
Goal: To help students identify a positive quality, characteristic or experience that that they have that Darnell may or may not have
Ask each student to write a positive characteristic or descriptive word about themselves on a sticky note and put it on the front of their shirts. Next, students are to walk around the room "hawking" their characteristics, and trading with others to gain something that they may not have. At the conclusion of the activity, have students discuss why they chose particular attributes, or traded them, and whether or not Darnell appears to display these. Discuss the impact of these attributes on college success.

I am SUCCESS

Class activity
Materials needed: flip-chart paper, markers, and dictionaries
Time: 20-25 minutes
Goal: To assist students in building a positive self image as a college student
Give each student a piece of paper and a marker. Ask them to think about positive words that either describes them now or how they want to be described in the future. These words should spell SUCCESS. At the top of the paper ask students to write: I am SUCCESS. Below that along the left side they should write *I am* _____ six times. The seventh line should end in I am SUCCESSFUL. For example a student might write:

> I am SUCCESS
> I am **S**trong
> I am **U**nafraid
> I am **C**ourageous
> I am **C**onnected
> I am **E**nthusiastic
> I am **S**tructured
> I am **S**UCCESSFUL

Ask students to share their statements with the class by starting with I am SUCCESS and ending with I am SUCCESSFUL. Dictionaries can be helpful, especially with the letter U! Some positive U words include unabashed, unafraid, unbreakable, unwavering, and undefeated.

8. What other activities can I incorporate to make the chapter my own?

In many ways, *FOCUS on Community College Success* teaches itself. It contains built-in activities, discussion and reflection tools, and a variety of features to motivate and engage students. Beyond what appears in the student edition, the instructor's version of the text is annotated. The annotations in each chapter provide helpful background information for you and contain a variety of suggestions for five ways to enrich the chapter. Separating the annotations into five categories helps save you time because you can scan for what you need as an instructor:

1) **Teachable Moments** (places to capitalize on a particular learning opportunity)
2) **Activity Options** (additional exercises to introduce or emphasize content)
3) **Sensitive Situations** (alerts about in-class discussion topics that may generate possible controversy, embarrassment, or discomfort among certain students)
4) **Emotional Intelligence (EI) Emphasis/Research** (research on EI that reinforces a tie between non-cognitive variables and college success, starting in chapter 2)
5) **Developmental Students** (provides insight and suggestions to working with students who may be enrolled in developmental education courses)
6) **Teaching with Technology** (suggests ways to use YouTube, teachertubes, or other technical or online resources to enrich learning)

If you are familiar with additional research about teaching and learning, capitalize on what you know in addition to what appears in this Instructor's Resource Manual; tailor the class to complement your personal expertise. For example, research indicates that instructors have a short window of time to actively engage students in learning. If students are not engaged early on, it may be impossible to reverse the situation. The more engaged students are, the more likely they will be to remember and apply what they learn.

Included here, all in one place, are Activity Options from the Annotated Instructor's Edition. Reflection, discussion, and writing or presentation opportunities are ways in which students can become active learners.

ACTIVITY OPTION (p. 4): This activity helps students to understand the differences between high school and college and subsequently the modifications that may need to be made. Have students brainstorm the differences between high school and college. If some of your students have been out of high school for a number of years or did not finish high school, simply change the activity to include the differences between work and college. Ask a volunteer to keep track on the board. Once the list is complete, ask the class to select five major differences and what adjustments they will need to make in order to be successful.

ACTIVITY OPTION (p. 5): Give students an index card and have them list their gender, ethnicity, background, age, occupation, talents, awards, or anything that might be unique to them. They should not add their names to the cards. Read the cards out loud. Ask a student volunteer to record on the board the commonalities in the group. Ask a second volunteer to record the differences. Are your students surprised by the diversity? Are they surprised to find they are not alone in the class?

ACTIVITY OPTION (p. 5): Divide the students into groups. Present them with this scenario: Your friend Tom is very shy. He comes to classes for two weeks. He feels that he has been misplaced in three of his four classes. Has done some homework assignments, but honestly, he does not feel they were done correctly. He things he should just stop coming to his classes and maybe try again some other time. Ask students to think about Tom's problem and decide what advice to give him. Have each group share responses with the class. Did the responses of the class have anything in common?

ACTIVITY OPTION (p. 6): Be sure that you do Exercise 1.1 along with your students. Remember, they want to get to know you too. Pair students and have them share their information with their partner student. Have the partner introduce the student to the class and report on two or three items (from the activity above) that were really interesting about the student they just met. Another activity is called "You Would Never Guess." Ask students to write something on an index card that no one would guess about them (non-embarrassing items that are appropriate). For example, a student might write on a card "I am one of nine children," "I played Annie in our high school play." Collect the cards and read them aloud. Have students guess who it might be.

ACTIVITY OPTION (p. 7): Depending on the resources available at your college, schedule a visit to the career center and/or advising center to learn more about careers and the types of degrees needed for particular careers. If this is not possible, consider asking an advisor/counselor to present to your class on the programs offered at your college and the differences between certificates and associate's degrees.

ACTIVITY OPTION (p. 10): As an extra-credit assignment, have students who will be transferring visit their advisor and get a transfer agreement or go online to research which courses will transfer to their desired transfer school. Student could also call or visit their desired transfer schools to learn this information.

ACTIVITY OPTION (p. 12): Even if you had an advisor visit class, it is still a good idea to have students make an appointment with an advisor to begin this important relationship. A variation on the index card is a brief reflection paper on what they learned during this visit (e.g., where the advising office is located; what it has to offer; how my learning style impacts my career goals; how important it is to have a career plan, etc). This can also be coupled with Exercise 1.2.

ACTIVITY OPTION (p. 13): Once students understand how to compute GPAs, they can immediately apply the skill to their situation. Many students may not have a calculator with them, but many have a cell phone with this feature. This activity is an opportunity to discuss your institution's probation/suspension policy, the impact of grades on financial aid eligibility, repeat policy and more. Have as many scenarios as you do groups, with each group discussing a different "student." For example, using your college's courses and grading system, have one student who is doing well, one who is struggling, etc.

ACTIVITY OPTION (p. 15): Teaching students to analyze their syllabi early in the semester can be an excellent way for students to prepare for their courses. Have them use the syllabus for this course and highlight title, instructor, e-mail, office phone, office hours, course description, textbooks, attendance policy and grading policy. A variation on this activity could have students bring in a syllabus from another class for analysis.

ACTIVITY OPTION (p. 19): The Resource Game is a fun, high-energy activity that helps students learn about important campus resources. Create index cards with one campus resource on each card. Divide the class into two groups for an in-class contest. This activity can be combined with the College Catalog Scavenger Hunt. This activity requires students to bring their catalogs to class and answer questions from information found in the catalog. Sample questions can include:

- Where is the Student Life office?
- When is Spring Break?
- How many credits are required for the Associate's degree in Electronics?

ACTIVITY OPTION (p. 21): Having a career focus can keep students motivated to stay in college. This activity helps students learn the basics of career research. Have students share what they have learned with everyone in class.

9. What homework might I assign?

Getting Involved
After reading about the PCP Syndrome (p. 17) assign students to sample the activities offered at your college. This can vary from attending a student club meeting to attending a concert offered on campus. Inform students where they can learn about student organizations as well as campus events. Ask them to choose one club or event to attend and write a brief summary of the meeting or event. Have them include not only the event and date but ask them to write about what they learned, what surprised them, and what they would do differently if they did the assignment over.

Jumpstart on Time Management
If you have bundled a Semester Planner with this text (see your Cengage sales representative) or if you have required students to have a planner, assign students to transfer important class deadlines and assignments from your syllabus to their planner. This assignment can help students manage their time as well as their non-college priorities. Ask that students complete the activity on page 10, "**How Full Is Your Plate?**" before getting started on this assignment.

Getting Connected
A major factor in college retention is whether or not students feel connected to something or someone on campus. Ask students to select one of their instructors and schedule an appointment with him/her. Brainstorm with the class the information they will need to gather from the instructor appointment. It could be information such as where did you go to college, what was difficult for you, did you play sports, etc. Assign this activity and

require students to complete a brief report with the answers, and ask students to present this report in class.

Journal Entry Options

One: Have students write a one-page journal entry, or send you an e-mail reflecting on the Readiness Check. You might prompt students by asking them to choose the three questions they responded to with the lowest numbers and how these questions relate to success in college. Ask students to explain if they have any control over their ability to improve their score on these items and to discuss why or why not.

Two: Have students write a one-page journal entry or send you an e-mail describing their plan for becoming a "professional student." What transformations will they encounter? What will be the result at the end of the term? How is this different from being a student in high school?

Three: Ask students to write a journal entry comparing their original response to the *FOCUS* Challenge Case about Darnell Williams, **"What Do YOU Think?"** with their final impression after reading the chapter to the **"NOW What Do You Think?"** section.

Four: Use the Insight → Action prompts as journal or blog assignments.

10. What have I learned in teaching this chapter that I will incorporate next time?

CHAPTER 2: BUILDING DREAMS, SETTING GOALS

1. Why is this chapter important?

This chapter sets the foundation for student learning: self-understanding. The desire to learn more about what makes us tick is a fundamental human trait, and students are no exception. But often students lack self-insight and are not always realistic about the personal and academic investment required to get a college degree. In the 2007 Noel-Levitz National Freshman Attitude Study of nearly 100,000 entering college students, 95% of these students had a strong desire to complete their education, with almost 75% indicating they would welcome help in developing their test-taking skills, 66% wanting career guidance, and 48% indicating they would like help in math. But, these same students often don't access the support services provided on campus or approach their teachers for needed help. According to the Community College Survey of Student Engagement (2008), 59% of respondents indicated their goal was to earn an associate degree, yet only 36% of students earn a certificate, associate or bachelor's degree in a six-year period. According to Survey of Entering Student Engagement (SENSE), 85% of new students at community colleges or career/technical schools believe they are academically prepared for college; however, up to one-third of these students will sabotage themselves by skipping class or failing to turn in assignment within the first several weeks of the term.

As instructors, we must help students learn more about themselves, so that they can reach their reported goal: attaining a college degree. Follow students' interests and get them thinking about who they are, about their attitudes, values, and behaviors, and help them make connections between these things and college success. Sometimes we assume "they get it"—that is, they understand college success skills conceptually. But understanding and acting on that knowledge are two different things. Remember that most of the students who enter college want to succeed. We have to help them to understand themselves, and turn their desires into real behaviors that propel them toward the finish line.

This chapter features Gloria Gonzales in the *FOCUS* Challenge Case. Gloria has big dreams but no plan to accomplish those dreams. Like many of the students in your class, Gloria needs help in setting realistic goals and creating a plan to achieve them. This chapter introduces students to how *FOCUS* can help them learn by understanding motivation and goal development.

Also, in this chapter students will begin to see the pattern of the text repeated from chapter 1 as well as an introduction of new elements. The chapter begins with a Readiness Check, then a *FOCUS* Challenge Case, followed by the introduction of the Challenge→Reaction→Insight→Action system and the Academic Intrinsic Motivation (AIM) Scale's C-Factors. These C-Factors (challenge, control, curiosity, and career outlook) will help students focus on what motivates them and why. As you and your students work through the text, it will be important to reference your students AIM scores from this chapter.

2. What are this chapter's learning objectives?

➢ How this book will help students learn
➢ What motivates students
➢ How students' attitudes can sabotage them
➢ Why students should distinguish between dreams and goals
➢ How students can develop goals that work

3. How should I launch this chapter?

You're most likely past your first week or so of class. Congratulations! Remember that research shows that these first few weeks can make or break the way that students connect to you and to each other. According to one study, students make assessments about instructors within the first five minutes of the first class (in this study, even *before* the syllabus was distributed). Furthermore, their initial reactions held until the end of the term! *The Chronicle of Higher Education* reports that when it comes to retention, attitude matters most. Entering students judge the "fit" between themselves and the institutions they choose to attend very early in the term.

If you encourage IMs or text messages, are you receiving them from students? Are your students e-mailing you? If you have a Facebook page for the course, have the students become "fans" or "friends"? If you are using Twitter, are they following you? Have students come to meet with you, one-on-one? If students have not responded to you or contacted you *and* they are not showing up for class, it's important to take action. Contact them directly by phone or e-mail, and if they don't respond, do some quick intervention. Be persistent! Check with their academic advisor to find out if they are attending other classes. If your institution has an "early alert" system for students, now would be a good time to sound the alarm or raise a flag. Remember: first-year students are "under construction," so go the extra mile! In addition to making sure that students are coming to class and are engaged, here are some things to think about for this chapter.

- **Make sure students know each other's names.** You probably already know everyone's name in the class, but students may not know each other. You can do a brief check by asking students to name a person in the room and something they remember about them. Chances are students remember at least something about everyone. By doing it this way, you don't put anyone on the spot by asking them to name everyone in the group. When a student names a person and says something about him or her, then it becomes that person's turn to name another. Do this until everyone is named. Make sure that you jump in and help out if it seems like a few people are left without anyone remembering their names. If you have a sense that someone might be left out, you should introduce those students—or start the activity yourself by naming a person that seems isolated from the other class members. If you have a large class, ask students to take out a sheet of paper, fold it long ways to make a "table tent," and write their name on it so that everyone learns everyone's name. Students are gratified and appreciative when others remember their names and details of their identities.

- **Create a Contract for Success in your class**. This activity is similar to Exercise 2.3 "The Ideal Student," but contains an additional element. At this point students have been exposed to a variety of students, instructors and instructional styles. Ask them to brainstorm on what qualities they believe successful students possess. Ask someone to record these on the board, and if possible ask someone with a laptop to record them in a document. After students have generated 10-20 success characteristics, ask them what qualities they like to see in their instructors. Compare the lists and point out similarities; does motivation appear on both lists? What about attitude and effort? Ask the students if they would be willing to sign a contract that says students will strive to attain and maintain those success characteristics. Ask yourself if you are willing to sign off on the instructor characteristics for success. Bring the contract back to the next class listing the student and instructor characteristics and have everyone, including you, sign the contract. Provide each student with a signed copy. Refer back to this contract as needed throughout the semester if students (or you!) begin to stray off course.

- **Remember the Readiness Check at the beginning of the chapter and the Reality Check at the end**. These activities help students focus on whether they are ready to read and learn. Again, students using *FOCUS* reported that Readiness Checks become a habit, one that they also perform, not just before they begin to read, but also mentally before each class begins. This habit also extends to their other courses, which is one of the activity's intentional goals. The chapters end with a Reality Check that compares students' expectations at the beginning of the chapter with the actual experience of reading.

- **Going beyond the book.** Ask a career counselor to present to your class on different ways students can create a Career Outlook. Your students may have ideas about careers but lack the skills to learn more about the academic preparation and future demand of their chosen career. If your campus has a career center, arrange for your class to visit the center and examine some of the resources available to help students research careers.

- **Developmental Students and Returning Adult Learners:** Many first-year students will need assistance in how to approach and read texts, and developmental learners are no exception. Ask students to skip to the Step 2: Reaction – "What do you think?" *before* reading Gloria's Challenge Case. This will help students as they read. Returning Adult Learners will most likely be interested in the Academic Intrinsic Motivation Scale. Some students will score low on this self-assessment. Consider meeting with each student, one-on-one, to discuss his or her scores. Remind the parents in your class about the *FOCUS* on Kids worksheets, available on the online *FOCUS* on Community College Success Resource Center. The Chapter 2 worksheet discusses how individuals can make their dreams come true.

4. How should I use the *FOCUS* Challenge Case?

Just as in chapter 1, the chapter begins with a *FOCUS* Challenge Case about a real student (or a composite of many students) that depicts a challenging situation college students often face.

In chapter 2, we meet Gloria Gonzales, a student who dreams of becoming a famous fashion designer. She enters her first class, thinking she knows everything she needs to know. School is not a top priority, and she is a first generation college student. Even though her family thought Gloria's older sister was the "smart one," she dropped out of college and is now out in the workforce earning money. Gloria plans to work about 45 hours a week while in school (a risk factor) at the store in the mall, where she is a successful sales person (not necessarily a skill indicative of potential talent as a fashion designer). Everyone said college was the "right thing to do," so she enrolled in a community college without much forethought or planning. Her parents wanted her to go to a four-year university and get a "real" degree in business so she would have a secure career, but Gloria has other ideas about her future.

Use the Gloria Gonzales story to get students to begin opening up and refer back to Gloria whenever you can. Ask students which of Gloria's qualities they see in themselves. Have them answer the "What Do *You* Think?" questions and pair up to discuss their responses, or ask students to work through the questions in small groups. Other suggestions for using Gloria's story:

- Ask students to review the visual clues in the chapter opening (e-mail list, work schedule, course schedule) and have the students tell you about Gloria.
- **Direct It!** Assign a "scene director" for the Challenge Case. Assign a student to role-play Gloria and another student to role-play her advisor and two other students to play her parents. The director can stop the scene at any point and redirect the "actors" as well as get input from the "critics"—the other students in class!
    o Scene 1: What would her advisor say about her dream and strategies for turning it into a goal?
    o Scene 2: What does Gloria need to tell her parents about her experience versus their expectations of her based on Gloria's older sister?
    o Scene 3: Ask students to write or develop a short skit on the end of Gloria's first semester. What did she learn, what changed as a result of taking the College Success class? What resources at your college would students suggest Gloria take advantage of?

In Step 3: Insight, ask students to create two endings to Gloria's story: one that demonstrates a performer's perspective and one that demonstrates a learner's perspective. Alternatively, you could give them examples of each and ask them to identify which is which. Examples could include:

- Gloria is wasting her time and her parent's money, she should just quit now (performer).
- Gloria should try to remain open about her career plans and use her first semester as an opportunity to experience college and examine different majors (learner).
- Gloria really enjoys her job and she should make that her priority (performer).
- Gloria could reframe her question of "Will I be successful?" into "How can I be successful?" (learner).
- Gloria will never be a fashion designer; she is wasting her time with college until she gets serious about a career (performer).

Show the chapter 2 FOCUS TV "Dreams and Goals" episode in class available on CourseMate or via the Power Lecture CD's FOCUSPoints. In addition to reading the FOCUS Challenge Case, show the chapter 2 "Inside the FOCUS Studio" episode featuring Gloria Gonzales. This talk show is based on the Emmy-Award winning Bravo series, "Inside the Actor's Studio," and this episode stars Debbie, who plays Gloria Gonzales in the book. The "Inside the FOCUS Studio" shows include brief comedy sketches, based on the chapter's content, and cover the chapter material in substantial depth, using a kinesthetic learning modality. Since many or even most of today's learners are kinesthetic, they will likely respond favorably to this format.

5. What important features does this chapter include?

Readiness and Reality Checks

In the beginning of each chapter students complete a Readiness Check and at the end they do a Reality Check. It is important to help students compare their expectations with their actual experience, because, among other things, it helps them to more accurately predict how long an assignment will take. Your students may not be experienced at reading texts, which may make this chapter more challenging for them. A writing assignment or class discussion can be used to share students' pre and post chapter results. You might even ask students to e-mail you a short reflection about their expectations and the realities they have come to understand by the end of the chapter. When students are able to go over material more than once and reflect, they begin to hardwire information.

Challenge → Reaction → Insight → Action prompts

This chapter introduces the learning system used in every FOCUS chapter: The Challenge → Reaction → Insight → Action system. Keep reminding students about this learning "chain reaction." Students need to understand that learning is different for each individual because it is based on what someone already knows about a subject.

In a Challenge → Reaction prompt in this chapter, students are asked to identify attitudes, beliefs, fears and values that could cause one to lose focus as well as maintain focus. At the end of this chapter, students are asked to create the conclusion to Gloria's case study. In addition, students are asked to identify a key learning from the chapter and how can they increase their motivation. Because this learning system is used in every chapter, make sure you spend a little extra time on these so that they become a very natural anticipated activity for all the remaining chapters.

Exercises and Self-Assessments

The AIMS assessment (Challenge → Reaction on intrinsic motivation) in this chapter sets up the book's C-Factors. Other activities—for example, "Your Academic Autobiography"—are great self-assessments. Take some time for students to share their stories with others. Often, students don't realize that others are in the same situation and finding commonalities can help your group bond.

C-Factors

Each chapter of *FOCUS* from now on contains features related to the four aspects of intrinsic motivation: curiosity ("Curiosity" a short article on something related to college success), control ("Control Your Toughest Task" allowing students to apply control to a tough class or on the job), career outlook ("Career Outlook" a career interview with a professional), and challenge ("Challenge *FOCUS* Case" and online quizzes help students to learn to adjust the level of challenge to keep their motivation high). These built-in features are intended to increase students' intrinsic motivation. Use them well!

FOCUS on Careers

This feature highlights a career related to the chapter's content. If students become really "hooked" on the information presented in the chapter, they can begin thinking about particular careers that may be possible fits for them. In this chapter, we meet Saree Robinson who introduces readers to the career of Fashion Merchandising.

How full is your plate?

How full is your plate? is designed to help students think about life management and how to make corrections when needed. Worrying about not having enough time to get everything done can cause time management problems. The activity featured in this section can be done alone or in a group setting, having students make suggestions for other students.

6. Which in-text exercises should I use?

Six exercises are built into this chapter. Here are descriptions of why the exercises have been included, how much time each one will probably take, and how you might debrief them.

EXERCISE 2.1 HOW DO YOU "SPEND" YOUR TIME?

Why do this activity?
This activity is designed to help students see the cost of missing class. Students are often surprised as to the actual cost of missing classes and this activity helps to illustrate this point.

What are the challenges and what can you expect?
This activity is relatively easy, however, be prepared to go through an example including the calculations so that everyone can see how it is done. You will also want to have tuition rates available for those who don't remember as well as examples of other expenses students might incur: childcare, food while at school, parking, gas, supplies, etc. Students will also want access to a calculator, so be prepared to ask students to share! Many cell phones have a calculator function.

How much time will it take?
It should take between 15-20 minutes and the only materials needed are the students' textbooks.

How should I debrief?
It's a good idea to ask students the following question when they are done: did anything they learn surprise them? You could ask each student to share his/her hourly rate and post on the board. Ask students if they think it is worth it to miss a class. Many students are tempted to work additional hours and may occasionally miss class to do so. How does their class hourly rate compare with their work hourly rate?

EXERCISE 2.2 HOW MOTIVATED *ARE* YOU AND *HOW* ARE YOU MOTIVATED?

Why do this activity?
This activity is the Academic Intrinsic Motivation Scale (AIMS) and measures intrinsic motivation to succeed in college. This exercise is critical to students' understanding of extrinsic and intrinsic motivation.

What are the challenges and what can you expect?
Developmental learners may need additional time to complete this activity, and it might be a good idea for all learners to complete this exercise outside of class. Students who are undecided about a major may have difficulty or get discouraged with the "major" and "chosen profession" statements. Encourage students to answer the questions honestly. A possible challenge with this activity is students with low scores. Have all students write a journal entry or e-mail to you and ask them why they think their scores were lower than expected. Also have them write on how they think they could raise their scores.

How much time will it take?
If it is done in class, plan on approximately 30-45 minutes to take and debrief. The only materials needed are the students' textbooks. If it is done outside of class, plan on 15-30 minutes to debrief.

How should I debrief?
Start with a conversation on the differences between extrinsic and intrinsic motivation. Ask students to list examples of extrinsic and intrinsic motivation and post those on the board under their respective headings: Extrinsic and Intrinsic. Engage the class in a conversation around motivation and optimism. For example, how are they related? Can your students provide examples of a time when they were optimistic they could do something? How were they motivated? As stated above, some students will score low on this assessment. A journal or e-mail activity can help students process their scores. This activity could also be the basis of a one-on-one visit with you to process privately.

EXERCISE 2.3 THE IDEAL STUDENT

Why do this activity?
This activity helps students identify behaviors that lead to student success and then commit to them. You can also use this activity with students to identify the learning outcomes that you want them to have for this course (as well as what *they* want to learn in the course) and can serve as the "contract" they have with you. Throughout the course, especially at mid-term, remind students of the contract they created and ask them whether or not they are meeting their goals and if not, why. Consider adding the Ideal Teacher component discussed earlier for a two-way contract with your students.

What are the challenges and what can you expect?
Regardless of how you structure this activity, consider assigning it for completion outside of class. This gives students an opportunity to come up with a more complete list of behaviors for themselves (and you!). It also emphasizes the importance of work done outside of class.

How much time will it take?
It should take between 20-25 minutes and the only materials needed are the students' textbooks (or you may simply read or e-mail the assignment to them).

How should I debrief?
Ask individual students to share their lists, and then make a master list as a class. Ask students to copy down the master list and put their initials next to each item they will promise to try to do during the term. Complete the activity by having students create a similar list for "The Ideal Teacher" (you!) and sign the items you will promise to try to do. As stated earlier, ask a student with a laptop to record the master list and print a copy for the next class session so everyone, including you can sign the "contract." Follow up with copies to everyone. Many of the behaviors students identify will be related to self-regulation and emotional intelligence (described in more detail in chapters 9 (Reading and Studying) and 11 (Building Relationships).

EXERCISE 2.4 YOUR ACADEMIC AUTOBIOGRAPHY

Why do this activity?
This activity is designed to help students reflect upon their educational experiences, to help them identify themes in their academic life that have made them the student they are, and to help them think about how these behaviors might help or hinder them in college. The assignment also gives you an initial, baseline assessment of students' writing skills and alerts you to any non-cognitive variables that might interfere with students' learning.

What are the challenges and what can I expect?
Students enjoy looking back to early reading and writing experiences. Often, they have not thought about this for a long time. Encourage students to look for themes that describe them as learners: some kind of reoccurring behavior, such as loving to read, struggling to sit still, or succeeding based on their connection with particular teachers, and how these factors might influence their work in college. Ask students to include

specific times and places in their examples, such as primary school, middle school, and high school, or particular subjects. Be sure that students don't simply submit a string of facts, but that they do some interpretation and speculation about how particular events affected them. For developmental learners or others who prefer other ways of communicating, this assignment can be done in a very visual way by using PowerPoint or a "Lifeline of Learning"—a visual timeline of learning themes.

How much time will it take?
This is a homework assignment that should take students about an hour.

How should I debrief?
Students really benefit from hearing how other students responded to this activity and often can identify with each other. Students might be assigned to read another student's paper and report to the group two significant facts that seemed to have shaped the way the student learned. Or if students write about sensitive issues—difficult home situations, for example—you may wish to keep their papers confidential.

EXERCISE 2.5 THEORIES OF INTELLIGENCE SCALE

Why do this activity?
Performers and learners view intelligence very differently, and both are present in your class. This brief activity allows students to determine what they believe about their own intelligence. Performers will agree more with the first two statements while learners will agree more with statements three and four. This understanding will help students in how they approach their classes.

What are the challenges and what can you expect?
This activity can be done in class as the foundation of a discussion on ability versus effort. Some learners may struggle with a few terms such as "cultivated," be prepared to define some words. This exercise can be introduced by defining and describing the terms "performers" and "learners" and how they relate to ability and effort.

How much time will it take?
This activity should take approximately five minutes not including time for discussion and the only materials needed are the students' textbooks

How should I debrief?
While most students will identify with one or the other, it is important that students see intelligence can be cultivated through learning. It is also important for students to see they have been both a learner and a performer. The Activity Option (p. 42) is an excellent way to illustrate this point. Ask students for examples when they were a learner, and then ask them for examples of when they were a performer.

EXERCISE 2.6 CORE VALUES SELF-ASSESSMENT

Why do this activity?
This exercise helps students to see their core values. Comparing students' core values should reveal that while differences exist, students are not really all that different in their values. This exercise helps to introduce students to values, dreams and goals.

What are the challenges and what can you expect?
Students may have difficulty ranking their top five values. Remind students that ranking five doesn't mean they don't have other values, it simply means these are the most relevant to them today. In six months or six years they might choose others as part of their top five values.

How much time will it take?
This activity will take 10-15 minutes and the only materials needed are the students' textbooks.

How should I debrief?
After giving students time to assess their values, ask students to share their top five. What did they learn about themselves? Did anything surprise them about their values? About other students' values? What similarities are present in your class? What values might be missing? As a closing to this exercise, read the quote from Lao Tzu at the bottom of page 42 out loud to your students. Have your students write a one paragraph reaction to the quote on what it means to them to know yourself and master yourself.

7. Which additional exercises might enrich students' learning?

"Life By The Book"
(based on Underhile, R. in Fetro J.V. & Drolet, J.C. (2000). Personal & Social Competence. ETR Associates).
Class Activity
Material needed: Copy of the poem "Autobiography in Five Short Chapters" by Portia Nelson, available at *http://www.mhsanctuary.com/healing/auto.htm*
Time: 25-30 minutes
Goal: To assist students in understanding where they are and in setting attainable goals. This exercise can also assist students with understanding locus of control.
Before class review the poem "Autobiography in Five Short Chapters" and determine emotions associated with the situations in each stanza of the poem. Divide the board into five sections for each stanza of the poem. Provide the poem and give students five minutes to read it. Ask students to write in the first section words that might describe the emotional state of the person based on the first chapter of the poem. How might someone feel who walks down the street and falls in a hole?

Repeat this process for the other chapters, recording words in each section on the board. Ask students to describe the progression of words from chapter 1 to chapter 5. How are the words in each column different—for example from chapter 1 to chapter 2, from chapter 2 to chapter 3, and so on? Focus the discussion on what streets college students walk down? What are the "holes" that college students encounter? How are the streets and holes related to the topics in this course? What chapter are you in your life right now, and where do you want to be?

Focus Learning System
Class Activity (or an out-of-class assignment where students work in groups)
Material needed: Old magazines, tape, markers, and flip charts
Time: 20-30 minutes
Goal: To help students understand the Challenge → Reaction → Insight → Action System

In groups, have students describe some challenge that they may encounter during college. Using photos from magazines, ask students to select faces of individuals that represent how they identify a *challenge*, another photo of a facial expression that represents their *reaction*, one that represents *insight*, and the final photo representing *action*. Using only these four photos as prompts, the groups share their challenge and subsequent responses and behaviors with the class.

"The Human Continuum"
(based on Staley, C. (2003))
Class activity
Materials needed: none
Time: 10-20 minutes
Goal: To help students place themselves on a continuum to predict their AIMS score

The following is an activity that asks students to *predict* their AIMS scores. However, the continuum is an activity to have students quickly respond to most any prompt related to course material.

- Identify one side of the room as one pole (High AIMS scores: 100-125) and the other side as the opposite pole (low AIMS scores: below 75) with the remaining scores in the middle.
- Ask group members to take a position that they believe will most likely represent their score.
- Ask each member individually to explain why he or she will probably score as predicted.
- Then ask students to fill out the instrument. They may be surprised because they believe themselves to be more intrinsically motivated than revealed by the instrument. Remember that actual scores on the instrument may get at sensitive issues. Having students report out is probably not a good idea, but this activity can be illuminating.
- Remind students that having a high level of intrinsic motivation is not necessarily a guarantee that they will be successful. They must translate their motivation into action.

8. What other activities can I incorporate to make the chapter my own?

While suggestions and activities are provided for you, this text is so rich that you can use all of the annotations, the Readiness and Reality Checks, the Challenge → Reaction → Insight → Action system in any way that is comfortable for you. Keep in mind the concept of student engagement and that the more involved the students are the more likely they are to learn.

Scan for particular annotations in the Instructor's Edition for ways to enrich the material for your particular group:

1) **Teachable Moments** (places to capitalize on a particular learning opportunity)
2) **Activity Options** (additional exercises to introduce or emphasize content)
3) **Sensitive Situations** (alerts about in-class discussion topics that may generate possible controversy, embarrassment, or discomfort among certain students)
4) **Emotional Intelligence (EI) Emphasis/Research** (research on EI that reinforces a tie between non-cognitive variables and college success)
5) **Developmental Students** (provides insight and suggestions to working with students who may be enrolled in developmental education courses)
6) **Teaching with Technology** (provides online or other technology options for reinforcing concepts from the chapter)

Included here, all in one place, are Activity Options taken from the Annotated Instructor's Edition.

If you are familiar with additional research about teaching and learning, capitalize on what you know in addition to what appears in this Instructor's Resource Manual. There are so many ways that you can make this chapter your own. For example, if your background is psychology, you have a great deal of information to share with the class about learning styles, motivation, and personality. If you are a business professor, share with your students how certain types make for ideal accountants or others ideal stock market traders. Share with students your background and area of specialty and refer to it in this chapter.

ACTIVITY OPTION (p. 31): Have students respond to the following challenge: It's Friday, and a student has a 10-page paper due on Monday. His best friend has invited him home for the weekend and the student wants to go. What are the possible reactions, insights, and actions related to this situation?

ACTIVITY OPTION (p. 34): Hand students cards that state something that might cause a student to lose focus in school. Cards may include items such as these: your roommate blasts music all day, your grandmother is ill, your books cost more money than you expected, your babysitter's last day is Friday, and so forth. Depending on the size and composition of the class, make as many cards as you need. Ask students to hold up cards that cause students to lose focus, but situations they can change and refocus. Ask them whether it's possible to have control over the situation and if so, how.

ACTIVITY OPTION (p. 35): Ask students to make a list of three things that motivate and three things that hinder them. Have students lead a discussion on which ones are extrinsic and which are intrinsic.

ACTIVITY OPTION (p. 37): Give each student 10 sticky notes. Ask students to write one phrase on each paper to fill in the blank: The ideal student _____ . Repeat this prompt 10 times, each time giving the students only seconds to fill in the blank. On the board, write, "student has control" on one side and "Student has no control" on the other. Have students put their sticky notes under the heading they believe is true of their statement. Some students believe that they have no control on issues that they really do. Let students lead the discussion. This activity pairs well with Exercise 2.3.

ACTIVITY OPTION (p. 37): Divide students up so that at least two students are assigned to each of the eight ways to adjust attitude. Ask students to describe a real-life example related to the numbered point they have been assigned.

ACTIVITY OPTION (p. 40): After a discussion on performers and learners, ask students if they think it is possible to be a performer in some situations and a learner in other situations. Have students apply these concepts to themselves by describing an example when they were a performer and an example of when they were a learner. This activity can be done in conjunction with Exercise 2.5.

ACTIVITY OPTION (p. 42): Divide students into groups and present each group with a different scenario that points out how a student has made a decision based on values. Ask students to identify how the values were used to make a decision.

ACTIVITY OPTION (p. 42): Ask students to answer the following question: "If I could spend one day with someone who has died, who would it be?" Have students share their choice and explain why. This activity demonstrates what values really seem to be important to that individual. Suggest reading Mitch Albom's book *For One More Day* (2006).

ACTIVITY OPTION (p. 42): To help students understand Carol Dweck's material, have them do the Step 3: Insight in this chapter in which they write a paragraph ending to the case study about Gloria Gonzales. Do their paragraphs give hints as to whether they themselves are performers or learners? ("Gloria will never be as smart as her sister, so she should just make a career for herself in retail at the clothing store she works at." versus "Gloria should just dig in and do her best or she'll never know what she's capable of.") Compare and contrast individual student's paragraphs to search for hints about their own views of intelligence.

ACTIVITY OPTION (p. 44): Put students in groups of three or four and assign each group two letters of the word *FOCUS.* Ask students to think of successful student behaviors that begin with the letters they are assigned. Ask them how these behaviors connect to goal setting. As a class, make a banner to hang in the classroom with the word *FOCUS* with successful student attributes under each letter.

ACTIVITY OPTION (p. 44): To help diminish the abstract nature of goal setting, ask students to complete this statement: I want to pass this class with a(n):_____(Insert

Grade). Does their goal have "FOCUS: Fit, Ownership, Concreteness, Usefulness, and Stretch?"

ACTIVITY OPTION (p. 45): Have students write a letter to themselves, their parents, loved ones, or a friend listing their goals for the semester and what they will do to meet them. Provide envelopes for students and seal their letters and return these to your students at the end of the term to see if they met their goals. Have them write a paragraph about why they did or did not meet their goals upon return of the envelopes.

9. What homework might I assign?

Generating Goals
Have your students create three goals for this semester that pass the *FOCUS* test: (1) **F**it (2) **O**wnership; (3) **C**oncreteness; (4) **U**sefulness; and (5) **S**tretch. Then, have them identify three obstacles that could prevent them from reaching their goals—and how they would work around these obstacles.

"A Letter for Later" by Staley, C. (2003).
Goal: To help students describe their own behavior, set goals, make predictions, and to see whether or not they met their goals and if not, why not. (Described briefly earlier.)

Have students write a letter to themselves answering some of the important questions in this chapter. Students are to describe who they are and what they want to become. They should describe what motivates them and their values, dreams, and goals. In addition, ask them to respond to the phrase "If it is to be, it is up to me," and how they might enact this phrase in all their classes during the term. Do they think they will make smart choices, set realistic goals, be able to monitor themselves, and create their own futures? If so, describe how, and if not, why. Students will place this letter in a sealed envelope and give it to you to return the envelope to the students at the end of the term. Responding to their original impressions could become the basis of their final class writing assignment.

Journal Entries
One: Have students write a one-page journal entry, or send you an e-mail reflecting on what they learned about themselves in this chapter. You might prompt students to write about their AIMS score and what they would like them to be if they are not satisfied with their score.

Two: Have students write a one-page journal essay or send you an e-mail describing one situation in which they were extrinsically motivated and one in which they were intrinsically motivated and how they felt about each. Ask them to connect the different kinds of motivation to college success.

Three: Ask students to write a journal comparing their original response to the *FOCUS* Challenge Case about Gloria Gonzales, "What Do YOU Think?" with their final impression after reading the chapter to the "NOW What Do You Think?" section.

Four: Use the Insight → Action prompts as journal or blog assignments.

10. What have I learned in teaching this chapter that I will incorporate next time?

_____
_____
_____
_____
_____
_____
_____
_____
_____
_____
_____
_____
_____
_____
_____
_____
_____
_____
_____
_____
_____
_____
_____
_____
_____
_____
_____
_____

CHAPTER 3: LEARNING ABOUT LEARNING

1. Why is this chapter important?

Changing behavior requires that you first become aware of what you are currently doing. As an instructor, do *you* know how you learn? Do *you* know what your VARK preference is and how that impacts your teaching? Information in chapter 3 is vitally important to you, too. In this chapter, both you and your students should fill out the VARK assessment that appears for your own benefit, but you should pay particular attention to the VARK activities that will reappear as potential assignments in every chapter. The VARK is based on information input and processing—Visual, Auditory, Read/Write, and Kinesthetic (sensory modalities). For a quick review of VARK including help sheets and the opportunity to take it online, go to http://www.vark-learn.com. The help sheets assist learners on how to Intake information, SWOT (Study without Tears) and Output.

After discovering their learning style using this instrument, students will have opportunities to reinforce their preferences and try different approaches in every chapter. VARK activities appear in this and each chapter of *FOCUS on Community College Success*, and by the end of the book, students will have been able to try eleven different approaches to their strongest preference so that they develop the skills to translate between the "language" used by their instructors and their own VARK learning preferences, a critical skill for college success.

As you will see in this chapter's *FOCUS* Challenge Case about Tammy Ko, students often encounter instructors and situations in which they will need to understand how they learn best in order to study and prepare for exams appropriately. As instructors, we can't adapt to every single learning style in a class (although we can certainly try to reach them all by varying our assignments and teaching methods). Students must learn to assume responsibility for adaptation themselves.

This chapter is also important because in addition to learning about themselves, it gives students an opportunity to learn about learning and the brain and multiple intelligences. Students may find it fascinating to discover how they can create conditions that are optimal for learning, and "ah-ha" moments may happen when students realize that what works for one person may not work for another. And, above all, when they understand that they have control over their learning, students are more confident that they can succeed. The response is transformed from "I can't learn because the teacher is boring" to "Okay, this isn't working; what can *I* do about it?"

Also, in this chapter students will begin to see the pattern of the text repeated from chapters 1 and 2. The chapter begins with a Readiness Check, a *FOCUS* Challenge Case, the Challenge → Reaction → Insight → Action steps, and the recurring C-Factors—all parts of the infrastructure of the book. These C-Factors (challenge, control, curiosity, and career outlook) that appear throughout the book, will help students focus on what motivates them and why. As you and your students work through the text, it will be important to reference your students' AIMS score from chapter 2. If a student has low to moderate intrinsic motivation, it is especially important to re-emphasize the C-Factors. Remind students that it's not enough to have the *insight*; they must take *action* to achieve positive change. So taken together (the 4C's and the Challenge → Reaction → Insight → Action steps), these features will help students see that by understanding what makes them tick, and by doing something about it, they are much more likely to have positive learning outcomes in all their courses.

2. What are this chapter's learning objectives?

- ➢ How learning changes the brain
- ➢ How people are intelligent in different ways
- ➢ How students learn through their senses
- ➢ How to become a more efficient and effective learner
- ➢ How personality type can affect learning style

3. How should I launch this chapter?

This chapter can be launched in a variety of ways. A great way to introduce learning is by asking students to think back to a time when they really enjoyed learning something. It could have been in school or even on the job. Ask them to describe what it is they learned, and to think about how they learned it. This discussion can then lead to the *FOCUS* Challenge Case and additional learning—about learning! This chapter is rich with self-assessments and activities; have fun!

- **By now students should be settling in, and you may begin to see some friendships emerging in the class**. You may also see some students who are sitting alone and struggling. They may be dealing with some of the issues that are addressed in this chapter. However, be sensitive to the fact that introverted students may naturally be reluctant to engage in class; however, this does not necessarily equate to being more at risk. Think about personality issues if (or when) putting students into groups. A sole introvert in a group of extraverts may have a hard time getting a word in edgewise. Create a climate where students are the most likely to be engaged.

- **Control: Your Learning.** This is a great activity to get students to zero in on the classes they are taking this semester. It's a reflective activity that asks students to describe their classes and compare them to the optimal conditions for learning that are listed in the text. Don't pass up this activity. It's a great way for students to apply what they are learning. It also might help them identify a class in which they have to make some changes or get extra help. This activity also works well as a topic for a one-on-one office visit with you.

- **Developmental Students and Returning Adult Learners:** How are your developmental students and returning adult learners doing at this point of the semester? Consider having all students schedule a "conference" meeting with you during your office hours or just before class to check in with them. Make a point of asking them how they are doing in other classes-as well as how things are going at home and work. One issue returning adult learners may face is feelings of jealousy from family members who are not in college. If your college has a student group focusing on adult students, make a referral. Also, if students express concern about this or any other issue, refer them to any campus or off campus resources that might be available. Don't forget about the *FOCUS* on Kids worksheets. The worksheet for chapter 3 helps kids learn how they learn best and compare their learning styles (informally) with Mom's or Dad's. The *FOCUS* on Kids worksheet can lead to an interesting discussion!

- **Help students find support.** This might be the time and place to ask students if they need help. After the "Control: Your Learning" activity, students might be a bit more aware of the realities of their college experience. Most college students need one kind of help or another at some point in college. Students who need help, but can't seem to find the time or the courage to take advantage of campus resources often become retention statistics. Remind them of the support services available on your campus that were discussed in chapter 1. They may have also learned about them during orientation, but sometimes if you don't need information at the time, you don't pay close attention. Now is a time to share some information about where they can go for help. Also, see if there are common concerns in the class. Students find comfort in knowing they are not alone. Find out if there are students who are doing well in classes where others are not and connect them with each other for informal tutoring from which both "teacher" and "student" can benefit. Help students taking the same classes to form study groups. Academic and social integration are two key components of a successful college career.

- **Remember the Readiness Check at the beginning of the chapter and the Reality Check at the end**. These activities help students focus on whether they are ready to read and learn. Again, students using *FOCUS* reported that Readiness Checks become a habit, one that they also perform, not just before they begin to read, but also mentally before class begins. This habit also extends to their other courses, which is one of the activity's intentional goals.

- **Going beyond the book.** Check with your career center staff, or academic advising center to see if the Myers-Briggs Type Indicator is available for students to take. This tool will give students a more in-depth look at their personality type, going beyond VARK and multiple intelligences. Also, encourage students to look online at the vast resources about personality type, including those on the VARK website. The *FOCUS on Community College Success* online Resource Center also includes chapter enrichment activities called, "Your Type Is Showing" focused on the chapter's topic and the MBTI.

4. How should I use the *FOCUS* Challenge Case?

Just as in chapter 1, the chapter begins with a *FOCUS* Challenge Case about a real student (or a composite of many students) that depicts a challenging situation college students often face.

In this chapter, we meet Tammy Ko, a first-semester student at community college. Tammy has found college to be hectic in large part due to her work schedule. She was excited to begin work on her associate's degree in criminal justice. Tammy's advisor suggested taking the Introduction to Criminal Justice to help her confirm her career choice. Her other career research has consisted of watching crime shows on television. But, her instructor, Mr. Caldwell, is not at all what she expected. She is frustrated, not doing well on tests, and does not understand why he only talks about theories of criminology. He is not exciting (hasn't bought an article of clothing in 20 years!) and they never talk about cases like they do on her favorite TV shows. It is guaranteed that this is a situation many of your students will face at least once in their college careers. By using this *FOCUS* Challenge Case, students will begin to see the connections between who they are as learners, and how this knowledge connects to their success in college.

Use Tammy's story to get students to begin opening up and refer back to Tammy whenever you can. Ask students if they think that Tammy will have challenges in other college classes and what those challenges will be. As a part of a group discussion, ask students if they have encountered this situation in college. Most likely they have. It's important that this discussion does not become a course complaint session or an instructor-bashing one. What's really important is that students come to understand that *they* are the ones who will have to make adjustments. Other suggestions for using Tammy's story:

- Ask students to review the visual clues in the chapter opening (program description with course listing, requirements for police applicants, Tammy's essay test) and have the students tell you about Tammy before launching into a discussion.
- **Direct It!** Assign a "scene director" for the Challenge Case. Assign a student to role-play Tammy and another student to role-play Mr. Caldwell. The director can stop the scene at any point and redirect the "actors" as well as get input from the "critics"—the other students in class!

  - o Scene 1: Tammy works with Mr. Caldwell to help her understand his style and to ask him for advice on how she can be successful.
  - o Scene 2: Tammy meets with her advisor and receives advice on support services available on campus. He reminds her that the class would teach her how to think and asks her how she is doing in her other classes.
  - o Scene 3: Tammy meets with a career counselor. She asks Tammy how her career vision could be very different from the real work?
- Before getting to Step 3: Insight, ask students to speculate how Tammy's first semester might end. What options do they see for her?

5. What important features does this chapter include?

Readiness and Reality Checks

Have your students complete the Readiness Check as well as the Reality Check at the end of the chapter. Consider having them do the **Activity Option** (p. 76) as an e-mail or journal assignment and ask them to provide an example of how they will use what they have learned to prepare for an exam.

Challenge → Reaction → Insight → Action prompts

Throughout the book, students will be reminded about the learning system used in *FOCUS*: The Challenge → Reaction → Insight → Action system. This learning system is part of the fundamental infrastructure of the text. The Challenge → Reaction in this chapter asks students to offer opinions on why Tammy is having difficulty learning in her Introduction to Criminology class. Furthermore, students are challenged to determine Tammy's sensory modality for taking in information. In the Insight → Action section, after students have reviewed key concepts on learning styles, they are asked if they would react differently to the initial questions about Tammy. Finally, students are asked how they will put this information into action for their own learning.

Stressed Out?

Sweating makes you smart and can reduce stress! Ask students to keep an exercise log for a week. Regular exercise helps reduce stress and takes care of physical needs so students can learn. Have students complete a short journal entry after 20 or so minutes of physical activity. How did they feel after exercise? Did it help to improve their mood? Were they able to concentrate more easily after exercise? Have students indicate their overall stress level for the day. An online exercise calculator can be found at http://www.prohealth.com/weightloss/tools/exercise/calculator1_2.cfm.

VARK Activity

This activity is designed to help students make connections between their preferred VARK learning modality and an actual assignment. Remind students that the reason they are doing this is to help them understand themselves and make the most of their preferences. If students are multimodal, recommend that they do more than one activity or that they vary activities from chapter to chapter. By the end of the book, students will have been introduced to 11 different ways to learn via their preferred modality or modalities.

Self-Assessments

This chapter has two key assessments: the VARK Learning Styles Assessment and an informal instrument on multiple intelligences. Your students may not completely comprehend how to apply their results to their coursework. Here is a good opportunity to use your own results in a "teachable moment." Connect your learning preference and multiple intelligences to your past learning experiences. There may even be a correlation between your chosen discipline and your results! In addition to these instruments, there is a self-assessment on a student's classes and optimal learning conditions. Also, students should begin to start connecting who they are with who they want to become. As students go through the text, each chapter presents a personal interview with a person in a certain career and highlights for students the most common skills for that occupation through the "Career Outlook" feature.

C-Factors

If you recall, each chapter of *FOCUS* contains features related to the four aspects of intrinsic motivation: "Curiosity," "Control Your Learning," "Career Outlook," "Challenge *FOCUS* Case" and online quizzes at the end of each chapter. Some of the C-factors are more prominent than others depending on the content for each chapter. Before much learning takes place people have to be curious about something. Many of the readings and activities cultivate curiosity, but a great one for this chapter is "Multiple Intelligences Self-Assessment" and the "VARK Learning Styles Assessment." Throughout the book students are asked to control their learning and think about their toughest task, either in terms of a class or on the jobs. Because this chapter is about learning, the focus is on what student can do to take control of their learning. More often than not, perhaps, students have more control than they think they do.

The "Career Outlook" is a great feature for each chapter and in this chapter we meet Mark Brown, NYPD Police Officer. Many students are interested in criminal justice careers. Make sure students are aware of and understand Officer Brown's advice that being a police officer is not like it is on TV. Through the use of this feature students will begin to make connections between themselves and careers, since they will be asked questions such as "What would you find most challenging about this type of career?" "What would you find most satisfying about this type of career?" and "What challenges would be present in this career?" Also, see the suggested homework assignment **Careers That Match Me!** below.

6. Which in-text exercises should I use?

Three exercises are built into this chapter. Here are descriptions of why they have been included, how much time each one will probably take, and how you might debrief them.

EXERCISE 3.1 WHAT IS LEARNING?

Why do this activity?
This activity is a great way to begin the chapter on learning. This activity is designed to assess student's beliefs about learning. Many students have a negative view of learning and will answer these statements as being true.

What are the challenges and what can you expect?
Instruct students to answer the questions honestly. Some students do not enjoy learning and have not had positive experiences in education.

How much time will it take?

This activity should take about 10-15 minutes to take and debrief.

How should I debrief?

This activity can be done in class with a group discussion on student's beliefs. It can also be done as a homework activity. Ask students to elaborate on the statements they marked as true. Why do they believe they are true? This exercise could also be used as a pre- and post-assessment for the chapter.

EXERCISE 3.2 MULTIPLE INTELLIGENCES SELF-ASSESSMENT

Why do this activity?

This informal assessment helps students discover how they are smart. It introduces the theory of multiple intelligences in a fun, practical manner. Upon completion, students have a better idea of their top three intelligence areas. Make sure you have done this exercise yourself as well.

What are the challenges and what can you expect?

Students typically need additional assistance in learning about the intelligence categories, particularly Interpersonal and Intrapersonal Intelligence. Students are sometimes surprised at their top three intelligences. Be prepared to debrief and consider asking students to journal about what they have learned from this exercise.

How much time will it take?

This activity should take 20-30 minutes depending on method of debrief used.

How should I debrief?

Ask students to determine your top three intelligences. List them on the board and have them provide you examples of why they think this is your intelligence. Reveal your three intelligence areas and provide specific examples for each of the three. Ask each student to list his/her top three. Were they surprised? Did they expect others to be present? Remind students this is an informal assessment, not a "scientific" instrument. Ask students how they study and have them compare their way to the list of suggested ways on page 64 of the text. Are they on track or do they have some opportunities to improve their techniques?

EXERCISE 3.3 VARK LEARNING STYLES ASSESSMENT

Why do this activity?

This activity helps students understand their preferred learning modality. By simply knowing the way they prefer to learn, and by using that preference in a variety of ways, learning will seem easier and certainly more efficient. Make sure you take this assessment, too. You may learn something about yourself that you suspected and now will get confirmation about.

What are the challenges and what can you expect?

All of us are curious to learn things about ourselves. This activity is easy, and students will enjoy adding up their final scores to see which of the learning styles they prefer. Many students will fit into the category of multimodal (having a preference for more than one modality). These students have more flexibly in learning than those students who have a strong preference for a single modality. However, to truly believe they have mastered material, multimodal learners will feel they have to make use of all their preferred modalities.

How much time will it take?

This activity should take about 20-30 minutes, depending on how much time you spend debriefing.

How should I debrief?

It's always a good idea to ask students if anything they learned by taking the assessment surprised them. Most likely students will feel validated about the way they learn. Most students agree immediately with their results although some may need more time to think about it. Ask students to share a learning experience that they feel was a good match for their learning style. See if you can get them to articulate exactly what the experience was like, why they think it is indicative of their preference(s), and what was especially positive about it. Be sure that you refer to Figure 3.1, which lists general strategies, study strategies, and exam strategies for each of the styles. VARK author Neil Fleming believes that people taking the VARK are in the best position to judge the accuracy of their scores, and that students should learn in college by engaging in "variations on a theme," using their preferred modalities in a variety of ways.

7. Which additional exercises might enrich students' learning?

Who Am I?
Class activity
Materials needed: Index cards with learning preferences written on them
Time: 30-50 minutes, depending on the size of the group
Goal: To help students identify the behaviors that are typically indicative of particular learning styles

In groups of three, students will role-play having a meeting over coffee. Each student will be given a card with a particular VARK preference or multiple intelligence and will act out their role in this casual meeting. The meeting could even be a meeting between a hypothetical instructor and student. After about five minutes the classmates who are observing are to write down the type of each character. It's okay to exaggerate! You might even use this activity for students to disclose who they are! You can guess along with the students.

Think/Pair/Share Activity
Class activity
Materials needed: none
Time: 10-20 minutes

Goal: To get students thinking about a class they are taking now where there is not a good fit between them and the instructor

Sometimes it's difficult to get a discussion going in class. This think/pair/share activity provides a mechanism for all students to get involved and can be used for any topic.

- **Think:** Individually have students identify a class, where their learning style does not match their professors' teaching style. (Note that a professor's teaching style may not be the same as his or her learning style, but it should be safe to say that learning style influences teaching style to some degree.) Also, students must identify one thing that they can do to help themselves succeed in this class. (3-5 minutes)
- **Pair** up with the student next to them and discuss their responses. The students will decide on one or two issues to bring up to the group. (3-5 minutes)
- **Share** with the class their responses and as a group the class will discuss some common responses that students encounter with their instructors as well as identify some techniques to help them succeed. (5-10 minutes)

Help Wanted!

Class activity

Materials needed: Newsprint for each group of 4-5 students and index cards with an occupation on it

Time: 10-20 minutes, depending on the size of the group

Goal: To help students recognize the skills connected to success in a career

Ask groups of four to five students to develop a help wanted ad with the learning type needed for a particular job. The jobs that each group will be given are artist, political candidate, president of a company, and social worker. Their job is to create a job description that would result in selecting a person who would work well in the job, using either VARK or multiple intelligences.

Help Is on the Way!

Class Activity (or an out of class assignment where students work in groups)

Material needed: none

Time: 40-50 minutes

Goal: To help students to problem solve a mismatch between a student and instructor

Present students with this challenge: Julia is attending a class on economics. The first day of class, the teacher says, "Okay students, you don't have to read your books, but the information in the book is on the midterm and final. In this class, it's all about real world economics. You will set up a business—it doesn't matter to me what kind—and at the end of the semester you must demonstrate your understanding of the key principles of economics as a result of this project. Class is dismissed for today. Come in next Monday with your proposal." Julia leaves the class in tears and tells her classmate, "I know I am going to fail, I just don't know what he wants or how even to begin!" In small groups, have students outline what Julia should do. In addition, have students speculate about the different VARK learning style Julia and her professor might have. Julia can't drop the class or change sections!

8. What other activities can I incorporate to make the chapter my own?

This chapter might present an opportunity to check in with your class to see how they are doing in their other classes. Developmental students might benefit from reflecting on how important it is to continue building the foundation for success. Adult learners may need to have time to discuss how they are adapting to college and how they are balancing work, home and school. Ask your students what is going on, and ask them if they need help.

Scan for particular annotations in the Instructor's Edition for ways to enrich the material for your particular group:

1) **Teachable Moments** (places to capitalize on a particular learning opportunity)
2) **Activity Options** (additional exercises to introduce or emphasize content)
3) **Sensitive Situations** (alerts about in-class discussion topics that may generate possible controversy, embarrassment, or discomfort among certain students)
4) **Emotional Intelligence (EI) Emphasis/Research** (research on EI that reinforces a tie between non-cognitive variables and college success)
5) **Developmental Students** (provides insight and suggestions to working with students who may be enrolled in developmental education courses)

Included here, all in one place are Activity Options taken from the Annotated Instructor's Edition.

Think about your own teaching style based on your VARK preference. Share this with students and while the best teachers are those who can teach to all types, this is not often the case. Make sure students understand this.

ACTIVITY OPTION (p. 51): Give students lengthy directions for a fictitious assignment that would be due in the next class. Give them instructions about where they would find an article to read about studying in college, and tell them that you want them to write a three- to five-page paper, then change your mind, and make it a one-page essay. Confuse them; change what you want. And then go right on to the next part of the class. See if anyone raises a hand for clarification. Someone should! If not, ask someone to repeat what is due. Discuss some of the strategies, if any, students used to clarify the assignment.

ACTIVITY OPTION (p. 55): Ask students to work in teams to build a learning tower. Draw a tower consisting of four blocks on the bottom row, three on the third, two on the second, and one at the top. The top block should be labeled "successful student." Students are to fill in what they need to know first before they are successful students. Each row should be a prerequisite to the next row.

ACTIVITY OPTION (p. 56): Determine whether there are any commonalities among the students' responses to this "Control Your Learning" exercise. Which courses do most students find the easiest? Which are the most difficult? Which are the least interesting? Have students share their responses so they can learn from their peers.

ACTIVITY OPTION (p. 59): Have students add up the number of checks they had in each category. Then group students according to their highest numbers. Give each group five minutes to share with each other their favorite classes (present or past). Ask students to find common threads in the classes they identified. Have the groups report to the class and discuss what they do to succeed in classes that they don't enjoy as much.

ACTIVITY OPTION (p. 62): Ask students to read the Intelligence-Oriented Study Techniques on page 64. Have them highlight the techniques they currently use and circle the ones they would like to try. Are they all in one intelligence type? Encourage your students to begin to develop some of the other types they are not as strong in. Doing so will help them in other classes where the teaching style may be very different from their more highly developed intelligence type.

ACTIVITY OPTION (p. 63): With their books closed, read the scenario out of the book on page 65 about a rich relative who has left you some money and you have decided to use it to buy a new car. What would you do? Ask students what questions they would need to consider to make their decision. Have students make a list of the steps they would take to get the car. Then have the students read the steps listed in the book a person would take based on their learning style. Ask them to compare notes. Did their process match any of the specific learning styles?

ACTIVITY OPTION (p. 66): On the board or on a large piece of poster board, list the four modalities (Visual, Aural, Read/Write, and Kinesthetic) and have students write their name and score of their top two modalities. For example, a student might put her name and a 10 under Visual and her name and an 8 under Aural. Are there similarities in the class? Do these students enjoy the same classes? Now ask students to put their dominant multiple intelligence next to their name. Are they beginning to see any patterns? Ask each student to describe one way in which they can use their dominant learning style and strong intelligence to help them in college (if there is not enough time in class, they can e-mail the class with their answer, or bring their response to the next class).

ACTIVITY OPTION (p. 67): Ask students to review Figure 3.1 (p. 67). Have students highlight the study strategies they presently use and circle the ones they would like to try.

ACTIVITY OPTION (p.70): Using the example in number 3 on page 67, determine the percentages of students in your class that are visual, aural, read/write, kinesthetic, and multimodal. Can you use this information to adjust your teaching style for the rest of the semester?

ACTIVITY OPTION (p. 72): Ask students to summarize their responses to the Reality Check and send it to you via e-mail. In addition, ask them to tell you the most significant thing they learned about themselves and give a specific example of how they will use what they've learned to prepare for an exam.

9. What homework might I assign?

Your students have gained a considerable amount of information about themselves by now. They know more about how they are motivated, their learning style, and their dominant multiple intelligence(s). Using the information they have, have students create a customized learning plan for their toughest course. Their plan should include how they will use their class notes, how they will read their assigned coursework, and how they will prepare for exams.

Who I am, what I know I can and can't do well, and what I am going to do about it
Goal: To help students to describe their own behavior, using their VARK preference
Assign students to do a PowerPoint presentation similar to the one described in the activity option above. Ask students to present to the class and report on one thing that they learned about themselves from this chapter, describe it in some detail, and identify how it will impact how they learn.

Careers That Match Me!
Goal: Students will use their VARK preference and top multiple intelligences to review possible careers, which might be a strong match for them.
Assign students this activity and let them know they can present the results in a way that matches their VARK preference. For example, visual learners may choose to submit a Power Point presentation. Aural learners may present a speech on their career matches while Read/Write may choose to do a 1- to 2-page report on this activity. Kinesthetic learners could choose to report out their on-the-job observations from their chosen career matches. Direct students to the Occupational Outlook Handbook at http://www.bls.gov/OCO/ for additional career information.

Journal Entries
One: Have students write a one-page journal entry, or send you an e-mail reflecting on what they learned about themselves in this chapter. You might prompt students by asking them to choose the three specific things that they learned about themselves. They can list their specific scores, but they must also indicate something that they currently do that reflects that behavior. Ask students to explain what about their particular learning style is a good match for college and what might put them at risk. What do they plan to do about any risk factors that are present?

Two: Have students write a one-page journal essay or send you an e-mail describing one situation in which they were really engaged in the class. What made it so? Can they also describe a situation where they were completely disconnected and explain why? How can they take what they learned about themselves in the first class and apply it to the second.

Three: Use the Insight → Action prompt as journal or blog assignments.

10. What have I learned in teaching this chapter that I will incorporate next time?

_____

_____

_____

_____

_____

_____

_____

_____

_____

_____

_____

_____

_____

_____

_____

_____

_____

_____

_____

_____

_____

_____

_____

_____

_____

_____

_____

_____

_____

_____

_____

_____

_____

CHAPTER 4: MANAGING YOUR TIME, ENERGY AND MONEY

1. Why is this chapter important?

There is probably no single topic discussed more often in student success courses than time management. This is a buzz word that we instructors hear often: "Oh, you teach a course on time management." And often we all at one time or another bemoan our own challenges in this area: "If I just had a few more hours in the day." Poor time management skills are one of the leading reasons why students are not successful in college. What is really important about this chapter is that simply making lists and prioritizing how to manage one's day or week is not the answer to time management. Successful students know what makes them tick, and learn it's more about managing your own behavior—how *you* manage your own time—than what you are doing at any given moment. Have you ever carefully analyzed how much time a project actually took you? Did you count the times you got up for a snack? How about looking out the window? Organizing your closet? Daydreaming about your upcoming break? It's not about the actual time, but what you are doing with your time on the task.

The chapter also makes a unique point among college success texts by discussing the relationship between time management, attention management, and energy management. Managing time becomes much less of a challenge when we manage our energy expenditure—when we are at our best physically, emotionally, mentally, and spiritually. When we're in balance, we're most productive.

Another really critical focus in this chapter is how to identify the common time wasters, and what to do about them. Just as students might have done in chapter 3 on other subjects, in this chapter students will be filling out logs and forms. Theses exercises aren't meant to be busywork and turned in for a grade, they can really help students get a solid handle on analyzing where and when they waste time. An important part of this exercise is to understand *how students are feeling during this process.* Are they wasting time because they really don't understand the assignment? Are they frustrated because the assignment is overwhelming? Of course, using the Insight → Action model, it is essential for students to actually change their behavior in order to reduce the amount of time they are wasting.

In addition, in this chapter the awful "P" word (procrastination) will be addressed with some strategies on how to avoid procrastination and just do it! Finally, students will address how to realistically balance work, school, and personal life.

2. What are this chapter's learning objectives?

➤ Why time management alone doesn't work
➤ How time management differs from energy management
➤ How to schedule a way to succeed
➤ How the P word can derail anyone
➤ How to realistically balance work, school, and personal life
➤ How to manage money

3. How should I launch this chapter?

This chapter could not come at a better time. In fact, it was planned that way. After experiencing a bit of a honeymoon period when it may have seemed to some students that they could do it all, stress sets in. They might have thought, "This is not so bad; I can manage everything," but around week four things begin to pile up. Their courses, which may have begun with review work they recognize from high school, have now taken off into uncharted territory. Now is the time to really tackle time management. And, students are ready to learn more. Begin your discussion of this chapter with a simple show of hands: Ask students if they are having trouble fitting everything in and managing time. Don't be surprised if all your students raise their hands.

- **Find out if a number of students in your class are taking other classes together.** Earlier the text discusses the value of working in groups. Especially for those extraverts in your class, working in groups may provide the help they need to get them on the right track. Students who are in the same classes will find that their approach to the same exam or quiz might be different. This is a good place to talk about quality study time—not just study time in general. Even if students prefer not to work in pairs or groups, students in the same classes can share their plans for how they will approach the upcoming tests and quizzes.

- **Developmental Students and Returning Adult Learners:** Returning adult learners (and all students) will have something in common with the *FOCUS* Challenge Case student Derek Johnson. Many students struggle with balancing school, work and home responsibilities, and this chapter is designed to give students some new tools to help with this balancing act. Encourage all students, but in particular developmental students, to read this chapter carefully and encourage completion of the activities and exercises. Remind students that all learners can become highly motivated and focused regardless of their current situation. The chapter 4 *FOCUS* on Kids worksheet will help your students with young children to teach them about time management and planning ahead. These worksheets are available in CourseMate.

- **Find out how many students have upcoming tests.** Take a few moments to see if anyone has several tests in the next week or so and how they are planning to prepare. Do a little survey in class to see how much time students plan to allot for studying for quizzes that are coming up. You will most likely find variation, so get a discussion going. Students may be surprised to learn how much time good students actually invest.

- **This is a time where you legitimately will find differences in students' schedules, and sometimes they are beyond the students' control.** Like the *FOCUS* Challenge Case student Derek, students' plates are often full. He may be a non-traditional college student, but most students have many outside responsibilities. A healthy step is to acknowledge the fact that there are some things out of our control. Using your good emotional intelligence skills, remind students that the one thing we can change is how we respond to situations. Sure, we could all cut back on an activity or two, but taking care of a sick mother, or working two jobs to support the family is sometimes something students must do. What these students can control is how they handle their challenging, time-consuming situations. Skilled time management and management of energy and emotions are keys to success.

- **Challenge your students to consider their energy management as well as their time management skills.** Often, students are so concerned with scheduling time to study that they forget about their energy management. Challenge students to take breaks during their study times. For example, encourage students not to read for several hours at one time. Instead, encourage them to study in 60-75 minute intervals. At the end of this study session, students should take a 15-20 minute break. This break is a great opportunity for students to grab a snack, walk around for a few minutes, or just relax. Their break should leave students feeling refreshed, which should allow them to easily refocus on their task.

- **Going beyond the book.** There are lots of resources about time management. For example, Steven Covey's book *The 7 Habits of Highly Effective People* (1990) might be one of the books that students in your class have read. Make sure that you tap the resources and knowledge of people in the class, especially if you have some adult learners in your class—ask them to share some of the tips they have learned from the workplace. Workplaces often have sessions on time and energy management, and these students might bring great tools to the table to share.

4. How should I use the *FOCUS* Challenge Case?

Derek Johnson is a student committed to getting his degree. He is pursuing an associate's degree in accounting, and he realizes that he has to get his degree in order to advance in his career. Five years after high school, he is ready. Or is he? He has a full time job, a wife, and one child with another on the way. He is heavily involved in singing in his church choir, coaching, and working out every day. He balks about the idea of a 12-page paper, and spends more time worrying about it than actually doing it. Derek seems to think that this 12-page paper is unreasonable. After all, he has a lot to do! Derek doesn't see anything that he can drop from his schedule.

Derek is not alone; most nontraditional students face similar challenges in balancing their responsibilities. It might be a good idea to point out the connection between attitude and motivation that was discussed in chapter 2 at this point. Ask your students what areas of Derek's life are interfering with his ability to complete his 12-page paper. One way to approach this challenge case is to break your students into groups of two or three. Ask each group to create a plan for Derek that includes all of his responsibilities: completing family tasks, going to his job and completing his project, and completing his paper—all in the allotted four weeks. After 10-15 minutes, ask each group to present its plan. You are sure to get different plans, which could help your students find a planning system that works best for them! Other options include:

- **Direct It!** Assign a "scene director" for the Challenge Case. Assign a student to role-play Derek, another student to role-play his wife Justine and another student to play Derek's boss. The director can stop the scene at any point and redirect the "actors" as well as get input from the "critics"—the other students in class!
  - o Scene 1: Derek needs to have a conversation with his wife about his commitment level to college. What could he say to Justine and how would she react?
  - o Scene 2: Justine wants to support Derek with his education, but feels he has too many things going on. What could she tell him that is both supportive and realistic?
  - o Scene 3: Derek needs support from his boss in order to be successful in school. What could Derek ask of his boss? What could his boss say to Derek that would encourage him to continue with his education?
- Ask students to review the images in the *FOCUS* Challenge Case. What story do the images tell?
- Ask students if Derek could reprioritize his commitments: working out, his brother's visit, coaching, etc.?
- What time and energy management techniques would students suggest for Derek?

5. What important features does this chapter include?

Again, you will see some of the important recurring themes in this book through these features.

Readiness and Reality Checks
This is a Readiness Check that students might be a little more willing to engage in, but they might not yet see the importance. If they are traditional students, they may not share some of Derek's responsibilities; however, they surely have many things to juggle, regardless. After students complete this Readiness Check, see if there are variations in the class responses. Is it because different students have different levels of things to manage? But the truth is, as any busy person will tell you, you will always make time to finish something that is important to you. Students may not know as much about money management or find it uncomfortable to talk about their situation. While students may think they know a lot about time management and their personal financial situation, the reality is that knowing is not necessarily doing. Most students are eager to learn more.

Challenge → Reaction → Insight → Action prompt
By now both you are your students are thoroughly familiar with the Challenge → Reaction → Insight → Action system. Each chapter is framed by these four steps. Students are again asked to describe the *FOCUS* Challenge Case issue and to create an ending for the case. In the Challenge → Reaction section students are asked to describe Derek's time management system and suggest three realistic ways for him to

balance his life. In Insight → Action section students are asked how they will apply what they have learned in this chapter to their own time and energy management.

Stressed Out?
A fourth dimension of energy interconnected with physical, emotional, and mental—spiritual energy—is important to many first year students. Four out of five new students are interested in spirituality. Take time with your students to help them explore their values, inner direction and ponder the meaning of life. Ask students how they slow down to think deeply about these issues.

Cultivate Your Curiosity: Choose to Choose
Is more giving us less? Are you a maximizer or a satisficer? We make many choices every day. Being inundated with choices causes individuals to invest great amounts of time and energy and can lead to self-doubt and dread. In this section students can review Schwartz's four recommendations to lower stress in a choice filled world. Make the choice to spend some time reviewing these recommendations and ask students to reflect on how they can choose to choose!

Careers Outlook
In this chapter, we meet Shaun Moreno, Accountant. Shaun held a variety of jobs on the path to becoming an accountant. Experiences in retail, customer service, and food service helped him understand business as a process. Shaun helps readers understand that this career can result in working longer hours during certain periods of the year. Take a show of hands: Who in the class is interested in becoming an accountant or accounting assistant? Why or why not?

VARK Activity
This activity is designed to help students understand that their preferred VARK learning modality even impacts the way they learn to manage time. You might even bring in a few different planners, and ask students to identify which they prefer and see if there are differences in what students chose, based on their preferences in learning.

When students return to class, they can group according to the activity they chose, take a few minutes and in one or two sentences describe to the rest of the class what they learned, what was helpful to them, and what was not. If time does not permit, just ask a few students to report what they learned, or have students send you a quick e-mail.

FOCUS TV: Procrastination
Even if you used the *FOCUS* TV segment on procrastination in chapter 1, it is a good idea to show it again with this chapter. Included in the FOCUSPoints, this humorous and informative segment discusses procrastination from the perspective of a life coach and a panel of students. This segment can be a great way to start a discussion of procrastination and how students can gain techniques to fight the "P" word.

6. Which in-text exercises should I use?

There are eight exercises built into this chapter. Included here are descriptions of why they have been included, what challenges you might expect, and how you might debrief each one.

EXERCISE 4.1 WHERE DID THE TIME GO?

Why do this activity?
This activity assists students in seeing how they spend their time. Some students will be amazed at how much time non-class activities take in a week.

What are the challenges and what can I expect?
No real challenges are evident with this activity. Some students will minimize the amount of time they actually spend socializing and hanging out. Remind students to be honest to get a true picture of where the time goes.

How much time will it take?
This exercise should take about 10 minutes to complete and debrief depending on method of debriefing.

How should I debrief?
This activity can be debriefed in a number of ways. Here are two: Ask students to record the amount of time they have remaining on the board, without their names. Some students will have very few hours remaining in their week; some will already be in deficit. Ask students how difficult it is to find time to study. Ask them how they can make adjustments in other activities to gain more time for studying. Another variation on debriefing this activity is to follow the Activity Option suggestion on page 81 and have students line up in a continuum from most hours spent studying to least. Ask them if they are satisfied where they are on the continuum, if not where would they want to be? What steps can they take to increase the number of hours they spend studying?

EXERCISE 4.2 TIME MONITOR

Why do this activity?
This activity helps students see the activities that make up their day. The Time Monitor lists a day's worth of time in 30-minute segments. This activity asks students to record how they believe they spent their day yesterday and how they are spending their time today.

What are the challenges and what can I expect?
Memory might be the biggest challenge to this activity in trying to remember yesterday. This exercise can be used as a homework assignment that is collected for the next class. By assigning it for completion outside of class, students can take the time needed to reconstruct what they did yesterday and have the time to log their activities for the present day.

How much time will it take?
Recording of yesterday's activities generally takes students about 30-45 minutes to recall and record. The recording of how they spend their "today" should take the entire day.

How should I debrief?
Collecting this assignment and making comments on each student's Time Monitor is important. Ask students how their memory of "yesterday" compared with their recording of "today." Remind students that no one is perfect in how they spend their time. What did they record that surprised them because it took as much time as it did? Ask students what would they change if they could.

EXERCISE 4.3 TERM ON A PAGE

Why do this activity?
It's essential that students get to see, on paper, the whole term at a glance. Also, they might not be aware of drop/add deadlines, or they will want to know when these dates are. When students were in high school, their schedules were more structured. They knew that they would be in class every day, and sometimes they even had a built-in study hall. Some high schools even have hotlines for parents or students to call in about what assignments are due. High schools often build in time management systems for students, but that's not the case in college. Some students are naturally good at managing their schedules, and others not. By seeing the entire semester after using their course syllabi to record tests, quizzes and papers, they might have second thoughts about going away for the weekend, for example, with a heavy week coming up.

What are the challenges and what can you expect?
One of the challenges of this activity is that not every instructor gives a detailed syllabus. Let's hope that is not the case, but if it is, encourage students to ask the professor for more information. The syllabus may say things like "there will be a number of tests and quizzes that will be determined" or "TBA" listed by assignments. Encourage students to be proactive with their instructors. Check to see if students in your class have the same course and instructors. If students go in pair or groups it may be less intimidating for the students, and more time efficient for the instructor to tell a group of students the same thing. Who knows, it might even motivate the instructor to get more specific about course expectations for students. If students are reluctant to write in their book, ask them to copy this page or recreate Figure 4.2 in a document or spreadsheet.

How much time will it take?
The amount of time this activity takes will depend on if students do this outside of class time (probably the best option) and report back to the class. If you choose this option, the in-class time is about 30 minutes.

How should I debrief?

You could debrief this activity a number of different ways. You can ask students to work in small groups to see if there are any common challenges. Most likely they will identify mid-term week as a busy one, right before Thanksgiving, and, of course, final exam week. Have each group identify one or two things that they will do to manage these busy weeks. Tell students it's not enough to say they will manage their time. Ask them specifically what they will do. Will they finish a paper before they go out for a few hours on a weekend night? Will they study with friends if they are in the same classes? Or, you might ask students to send you an e-mail to identify their biggest time management challenges and what they will do about them. Again, ask students to be specific. Or, you can simply have a class discussion about the benefits of planning. This discussion can lead into one about using planners and the different types available.

EXERCISE 4.4 SO MUCH TO DO—SO LITTLE TIME

Why do this activity?

It's important to show students that they really do have choices in how they spend their time. Like Derek, who didn't seem to think he had much control over his schedule, students think they just can't eliminate things. Also some students put priorities in the wrong place; sometimes putting others' needs before their own. Having students identify the criteria they use to assign items an "A, B, or C" and striking through what's not urgent or important is valuable and because it's not *their* list, they might be able to make harder choices and then incorporate the time management principles they've used into their own schedules. Consider having pairs work on this activity together so that they can discuss their choices.

What are the challenges and what can you expect?

There should not be many challenges in this activity. Students simply have to place a letter before each statement or cross it out. However, there may be differences of opinion between students, which can generate productive discussion as students discuss their rationales.

How much time will it take?

It's a quick in-class activity that can be discussed on the spot.

How should I debrief?

Divide the class into four groups and assign each group a letter, A, B or C, and the final "cross out/not urgent or important group." Groups identify and list only the statements they are assigned to. Groups report out and describe why they identified certain statements and other members of the class add or subtract to the list. When students add or subtract, they must identify why. A good class discussion about priorities should evolve.

EXERCISE 4.5 ARE YOU A PREEMPTIVE, PEOPLE-PLEASING, PERFECTIONISTIC PROCRASTINATOR?

Why do this activity?
This activity is designed to help students understand the four kinds of common problematic time management. Before beginning this activity, it might be helpful to think about yourself in relation to the 4 Ps-how would you describe yourself and what techniques do you use to overcome them? Share this with the class and ask if they can identify one or more Ps for themselves.

What are the challenges and what can I expect?
There are no real challenges associated with this activity. Ask students to brainstorm either as a large group or in small groups to review ways these individuals can improve their time management skills.

How much time will it take?
This activity should take 15-20 minutes including time to debrief.

How should I debrief?
If done in small groups, ask the groups to report out on the advice they would give each type of individual. If you did not disclose your problematic P type, now would be a good time to do so. Share with the class how you improve your time management skills.

EXERCISE 4.6 WHO, ME, PROCRASTINATE?

Why do this activity?
This activity asks students to review a list of 10 items and check the degree to which they normally procrastinate. The first five are typical procrastination items, the last five are generally prioritized much higher! This activity helps students to see the layers of procrastination and some of the reasons for procrastinating.

What are the challenges and what can I expect?
There are no real challenges associated with this activity. You could also encourage students to come up with a personalized list of tasks they often procrastinate in completing.

How much time will it take?
This activity should take 15-20 minutes including time to debrief.

How should I debrief?
Ask students to report out their "Always" list and if you asked them to develop their own lists, add items to the board to see if students share common procrastination items. Also ask students to share their reasons for procrastination. Alternatively, you could ask students to journal about these reasons or write a short paper on their results.

EXERCISE 4.7 HOW FISCALLY FIT ARE YOU?

Why do this activity?
This quick checklist will help students take stock of their financial planning. Students often learn money management from their families, either good skills or not so good skills. This checklist asks students to think about 10 common fiscal practices and then rate themselves on the practice.

What are the challenges and what can you expect?
While there are no challenges with this activity, students come from a variety of financial backgrounds, and it is best not to discuss students' results openly.

How much time will it take?
This activity should take students about five minutes to complete, and another 10 minutes to debrief.

How should I debrief?
After students have completed the checklist, ask them to respond in writing to three questions. What surprised me about this activity? What is one thing I am most proud of from this activity? What is one thing I am going to change? Ask students to turn their written responses in to you for review.

EXERCISE 4.8 CREATE A SPENDING LOG

Why do this activity?
Where does the money go? How many times have you heard this question (or asked it yourself)?! After students review a sample spending log, ask them to take one day that is representative of any day to track their spending.

What are the challenges and what can you expect?
This activity should be assigned outside of class to complete. Ask students to bring their log back to class for review and discussion.

How much time will it take?
The log should take students one full day to complete and about 20-30 minutes to debrief in class.

How should I debrief?
Ask students to share their logs. What could they have done without? How could they be wiser shoppers? If students planned better, how much could they save?

---

7. Which additional exercises might enrich students' learning?

<u>Just Say No!</u>
Class activity/role play
Materials needed: None
Time: 15 minutes

Goal: To help students understand that they just have to say "No!" sometimes

Ask for two volunteers from the class. Student A and Student B are good friends. Student A has two tickets to a sold out concert for tonight. The other student (B) has a midterm at 8:00 a.m. tomorrow and has to study but agrees to go out. Student A's job is to get student B to go out to dinner, and then the concert, and then out for coffee, extending the night as long as he/she can. At what point will the student say "no"? (Student B is not to be told of the plan to extend the evening.). Ask students if they have ever been in a situation like this and what they did about it.

The Ten-Minute Teller

Class activity: Discussion after students do this activity at home

Materials needed: Timer

Time: 20 minutes

Goal: To help students break down tasks into small increments and stay focused

Sometimes when tasks are not pleasant or seem as if they will take forever, if they are broken down into smaller segments they seem much more manageable. For homework, ask students to do some activity that they don't want to do. Break it down into three ten-minutes segments. Segments don't even have to be back to back. At the end of 10 minutes, students can take a break or continue. Before they begin the next segment, ask students to take a few minutes to record what they accomplished in the previous segment. Have students come to the next class to discuss what they chose to do, and if the 10 minute segments helped them to stay focused. Did they accomplish more than they thought they would? Once they got going, did they feel better? Sometimes just beginning something is all students need to avert procrastinating.

Help Me with My Bad Habits!

Materials needed: nothing

Time: 30-50 minutes, depending on the size of the group

Goal: To help students to identify bad habits they have that cause them to waste time and come up with strategies to help

Divide the class into two groups. Each group is asked to come up with five bad habits for wasting time. For example, a student might be ready to sit down to work on the computer and start to surf the net, or play solitaire. After five minutes each group gives the other group the five habits they identified. It might be a good idea to create a "master" list of all the bad habits. Give each group another five minutes to come up with suggestion on how to "break the habit."

My Favorite Planner

Class activity

Materials needed: Students need to bring in their planners

Time: 30 minutes, depending on the size of the group

Goal: To help students see the different kinds of planners and how people in the class are using them

Ask students to bring their planners to class and take turns coming to the front of the class, and in two minutes describe why they like the planner (or not). Also, ask students to show what they write in their planners. You might bring in the college planner, if one is given out to students during new student orientation, for example, and they have forgotten that they have it. These planners are helpful since they include dates that are important on a particular campus. Students may be surprised to see that there are day planners, week at a glance, month at a glance, and ones that combine many features. Students must feel comfortable with their planner, and feel that it is helping them. If not, they just won't use it. Also, many students use the scheduling function on their cell phones as a planner. Discuss the pros and cons of this method of time management.

Assignment Calculator: You _CAN_ Beat the Clock!
Materials needed: Students need access to the Internet and a printer, and an assignment from another class to use in planning
Time: 20-30 minutes to complete outside of class, 20 minutes to share in class
Goal: To help students understand the importance of planning for the completion of a major paper or other assignment
Direct students to have an assignment that is due at some future point of the semester and have them to go to www.lib.umn.edu/help/calculator/ and complete the Assignment Calculator. Students can set up emails to remind them of critical steps and print out an easy to use checklist. Have students bring in their checklists and present to the class on how they could use this for future assignments.

8. What other activities can I incorporate to make the chapter my own?

Take full advantage of the activities that are part of the annotations in the text as well as lists and activities in the chapter such as "How time flies!," "To do or Not to do," or "Lame excuses for blowing off class." Consider assigning students to lead particular activities. You can even break your class into segments—some segments you lead the class, and have students lead other segments. Allowing students to lead the class is one way to engage your introverted students. Plus, you can sit back, relax, and enjoy watching. Think about putting these activity options from the annotations included here on a small sheet of paper and have students pick from a basket. Since control is an important C factor, give students some flexibility in how they interpret their "chosen" activity!

Included here, all in one place, are Activity Options taken from the Annotated Instructor's Edition.

ACTIVITY OPTION (p. 78): Ask students to make a list of excuses they think are good reasons for missing class or an assignment deadline. Discuss these excuses with the class. Sometimes students don't understand that their education should be one of their first priorities, and they need to be reminded that some reasons are really excuses that will derail their education.

ACTIVITY OPTION (p. 78): Have students review Figure 4.1 _The Dynamics of Energy_. Ask students to highlight the characteristics that are most like themselves. Then ask them to circle the quadrant which has the most characteristics they possess. Ask them what actions they can take to develop more positive characteristics.

ACTIVITY OPTION (p. 79): Give students a chart with times for a full day (twenty-four hours). Have them quickly list their high-energy times. Come together as a group and compare. Are there common times among the group? You should see differences among the students. Now, ask students to volunteer to tell you when they typically study. Are they doing it during peak energy times?

ACTIVITY OPTION (p. 79): Have students research healthy, high-energy foods on the Internet. Have students share their ideas and create a master list. A variation on this activity is to research quick, healthy, high-energy recipes and ask each student to bring a recipe to class to share and combine in a "Class Cookbook." Remind students to give credit for the recipes.

ACTIVITY OPTION (p. 81): Students can share their responses to Exercise 4.1 with each other. If students are willing, you can line them up on a continuum for a quick class check. Have students line up from most hours spent studying to least. Why are they standing where they are? Are some students taking more classes than others? Are some students totally on their own financially? Remind students that time in the library does not always equate with learning. Line up students again with those who stay focused for most of the time they study on one end and those who are distracted throughout the time on the other. Have focused students share their tips with others.

ACTIVITY OPTION (p. 82): Ask students to calculate how much time they spend online for things that are not school-related. How many times in the middle of working on the computer for some school-related activity do they respond to an IM or check their e-mail? Often? If this behavior is fairly typical, would they like to change? What could they do to improve their online habits? Give students about ten minutes and then have them report to the group. The goal is to compare notes on how to improve online habits.

ACTIVITY OPTION (p. 84): This is a great opportunity for students to share with each other their plans for the term. Some students will have lots of details on their calendars while others will have just a few bullets. Pair up students. What do they learn from each other? Ask students if they have a planner and if they use it every day. Students will begin to see that even if something is not natural, with practice they can develop productive habits, like good planning. Developmental students may need lots of encouragement to begin to use a planner and may need continued encouragement to continue using it.

ACTIVITY OPTION (p. 90): Make two sets of index cards with the same tasks as listed in Exercise 4.4. Divide the class into two groups and have them decide as a group which time zones to put each task into. At the end of 15 minutes, have one member of the team report the criteria used to place the cards in the zones to the class, what was eliminated, and what they observed about the different members in the groups. Then give each one of the fifteen cards to an individual student, and have him line them up from left to right to indicate how he would organize the day. He'll likely have to negotiate his positions.

ACTIVITY OPTION (p. 97): The five strategies listed here can help students use real-life techniques to balance multiple things. Write these five techniques on index cards, one per card, and make as many sets as you need so that each student in the class has at least three cards. Hand out the cards and ask students to work in pairs or small groups to come up with real-life examples and solutions for the technique on their card to present to the class.

ACTIVITY OPTION (p. 99): It may be beneficial if students share their responses. Group students by their spending from zero to $10, $10 to $50, and above $50. Have the groups identify items that they could have done without. Have students tally the cost of the items they could have done without. Ask students what they would do in the future to be wiser shoppers. If you have students with very different income levels, sharing this information could be a sensitive situation.

ACTIVITY OPTION (p. 100): As a class, develop some fiscally fit ideas. Print out the ideas. Have each student highlight the ideas that would help him/her the most. Encourage them to put the ideas into action.

ACTIVITY OPTION (p. 100): Have students develop a five-slide PowerPoint presentation for the class. Slide one should describe the most important thing they learned in this chapter about managing time and energy. On the second slide they must include one challenge that they're facing and on the third, a specific activity they will do to help them manage the challenge. In the fourth slide they should describe a possible pitfall they may have to completing the activity and on the last slide what benefit they will derive if they stick to their plan.

9. What homework might I assign?

Essay
Students can write a one or two page essay on the follow topic: What I Learned and What Time Management Strategies I Will Incorporate and Why? Goal: To help students to describe some of the challenges they are facing in college, and what information from the chapter they will use.

Video Review
In addition to the *FOCUS* TV video on Procrastination, students may find the Academic Skills videos from Dartmouth College helpful in learning about time management and goal setting. Students can view the video on time management online at www.dartmouth.edu/~acskills/videos/index.html. This video is approximately 18 minutes and is available with captions. Ask students to view the video and write a two-paragraph review of the video. Students should answer the following questions:

> *What did the students in the video understand about time management?*
> *What are the benefits of using a term/semester planner?*
> *What did I learn from this video?*

My Budget
Assign all students in the class to develop a budget for where they are right now and a future budget for where they want to be after they have finished their formal education

and are on the job. Students can use whatever program they wish: Microsoft Excel, Quicken, or any word processing program. Students could also use an online planner (see: http://au.pfinance.yahoo.com/calculators/budget-planner.html) to assist them with categories. Students should come back to the next class prepared to discuss this. The goal is to help students understand the importance of planning and budgeting and gain the knowledge of how financial management impacts college success.

Journal Entries

One: Have students write a one page journal entry, send you an e-mail, or blog describing something they do to procrastinate. Students must identify a situation when this has happened and what repercussions procrastinating had. Then, ask them to identify an upcoming assignment where procrastination might derail them, and have them describe to you how they plan to overcome the temptation. They can choose from the "Top Ten Procrastination-Busters" list or identify one of their own.

Two: At this point in the semester, students may need some additional motivation. Have students generate a reward system for themselves. Ask students to list five or six activities that they enjoy, but that they don't have time for. Ask students to identify three activities that they must complete this week. These activities could be reading all their assignments, studying for an exam, working on a research paper, etc. Ask them to commit to completing these assignments. If they do, they get three rewards. At the end of the week, have students prepare a three-slide PowerPoint presentation on their experience.

Three: Use the Insight → Action prompt as journal or blog assignments.

10. What have I learned in teaching this chapter that I will incorporate next time?

_____

_____
_____
_____
_____
_____
_____
_____
_____
_____
_____
_____
_____
_____
_____
_____
_____
_____

CHAPTER 5: THINKING CRITICALLY AND CREATIVELY

1. Why is this chapter important?

So what does thinking really mean? According to Staley, thinking is defined as a focused cognitive activity you engage in purposefully. You are focused on something and not simply daydreaming. When thinking critically, we use standards by which to judge things and don't just jump to conclusions and believe everything we read or hear. When we think creatively, we come up with different ways of thinking about the same thing. Creative thinking often uses the words "what if?"

Really, no one can expect first-year college students to have fully developed critical thinking skills. In fact, the world is pretty black and white according to most of them. In their minds, there are right ways to do things, and wrong ways, and not too much in between. Sometimes, students have been raised in very sheltered environments; some have been raised in complicated families or even have troubled backgrounds. Students come together from small towns and large cities, and often find that their thinking is challenged. They find out that there are some grey areas in life and that sometimes the context or the situation must be considered. What students experience, read about and study about in college will require them to use thinking strategies that they may have never used before. But, without making this critical leap from dualistic thinking to critical thinking, succeeding in college will be difficult, if not impossible.

This chapter brings with it some sensitive situations that you should be aware of.

- **Be sensitive to the fact that you will most likely have students who feel very differently about a number of topics based on their age, experiences, and upbringing.** Just like Desiree Moore, who feels uncomfortable about not having "the right answers" in class, the level of discomfort around controversial topics is common among first-year students. For some, they have left their comfort zones and the ways they were raised, and their fundamental beliefs may be challenged. Even though their original beliefs may be strengthened through testing in college, they may feel threatened by broaching particular topics. Because your goal is to get students to *think,* be sure that you create a safe climate. Your students should feel that your class is a place to test their thinking and reasoning without judgment or criticism.

- **Be careful how you approach students who demonstrate faulty reasoning.** You may find flaws in students' arguments or faulty reasoning. Instead of directly challenging these students, it's important to make sure that your response is something like "I never thought of it that way—have you ever thought about…?" Just don't make students feel attacked, because then they will shut down. Also, don't let students shoot each other down, but model for them how to disagree and challenge each other appropriately with questions like "what if…?, have you ever thought of…? did you know that…?"

- **Be aware that research identifies gender differences in how students relate to academia.** As first-year students, males are more likely to interact more with their instructors. However, females are more likely to take notes and study to do well. Later in their academic careers, females rely on other's opinions and collect ideas to construct their own knowledge. Males see the opinions of others as opportunities for debate or challenge. Finally, while females often have their own ideas, they also value the ideas of others. Males tend to process ideas more independently. It is important for you to design a classroom environment that allows both men and women to feel safe, while being appropriately challenged.

2. What are this chapter's learning objectives?

- ➢ How focused thinking, critical, and creative thinking are defined
- ➢ How a four-part model of critical thinking works
- ➢ How to analyze arguments, assess assumptions, and consider claims
- ➢ How to avoid mistakes in reasoning
- ➢ What metacognition is and why it's important
- ➢ How to become a more creative thinker

3. How should I launch this chapter?

A good way to launch this chapter is to get students thinking about thinking! That may sound redundant, but you could begin by asking students to identify the kinds of questions they will answer in college. Questions could range from topics as far-reaching as these: "What is the capital of Iran?" to "Should stem cells be harvested?" to "How important is ethics in today's business world?" Students need to understand that when we make a decision about something, we have facts to take into account, opinions about things, our own experiences, as well as ethical and moral values that underpin how we think and respond.

Think about beginning this chapter with a discussion about the media. How do you know what you see on the news or read in the newspaper is true? If you are not sure, how would you find out?

- **Begin a discussion about why people may have very different responses to the same question.** Ask for a show of hands.
    - Whose hometown is in the same community as this college?
    - Whose favorite color is blue?
    - Whose favorite ice cream is vanilla?
    - Who agrees that small colleges are better than large universities?
    - Does freedom of religion really exist in the U.S.?

Ask students about the differences in these questions. Clearly some questions were just factual. Either their hometown is in the same community as their college or it's not. Favorite ice cream and colors are based on opinions, and it really doesn't matter, does it? Maybe the question of the size of a college gets a little more controversial, but when it comes to freedom of religion, the question becomes much more controversial, and one's response may be rooted in faith as opposed to logic. Students should understand that good critical thinkers are aware of the differences between facts and opinions, and if they come to an emotional response to a question, they are aware of why. For example, someone may know an individual who has been persecuted for religious reasons, or they are horrified (or aren't) that Christmas decorations have become controversial. Challenge students to be active participants in their own thinking: they should be prepared to defend their thinking *process* as much as their individual opinions.

- **Developmental Students and Returning Adult Learners**: In some ways, Desiree Moore could be a developmental student and a returning adult learner. She has had difficulty in developing her critical and creative abilities and looks for the "right" answer. Developmental students (as well as all students) should be encouraged to think of different ways to solve problems. Developmental students may need to be reassured that the classroom is a safe place to try out new ideas and new ways of thinking. Returning adult learners may need the same reassurances. These students should have practical examples of how they have used creative thinking. Ask students if they have had to find childcare at the last minute or had to make a decision that they are proud of. There can be many examples of critical and creative thinking in your class! The chapter 5 *FOCUS* on Kids worksheet provides a puzzle for your students' children to introduce the concept of critical thinking and problem solving with puzzles.

- **Remember the Readiness Check at the beginning of the chapter.** Instructors could assume that students think they know a lot about thinking. But do they? Out of all the Readiness Checks students have completed so far, how interested are they in this particular chapter? Are they less motivated to read it because they believe they already know a lot about thinking or because the chapter sounds too abstract to them?

- **Going beyond the book.** There are a number of terrific opportunities for students to learn more about critical thinking in this chapter. They might even enjoy their logic, ethics, or philosophy classes if they were more prepared for the challenge. This is a good time to talk about some of the skills that are needed in courses such as these. Engage students in a discussion of careers that rely on strong critical and creative thinking, such as Legal Assistant, Lawyer, and Law Enforcement, not to mention careers in art, music and others. Also, consider getting students to read a bit more about emotional intelligence now. Strong emotional intelligence requires good analytical skills. In order to be realistic about something, which is a critical EI skill, you have to assess what is really happening. To know how to respond effectively to others, you have to know yourself. And effective problem solving is really a trial (and sometimes error), step-by-step approach to figuring out what is important and what will work.

4. How should I use the *FOCUS* Challenge Case?

Desiree Moore has been described as "detail-oriented" and "compulsive." In high school Desiree turned in assignments late (if at all) because she was always looking for the "right" answers. For 12 years she has bounced from job to job and has realized that she must go to college to get some skills to obtain a better job. Desiree has decided to enroll in the paralegal program at her community college. One of her two classes is proving to be a challenge. Desiree's Paralegal Ethics instructor, Mr. Courtney, emphasized the importance of critical thinking in his very first class. Mr. Courtney asks an endless chain of questions, none of which seem to have a *right* answer. Desiree is challenged by his style because she believes "the instructor knows the right answers." You might begin by asking the class if Mr. Courtney's style is an effective teaching method. What you will probably find is that you will have some differences of opinions in the class. This is a good opportunity to ask the class what is the right answer? There really is not a right answer. And that can be very frustrating for students. Exploring the Socratic Method, how it relates to critical thinking, and Desiree's reaction to it, might be another good way to launch the chapter. Other options for this case include:

- **Direct It!** Assign a "scene director" for the Challenge Case. After students review the Challenge Case, assign a student to role-play Desiree and Mr. Courtney. The director can stop the scene at any point and redirect the "actors" as well as get input from the "critics"—the other students in class!
    - o Scene 1: Direct Desiree to visit Mr. Courtney during his office hours. What questions would Desiree ask? How could Mr. Courtney help Desiree adapt to his style of teaching?
    - o Scene 2: A second year paralegal student and Desiree have a conversation. Desiree discusses her difficulties in Mr. Courtney's class. The second year student is empathetic, but essentially tells her she will have other courses like his. What advice does he give Desiree? What resources on campus might help?
- Ask students if they agree with the professor's statement "Learning to think is what college is all about?" Why or why not?
- Thinking back to the 4-Ps from chapter 4, what type of procrastinator is Desiree?
- What advice would you give Desiree to help her adjust to this professor's teaching style?
- If Desiree cannot overcome her perfectionism and search for the "right" answer, what challenges will she face in her program and profession?

5. What important features does this chapter include?

By now, students should be fairly used to the recurring features in the book. You might even be at a point, especially if your class only meets a few hours a week, to begin putting students into groups and assigning some of these features for homework and have them report on different ones in class. For example, you may assign the Challenge → Reaction steps to Group A, and the VARK Activity to Group B. Ask each group to prepare a two to three minute presentation on their assigned activities. As the course continues, keep track of which activities each group has already reported on. If you try this technique, be sure that each team has a chance to do a number of different features.

Readiness and Reality Checks

This Readiness Check may prove to be an interesting one. We might safely assume that a number of first year students have never even thought about thinking, or much less how to do it critically and creatively. They thought they *were* thinking! You might consider doing a pre- and post- comparison on this chapter. Guesses are that responses to the Readiness Check at the start will be different from the Reality Check at the end.

Challenge → Reaction → Insight → Action prompt

The Challenge → Reaction → Insight → Action steps in this chapter, or in any chapter, can be used in quizzes, journals, or class discussions. You might even consider taking all of the Challenge → Reaction → Insight → Action prompt questions, putting them in a basket, and have students pull them out and respond for an in class quiz. Try doing this in pairs and point out the wisdom of this method of learning in the group. Another way to use these questions is as a class opinion poll. For example, take the Step 2: Reaction question, "Do you agree with Mr. Courtney's statement "there aren't always right answers"? If that's true, why is getting a college education so important?" Ask students to answer this question on 3 x 5 index cards and turn them back in to you. Sort the answers into piles, based on similar answers. Then, report back to the class the similarities and the differences in their answers. This could form the basis for an interesting discussion on how multiple answers to a question could all be right!

How Full Is Your Plate?

Reorganizing one's "to-do" list can be very important. How flexible are your students? Sometimes developmental students and returning adult learners can seem pretty inflexible, but developing flexibility can be paramount in college success. Lead students through a "to-do" list reorganization. Were your students surprised by the results? How can they extend this flexibility to home, work, and relationships?

C-Factors

The feature "Control: Your Toughest Class" asks students to examine creative thinking in the context of a tough class. "Career Outlook" looks at the profession of legal assistant. "Challenge Yourself Online Quiz" is also available via CourseMate.

Career Outlook

The career focus in this chapter is on legal assistant Shaun Pilcher, and careers such as his. Shaun's original career path was law enforcement, but because of physical factors he researched other fields in criminal justice and decided to become a legal assistant. Shaun's advice to students is very important: get real world experience. He advises students to volunteer or do internships that will allow them to see the field first hand. Take a show of hands: who in the class would find this career satisfying? Who would find it challenging? Why or why not?

VARK Activity

This activity is designed to help students understand the value of capitalizing on their preferred VARK learning modality. This activity encourages students to relate their preferred VARK learning modality with particular study skills. Visual learners should use the white space in this chapter to write a personal response to each section of the chapter, while aural learners should discuss the key concepts with a friend. Read/write students will summarize a controversial article, and kinesthetic learners should interview other students on creative thinking.

FOCUS TV: Critical Thinking

This short segment, available in the FOCUSPoints teaching tool, provides students with a quick introduction to critical thinking. The segment will help to reinforce the Critical Thinking Pyramid found in figure 5.2.

6. Which in-text exercises should I use?

Three exercises are available in this chapter. Included here are descriptions of why these in-text exercises have been included, what challenges you might expect, and how you might debrief each one.

EXERCISE 5.1 AND JUST WHY IS CRITICAL THINKING IMPORTANT?

Why do this activity?
This activity is simple and quick and could be done in class. While it's in the format of a brief survey where students respond to statements about why critical thinking might be important, it's really a teaching tool to point out why critical thinking *is* important and what aspects of life it connects to.

What are the challenges and what can you expect?
When you take a look at the prompts they begin with "would you like to…become a better citizen, a better employee" for example. Students might tend to rate them all high. Of course, the point is exactly that. All of the reasons stated are essential reasons for developing critical thinking skills.

How much time will it take?
This activity should take about 30 minutes.

How should I debrief?
Because you will probably find that students score high on most of these, it's probably best to just have a general discussion about how critical thinking applies to all important aspects of life. You might start out by asking students which of the statements is not important. Let's hope they say something like "they are all important reasons for development strong critical thinking skills." If they don't, ask them to defend their answers as to why a particular statement is not important.

EXERCISE 5.2 ASPEN COMMONS APARTMENT COMPLEX CASE STUDY

Why do this activity?
Not only does this exercise relate directly to today's traditional students and help identify issues that can spark debate, it's a great example to bring in discussions about binge drinking and the possible consequences. Alcohol abuse is a societal issue, and chances are students of any age have been touched by its consequences somewhere in their lives. By looking at the letters to the editor from six different individuals and their reactions to a death of a college student from alcohol poisoning, students get a chance to try to sort out facts from claims, and the criteria for logical explanations versus self-serving motives.

What are the challenges and what can you expect?
You can expect that students will be interested in reading this. They will be pulled into the material and although they may not reveal what they really think since they may believe it's not what you would want to hear, they will likely be highly engaged. Be sure to reiterate that there are no right or wrong answers, so they will know you are not expecting a particular answer. Emphasize that you really *do* want to know what they think, not parrot back your own ideas.

How much time will it take?
This activity could take up a full class period or at least 50 minutes.

How should I debrief?
Two questions appear at the end of this exercise. Divide the class into two groups and assign them to one of these questions. Have groups report out and lead a discussion. If there is not time in class for this you could ask students to respond to the questions as a homework or e-mail assignment. Not only is this information relevant for students, it provides great examples for finding faulty reasoning, examining claims versus facts, and evaluating individual's opinions.

EXERCISE 5.3 PROBLEM SOLVING FOR YOURSELF

Why do this activity?
This activity provides students with an opportunity to try out the seven-step problem-solving model. Students should think of a problem they are currently facing and fill in steps one through seven.

What are the challenges and what can I expect?
There are no real challenges in this activity except for the students who may not be able to think of a current problem. Encourage students to steer clear of issues they cannot control (world hunger!) and concentrate on their own situation.

How much time will it take?
This activity could be done in class or as a homework assignment. If done in class, allow 20 minutes for completion and processing.

> **How should I debrief?**
> Rather than have each student discuss his or her problem, you might ask students which step was most challenging for them and why. Consider having students turn this assignment in for a grade and provide them feedback as needed.

7. Which additional exercises might enrich students' learning?

Critical Thinking—Critical Searching

(Adapted from Staley (2003))

Materials needed: Website links and a comparison chart

Time: 45 minutes to an hour

Goal: To help students critique websites for academic uses

Ask students to find four websites that relate to binge drinking for college students. Ask students to assess the four websites according to the criteria listed on the chart below. Then, ask them to present the most credible site to the class. Insist that students are able to logically defend their choice.

	Accuracy	Authority	Objective/ Perspective	Currency	Coverage/ Scope	Purpose	Access
1							
2							
3							
4							

The Best News of the Day

Class activity: Discussion in class, after students have reviewed the news articles at home

Materials needed: Two different news articles about of the same incident that you provide

Time: 45 minutes

Goal: To help students see that presenting slightly different information can alter one's perception of the same incident

For homework give students two short articles on the same topic. Maybe your town has more than one newspaper—taking an article from each would be ideal. Or you could use your college paper and the local one, or *USA Today*. Ask students to evaluate which version of the article they preferred and why? Was it because one was more sensational or gave more facts? This should lead into a discussion of what really sells the news. Is it just the facts?

Good Thinkers Please Apply

Materials needed: Large newsprint and markers

Time: 30-50 minutes, depending on the size of the group

Goal: To understand and describe the thinking skills necessary for success in careers

Divide the class into two groups. Each group comes up with a job description and want ad for a good thinker. Groups put their ads on newsprint for the class to see. Classmates vote on which is the better description. For example, the description might read "Wanted: An individual who is able to help bring our company to the number one position among our competitors in the nation. Applicants must be able to work effectively in teams, understand the steps involved in solving complex problems, etc."

8. What other activities can I incorporate to make the chapter my own?

At this point in the course you probably have a sense for whether you have a group of self-starters or students that you have to constantly draw into the conversation. You are probably getting comfortable with the students and now it might be fun to do something a little different. Remember that there are some people that don't like change, so make sure you still keep the same activities and assignments that were planned or put on your syllabus.

Included here, all in one place, are Activity Options taken from the Annotated Instructor's Edition.

ACTIVITY OPTION (p. 106): Divide the class into three groups. Choose three of the questions from "What Do *You* Think?" and ask students to work in groups to answer the question and report to the class. As a variation, ask students to do the same for homework and compare answers in the next class or discuss their responses in an online threaded discussion or chat.

ACTIVITY OPTION (p. 109): Have students listen to a lecture and then divide the students into groups. Have them create a list of questions related to the lecture to see how much they understand the material. Assign one group to ask questions at the end of the lecture, one group to disagree with a major point, one group to agree with another major point, and one group to summarize the lecture. If your college posts class lectures on YouTube, this can be an excellent way of having all students see the same lecture at the same time (if not, see www.youtube.com/user/grcctv for possible lectures that can be used).

ACTIVITY OPTION (p. 109): See if you can get your hands on a video of this *Monty Python* sketch for the class to watch or go to YouTube and watch it online (www.youtube.com and search *Monty Python Argument*). After viewing it, divide the class into two groups to discuss the difference between an argument as defined in this chapter and a contradiction.

ACTIVITY OPTION (p. 110): Divide students into groups and give each group a worksheet, which lists a series of arguments. Have students identify each argument with an "I" for inductive or "D" as deductive. Have each group write three arguments on the back of the worksheet. Have students switch papers to see if the other groups can identify the arguments correctly.

ACTIVITY OPTION (p. 111): Give students a list of arguments. Have students read each argument and list "U" if the argument is unsound and "S" if the argument is sound.

ACTIVITY OPTION (p. 113): This is another opportunity to take an article from the newspaper and look for arguments that support a fact (or not). Bring a short newspaper article to class (short and current is best, and something that will engage students). Follow the pyramid in Figure 5.2 to explore the reasoning. The class can work as a whole, or in small teams. This activity could also be used for homework.

ACTIVITY OPTION (p. 113): Play the "How Do I Know This Is True?" game. Bring in some headlines from the student or local newspaper. Put them on a PowerPoint slide or overhead, and show them to the class. Go around the room and have students fill in the following: I know this is true because _____. Any student can say "NOT" and then explain why it is not true. If it is true, and no one challenges, students just keep adding to why it's true.

ACTIVITY OPTION (p. 114): Alcohol use and abuse by college students is a hot topic. Use this opportunity to talk about this issue and how it pertains to your campus. Brainstorm a list of questions that students would want to know about alcohol use and abuse. Divide students into groups of two to three and give them a specific question from the list they just generated. Tell them to find the answer and bring it to class next week. Make sure that they tell you the source, and why they thought it was credible.

ACTIVITY OPTION (p. 116): You may wish to have students do the VARK exercise on critical and creative thinking individually instead.
V: Look over the letters to the editor. Make notes in the margins about as many faulty arguments as you can identify.
A: Discuss this simulation in class or with a friend. List three points you hadn't really thought about that your partner helped you see.
R: Summarize the case into a single paragraph. Summarizing is a great critical thinking tool!
K: (Use the same K activity.) Would actually serving on a task force help you or other kinesthetic learners become engaged and learn more? Why and how?

ACTIVITY OPTION (p. 123): Have each student bring in an idea-something they want to learn or an innovative idea. Then divide students into groups and have each student explain the idea and have the group help the student brainstorm ideas of how this could become a reality.

ACTIVITY OPTION (p. 123): Have students divide into groups based on their majors. Have groups make a list of how they would need to think critically on the job.

ACTIVITY OPTION (p. 124): Bring a pillow to class! Write some common first-year student statements on cards (friend or family concerns are good ones) and ask students to come up in pairs and use the Pillow Method to address the problem.

9. What homework might I assign?

Because there are many exercises and teachable moments in the chapter, any one of them could be used for a homework activity.

Journal Entries
One: One of the topics in this chapter is metacognition—thinking about thinking. Have students write a one-page journal entry, describing the three elements of metacognition and how improving their metacognitive skills could make them a better learner.

Two: Ask your students to find a news item that is interesting to them and examine it from at least two opposing viewpoints. Then, ask them to describe their own opinion on the subject. Be aware that this could lead to a sensitive situation, as your students may be hesitant to examine their own ideas.

Three: Use the Insight → Action questions as journal or blog assignments.

10. What have I learned in teaching this chapter that I will incorporate next time?

CHAPTER 6: DEVELOPING TECHNOLOGY, RESEARCH, AND INFORMATION LITERACY SKILLS

1. Why is this chapter important?

Are you among the 220 million Americans on the Internet today? Chances are good you are online and so are your students! Are your students using the Internet for research and writing or are they busy updating their Facebook status and checking sports scores? Students have numerous choices online, but do they know which sites are legitimate and how to use them for research and writing?

The answer to the last question is probably, no. Many recent high school graduates as well as returning adult learners may lack the skills necessary for information literacy. This chapter focuses on providing students an overview to the impact of technology and how to use it in an academic setting. In the section, *The Internet: The Good, the Bad, and the Ugly*, students will examine positive and negative sides to the Internet. In addition to lacking information literacy skills, some of your students may lack technology skills. Wikis, blogs, YouTube, MP3 and PDF—What does it all mean? This chapter will help to demystify technology lingo for students—and perhaps us as well!

How many of your students are either currently in an online class or have taken an online course in high school? Some students may be surprised to learn of the different demands of an e-learning environment. This chapter outlines tips for success in an e-learning environment and describes the differences between e-learning and c- (classroom) learning.

Information literacy is critical for college and life success. Many students lack the skills necessary to be information literate. Quite simply they cannot tell when they need information, they don't know where to find it, don't understand what it means, can't tell whether or not it's accurate, and don't know how to use the information once they have it. This chapter introduces students to a six-step information literacy model that will help them with any research, presentation and/or writing assignment. Finally, this chapter introduces (and reintroduces) students to plagiarism, both intentional and unintentional, and provides realistic solutions for avoiding plagiarism.

2. What are this chapter's learning objectives?

  - ➢ How technology impacts everyone's lives
  - ➢ How to use technology to be more academically successful
  - ➢ How e-learning (online) is different from c-learning (classroom)
  - ➢ How to cultivate research skills
  - ➢ What information literacy skills are and why they're important
  - ➢ What plagiarism is and how to avoid it

3. How should I launch this chapter?

Many students generally think of themselves as "Net savvy." But are they? Get a sense of your students' comfort with being online and using the Internet as a research tool. You could do this by asking for a show of hands: "How many of you are good at using the Internet to do research for a paper or presentation?" If students raise their hands, quickly ask them to explain what they do well and why they perceive this as a strength. Ask students for specific examples. Some students may have developed some fairly strong skills at using the Internet for research, while others may have developed some poor habits. Other students may lack basic skills of using a computer or doing research online. The point of this is not to criticize students, but rather to illustrate that everyone can learn new skills for technology and research.

- **Ask students to take a few minutes to describe their first writing experiences.** Take a few minutes to go around the room to have students share what they remember about their earliest writing projects. Were they on big lined paper, where they learned to shape their letters and write their name? Was it a story they wrote about a made-up character or their first book report? Sometimes these very first experiences are very powerful memories that are extremely positive or very negative. However, most young children enjoy writing stories and don't suffer from "writer's block." But don't be surprised if a student explains a primary, middle, or high school situation in which they worked very hard but did not get a good grade. Did it have an impact on how they think of themselves as writers now?

- **Find out if other students have research papers or projects they are working on currently for other classes.** Place students into groups of two or three making sure each group has at least one student who might be stronger with research skills. Ask students to discuss with each other the type of research they are required to do and how they are researching their topic. Ask students to report out what they learned and their suggestions for their classmates of what they could do differently or in addition to what they are already doing.

- **Developmental Students and Returning Adult Learners**: This chapter could cause anxiety for both developmental students and returning adult learners. Explain to students the topics covered in this chapter will help all students, at all skill levels, learn to better use technology and gain research and information literacy skills. The purpose of the chapter is not to teach students how to write; rather it will teach them new skills in researching and using technology. The skills learned in this chapter will complement what they are learning in other classes. For your students who are parents of young children, don't forget to suggest the *FOCUS* on Kids worksheet for this chapter. The worksheet helps young ones understand how computers help us learn. These worksheets are available in CourseMate.

- **Going beyond the book.** Schedule a tour of your campus library for your class. Ask the librarian to show students where the reference section is located. Use the Library Research Worksheet (see below: **9. What Homework Might I Assign?**) for students to complete and turn in after the tour, or modify the worksheet for your own needs. Another possibility is to take a tour of your campus writing or tutoring center to make sure students know that it is not only okay to ask for help, but where the help is located.

4. How should I use the *FOCUS* Challenge Case?

Dario Jones enjoys computers and being online. He has been called a "geek" ever since grade school. After spending some time working in his father's auto body shop, Dario has decided to go to his community college and study web design. His big surprise came quickly when he discovered playing with computers and studying computers are really quite different. Dario has also learned that he has no idea how to research a topic for his paper on Globalization and Internet Commerce. He quickly understands that he is not information literate. At the last minute, Dario decides to cut and paste related articles from his Internet search, while wondering if he has done anything wrong. Dario is pessimistic about his academic career, yet does not want a real-life career in the auto body shop. Consider the following discussion options:

- **Direct It!** Assign a "scene director" for the Challenge Case. After students review the Challenge Case, assign a student to role-play Dario and Dr. Otis. Another option is to have someone role-play a librarian to assist Dario. The director can stop the scene at any point and redirect the "actors" as well as get input from the "critics"—the other students in class!

   - o Scene 1: Direct Dr. Otis giving feedback to Dario on his paper. What should Dr. Otis say to him? What questions should Dario ask?
   - o Scene 2: Assuming Dr. Otis allows Dario to rewrite the paper, direct Dario to work with a librarian. Given what your students know about the library and how to research and write a paper, what advice does the librarian give Dario?
- After reviewing this case with your students, ask them if they feel Dario has done anything wrong. Why or why not?
- Another aspect to this case is struggling and not asking for help. Have your students ever been in this situation?
- Given the resources on your campus, what suggestions would students have for Dario?
- What questions would they want Dario to ask of his teacher?
- Why do you think Dario's instructor indicated they could not use Wikipedia?
- What should Dr. Otis do about Dario's paper?
- What assistance could the campus library have for Dario?

This *FOCUS* Challenge Case is a good way to begin to explore academic resources and policies in a deeper way. Students often enjoy getting outside of the classroom and having an "insider" tour of the library and writing/tutoring center. As you work through this chapter, refer back to Dario and review with your students the options for help they have at your college.

5. What important features does this chapter include?

This chapter is loaded with features that will help students gain a better understanding of technology, research and information literacy skills. If you are using a Facebook page for your class, consider using the Reaction questions for response on the group's wall. If you assign Exercise 6.4 Technology Project: Group Ad, have students post their assignment to the wall of the class page. Another option would be to have students post their video reactions to any of the assignments on YouTube for review by the entire class. There are many technology options available for your students!

Readiness and Reality Checks
This Readiness Check could be done as nongraded quiz on Blackboard (or whatever course management system your institution uses) or it could be done as a survey on Blackboard. This will allow your students a degree of anonymity while allowing you to see where students honestly rate themselves on this topic. Follow this up with the Reality Check at the end of the chapter.

Challenge → Reaction → Insight → Action prompt
The Challenge → Reaction steps in this chapter could be used to begin the classroom discussion. It might be interesting to divide your class into two groups, those who believe Dario plagiarized, and those who believe he did not plagiarize. Have each group come up with their arguments. Ask each group to choose one or two spokespersons and ask that each side present their case. This could lead to a discussion of your institution's policy on plagiarism. Using this same process, at the end of the chapter, ask the two groups to complete the Insight → Action questions by concluding Dario's story and deciding what actions Dario (and they) can take when using technology and doing research.

Stressed Out?
The Internet, much like some of your students, never sleeps! Other students may not be getting enough sleep due to work or family obligations. Ask students to complete this simple sleep log to determine how many hours of sleep they are getting. If students fall below 49 hours per week, ask them to develop a new strategy for getting enough sleep. This could make an interesting journal entry as well as a wall writing assignment for Facebook.

Curiosity: Are You Caught In The Net?
Internet addiction is a serious fact of life in our online world. Some of your students may be facing this addiction and do not realize it. Consider having a counselor come to class to discuss Internet addiction. If this resource does not exist on campus, a local community mental health agency may have someone available who can speak to your class.

<u>Careers Outlook</u>
In this chapter we meet Thomas P. Scola, web designer. Thomas advises students to get as much experience as possible, or even work for free if necessary to build up a portfolio. Can students prepare for this career at your institution? If so, consider having an instructor from the program speak to your class about careers in web design and Internet security. If not, what transfer options exist for students and what courses should students take to prepare for this transfer and career?

6. Which in-text exercises should I use?

Six exercises are available in this chapter. Included here are descriptions of why these in-text exercises have been included, what challenges you might expect, and how you might debrief each one.

EXERCISE 6.1 HOW TECH-SAVVY ARE YOU?

Why do this activity?
This activity is quick and provides students with a visual and terminology-based matching activity. This exercise will help all students, especially those who are not as tech-savvy, understand the variety of online sites encountered.

What are the challenges and what can you expect?
Although some students may not have well-cultivated computer skills, there are no real challenges to this activity, and it can be done in class or assigned as homework. A variation of this activity would be to assign it as homework and ask that students e-mail you a link to an example for every one of the descriptions.

How much time will it take?
This exercise should take between 5 and 10 minutes to match the example with the description. If you choose the variation listed above, it could take students 20-30 minutes.

How should I debrief?
The standard activity could be debriefed by asking students to discuss the validity of information found on different Internet domain extensions. For example, a claim made about a drug on a website that ends in .gov would be different than one found on a .com site. If the e-mail activity is assigned, you could ask students to present one or two examples from the eight descriptions and to discuss what they learned and/or what surprised them.

EXERCISE 6.2 HOW NOT TO WIN FRIENDS AND INFLUENCE PEOPLE ONLINE

Why do this activity?
Many students are not skilled at composing appropriate academic e-mails. This activity helps to reinforce some of the Netiquette rules from this chapter. This activity is well suited to do in class and discuss what rules were broken as well as what an appropriate e-mail response would look like.

What are the challenges and what can you expect?
It might be useful to divide the class into four groups, one for each e-mail example. Then have each group review their e-mail and come to some agreement on which rule was violated.

How much time will it take?
This activity should take approximately 20-25 minutes to complete and debrief.

How should I debrief?
Ask each group to present their e-mail and the rule they believe was violated. It might be useful to ask the entire class if they agree with the finding. Also ask each group to draft an appropriate e-mail for their student. The drafts could be written on the board and the entire class could be encouraged to provide feedback.

EXERCISE 6.3 CRITICAL SEARCHING ON THE INTERNET

Why do this activity?
This activity is designed to get students comfortable with evaluating online information for currency, accuracy, authority, objectivity, and coverage.

What are the challenges and what can I expect?
Developmental students and students who are unfamiliar with the Internet may need to be reminded that not all websites contain information that can meet the five criteria listed above. This activity is best done as a homework assignment. After students have chosen either Assignment 1 or 2, they should list one website at the top of the page and then evaluate it for each of the five criteria. The last page would be one to two paragraphs answering the questions for their particular assignment. Students would then hand in three pages for their three websites and one page for their summary.

How much time will it take?
This assignment will take students about one hour to complete.

How should I debrief?
In addition to turning this assignment in for a grade, students could be asked to prepare a short (2-3 minute) presentation on what they learned from this experience. Did they find websites that lacked all five criteria? Which ones were not objective? Which websites got high marks for all five criteria?

EXERCISE 6.4 TECHNOLOGY PROJECT: GROUP AD

Why do this activity?
This group project appeals to all learning styles and gives students hands-on experience with using a variety of technologies. It also provides students with an opportunity to use the six-step process of information literacy.

What are the challenges and what can I expect?
This project can be done in class, however, it would be best as an assigned out-of-class, team-building project. If you have students who feel as if they do all of the work, structure the assignment by giving students specific roles. Make sure that each group has a member that has access to technology, or that everyone is fully aware of the technology available on your campus. At minimum, students will have access to PowerPoint. Students do not need a video camera to complete this project. Students can import video clips (remind them to give credit!) from the web, and many cell phones have a video camera that could provide them with clips to insert. Still images can also be used to create the television ad for this course. In addition to PowerPoint, students might use Windows Movie Maker, iMovie on Macintosh, and Flash.

How much time will it take?
This project could take one to three hours, depending on how in-depth the group gets and the medium selected. Plan on another 30-45 minutes (or longer, if your class is larger) to showcase the ads in class.

How should I debrief?
Just as you do with other activities, ask students when they are done, what they learned by doing this activity. Did the Six Steps to Information Literacy work for them as they completed this assignment? Did anyone learn to use technology they never used before? Consider posting the advertisements on your Facebook group site or Blackboard.

EXERCISE 6.5 PLAGIARISM SURVEY

Why do this activity?
This activity is designed to be done independently and then serve as a basis for a class discussion. It helps students to begin thinking about plagiarism and how to avoid it.

What are the challenges and what can I expect?
Make sure you point out your institutional policy on plagiarism. It is a good idea to provide students with a copy of this policy. If you included this item in your Student-Teacher Contract at the beginning of the semester, now is a good time to reference this point.

How much time will it take?
This activity should take less than 10 minutes for students to complete.

How should I debrief?
After students have answered the questions and read the section that follows, engage the class in a group discussion on the questions. You could combine this exercise with Exercise 6.6. A great online resource for this topic as well as providing quick, easy to follow style tips for APA and MLA is the Online Writing Lab (OWL) at Purdue University available at http://owl.english.purdue.edu/

EXERCISE 6.6 PLAGIARISM OR NOT?

Why do this activity?
This activity gives students practical experience at reviewing an example of plagiarism.

What are the challenges and what can I expect?
Ask students to compare the Original passage with the Student paper and determine if the student has plagiarized.

How much time will it take?
This exercise should take 5-10 minutes and can be combined with the previous exercise (6.5)

How should I debrief?
Ask students if they believe the student has plagiarized. Why or why not? How would your students change the passage to avoid plagiarism?

7. Which additional exercises might enrich students' learning?

Searching the Web—Even to Learn about your own Campus Library
Class activity
Materials needed: computers
Time: 30-50 minutes, depending on the size of the group
Goal: To help students use the Internet to identify resources both on the web, and in the campus library
In small groups of two to three students, assign groups the task of identifying as many varied, credible resources to do a research paper on the topic of "college student debt" on the Internet. Be sure that students include a varied list of sources, including online database articles through your library as well as web sites. At the end of 30 minutes, have groups report what they found, including the most user friendly search engines and databases.

Under Cover
Out of class activity
Materials needed: computer
Time: 30-50 minutes
Goal: To help students identify Internet profiles of current college students with information that might lead to trouble
Individually, students are to browse a social networking site like MySpace, Facebook, or Second Life and find two profiles that indicate exactly where students will be and when. Have students identify what controls are in place to prevent potentially dangerous situations from developing. Students will also describe what features their chosen social networking site has that may be different from other Internet social networking sites.

Is E-Learning Right For Me?
Out of class activity

Materials needed: computer
Time: 10-15 minutes
Goal: To help students examine if they are ready for an e-learning course
Provide students this web link: http://www.grcc.edu/dlreadiness or
http://goml.readi.info/assessmentpublic.whatisreadi and ask they complete the online
readiness assessment. Once complete, ask students to write 1-2 paragraphs about their
level of readiness for e-learning.

Google Me!
Out of class activity
Materials needed: computer
Time: 10-15 minutes
Goal: To help students review, use and understand the five criteria to evaluate
websites
Ask students to do a Google search on their full first and last name. Even if they don't
appear in the results, chances are good someone else will that shares their name. Ask
them to select a website from the results and evaluate it using the five criteria: currency,
accuracy, authority, objectivity, and coverage from the text. Ask students to record their
responses on paper and include the full URL of the website they are reviewing. Did the
fact their site was a .com, .edu, .gov, etc. impact their responses on the criteria? What did
they learn about using the five criteria?

8. What other activities can I incorporate to make the chapter my own?

Many students initially struggle with research as Dario did. The activities and
assignments available in this chapter are designed to help students bridge the information
literacy gap. Based on the needs of your students, try several of the activities and don't
forget about the importance of taking your class to the library for a tour.

Included here, all in one place, are Activity Options taken from the Annotated
Instructor's Edition.

ACTIVITY OPTION (p. 132): In small groups have students review the ISpy web page
on page 133 and decide what parts of the profile should be eliminated to protect one's
identity. Have groups share in class what was left on the profile. Could anything still
identify this student? Remind students of the benefits of setting their profiles to private on
sites like Facebook and MySpace.

ACTIVITY OPTION (p. 139): Have the students complete exercise 6.2 individually
and submit responses to you. Total the responses for the four examples and have the class
discuss and see if all the students agree on which rules were broken.

ACTIVITY OPTION (p. 145): As an assignment for the next class, encourage students
to research a career that is of interest to them. Ask students to find three Internet sources
and three articles or books they can use as research references. They do not need to write

the paper, they only need to bring in a list of resources (this activity is repeated on the Library Research Worksheet in section 9 below).

ACTIVITY OPTION (p. 149): Students often have difficulty formulating a good thesis statement. Provide students with a template sheet to use to write a good thesis statement. Give students ten possible topics and ask them to write a thesis statement for each.

ACTIVITY OPTION (p. 151): Divide students into teams and number each team. Give each team the same paragraph with a variety of 12-15 errors. Ask students to find, circle, and correct the mistakes. As the teams finish, write their numbers on the board. When all of the teams have finished, have the first team finished identify the error and the correction. Is the fastest team the most accurate?

ACTIVITY OPTION (p. 152): Provide your students with a copy of the institutional policy on plagiarism. Have them highlight the consequences and discuss them. Make sure your students understand this policy. If your institution has a Conduct Director or Dean of Students, invite him/her to your class to discuss plagiarism and the possible outcomes of students found guilty of violating this policy.

ACTIVITY OPTION (p. 152): Remind students that different disciplines use different style sheets. When writing a paper, it is best to check with the instructor to determine which style sheet to follow. A great online resource for this topic as well as providing quick, easy to follow style tips for APA and MLA is the Online Writing Lab (OWL) at Purdue University available at http://owl.english.purdue.edu/

9. What homework might I assign?

This chapter provides multiple options for homework that will serve to reinforce the learning in this chapter. **Exercise 6.4 Technology Project: Group Ad** makes a great homework assignment. In addition, the **Activity Option** on page 145, having students list resources for a career, could be steps one and two in the Five Steps to Information Literacy that would culminate in Chapter 12: Choosing A College Major And A Career, by having students complete a paper and presentation on their chosen major.

Journal Entries
One: Have students write a one-page journal entry, or send you an e-mail describing an assignment that involved technology or research that was very difficult for them in the past few weeks. If they didn't have a particularly challenging assignment within that time frame, ask them to describe any challenges they have had in the past with technology or research.

Two: Use the Insight → Action questions as journal or blog assignments.

Library Research Worksheet

The worksheet that follows on the next three pages can be assigned to students as homework with or without a library tour. Depending on your needs and resources available, you may want to add other elements to the worksheet.

Library Research Assignment

General directions: It is best to complete this assignment in the college library. Many questions can be answered from any Internet connected computer, but some sites and questions may require you to be on campus.

Part I

Review Chapter 6, pages 142-144 on *Research Skills and Your College Success*. Also review the five criteria to evaluate websites on page 147. Then complete the following activities:

Use Google (www.google.com) to search for the following terms:

1. **Learning Disabilities** How many results did this search return? _____

   List two website addresses that are .org or .edu

   _____

   _____

2. **Dyslexia** *Select a Sponsored Link (make sure it is a .com) and list below*

   _____

   What purpose would a group have for sponsoring (paying for) their link to pop up when you search for a term?

   _____

Now, use Google Scholar (http://scholar.google.com/) to search for those terms:

3. **Learning Disabilities** *Did you find more or fewer websites?*_____

   How are these results different from your previous search using Google.com?

   _____

   _____

4. **Dyslexia** *What is the difference between this search and the one you did using Google.com?*

   _____

Part II

Think of a common topic, perhaps one you need to begin working on for an assignment and use Google (not Google Scholar) to search for it.

Choose a common topic_____. Number of sites Google comes up with_____.

Pick three off-the-topic links you found and write a thesis statement to a paper that would require you to use these leads in your research.

_____

_____

_____

In all likelihood, your thesis statement makes little sense. What does this tell you about the need for critical thinking and information literacy when using Google and other search directories and engines in your research?

_____

_____

Finally, open your mind to the creative possibilities your research uncovered. Did any of the Web sites spark ideas about your topic that you had never considered? Write down two ideas you never thought of before.

1._____

2._____

Part III

Answer the following questions using your college library's resources. Some questions can be answered from your college library web page, others may have to be answered during a visit to the library.

1. Name a database one would use to research a controversial issue?_____

2. Name a database one would use to research classical music?_____

3. Name a database one would use to research careers?_____

4. What are the operating hours during the semester?_____

5. What do students use for a library card?_____

6. How long can you check out a book?_____

7. Which Library Staff Member would you contact for assistance with Interlibrary Loans?_____

8. Can you check out videos from the library? If so, how long?_____

9. How many subscribed periodicals does the library hold?_____

10. Is this library connected to or affiliated with any other libraries?_____

   If so, how many?_____

Part IV

Career Research: During your visit to the college library, take some time to research a career that interests you.

1. Name of Career:_____

2. Using the library electronic resources, list three Internet sources about your career:
   a. Name of Source_____

   b. Name of Source_____

   c. Name of Source_____

3. Using the library's card catalog, find three articles or books related to your career you could use for a research paper:
   a. Name of Source_____

   b. Name of Source_____

   c. Name of Source_____

10. What have I learned in teaching this chapter that I will incorporate next time?

_____

_____
_____
_____
_____
_____
_____
_____
_____
_____
_____
_____
_____
_____
_____
_____
_____
_____
_____
_____
_____
_____
_____
_____
_____
_____
_____
_____
_____
_____
_____
_____
_____
_____
_____
_____
_____

CHAPTER 7: ENGAGING, LISTENING, AND NOTE-TAKING IN CLASS

1. Why is this chapter important?

You can't open a college success book without seeing a whole chapter devoted to being involved in class, paying attention, and taking notes. In fact, if you "Google" note-taking, you'll find thousands of hits, along with books completely dedicated to the subject. So why do so many students still struggle with taking notes when so many resources are available?

Note-taking is actually a complicated process. You must listen, write, and decide what's important at the same time. Students often don't know how to focus on the main ideas and what signals to look for in the text or listen for from their instructors that say "This is important!" When you come right down to it, most students are never told how to *attend* class—not just show up, but participate in the learning process. Being engaged in class is an essential component of college success. While it is important for students to be *physically* present in class, it is even more important for them to be *mentally* present.

Students also have probably never thought about the fact that the way an instructor teaches may or may not be a good fit for the way they learn. They may simply report that they dislike Professor X or they find Professor Y to be boring. Many students never think about the relationship between how their teacher teaches, how they learn, and how to take effective notes either when reading a text or listening to a class presentation. By empowering students with the knowledge of how to learn optimally, they can easily translate their instructor's teaching style into their own learning style. This enables students to take control of their own learning both inside and outside the classroom.

Think back: Can you ever remember anyone telling you that when you go to class you really have to train yourself to pay attention? Maybe for a few students it feels natural to go into the classroom, sit in the front, tune out everything else that is going on, ask questions to stay engaged, and take good notes. However, that's not the case for most students. Students may have to be reminded that listening effectively requires learning about the process and then practicing the skills. Some really important tips are to sit in the front of the room, ask questions, and practice good note-taking, but also skimming the material before class is a key strategy for being prepared to focus. It sets the stage for knowing what the professor is going to discuss. Encourage students to get to class early, and stay late (to foster relationships or ask further clarifying questions). Remind your students that it is important to be physically and mentally prepared before class begins. Often instructors give an outline of the day's session at the beginning of class, and at the end, they tend to summarize. So it is vital for students to tune in right away.

It's really important that students make the connection that some of their successes or failures in school may be connected to the way they learn and the fit with their instructor. Students can't control the way an instructor teaches; they can only control what they do about it. However, many students excuse their lack of learning by criticizing the way their instructors teach. Emphasize that it is always the students' job to adapt to their instructor's teaching, *not* the instructor's job to customize their teaching to each student's learning preference.

2. What are this chapter's learning objectives?

- ➤ How to get engaged in class
- ➤ How to listen with focus
- ➤ How to vary listening styles according to lecture styles
- ➤ How to take good notes
- ➤ How to vary note-taking systems and why
- ➤ How to ask questions in class
- ➤ How to use notes to achieve the best results

3. How should I launch this chapter?

This chapter (like every chapter of *FOCUS*) is vital to students' college success. Anecdotally, many instructors report that today's students appear to take fewer notes—perhaps because they find it too taxing, perhaps because they are largely kinesthetic learners, or perhaps because they've never learned how to do it effectively. Here are some suggestions you might try to launch this chapter.

- **Ask students to take a few minutes to think about an instructor whose lectures they find easy to understand.** Because awareness is a really important part of this chapter, ask students to spend a lot of time this week observing their professors and identifying those whose lecture styles they can easily understand and those whose styles are more difficult for them. This may even help them develop a habit of tuning in to professor's styles. Of course, the level of interest a student has in the course material will figure in, but at some fundamental level, students need to discover what works best for them and learn to develop "coping strategies." For example, if students are extraverts who enjoy lively discussion, but that is not the style of the professor, they might ask a classmate to discuss the lecture over lunch. You may have to encourage your students to try many different classroom strategies. By asking your students to become hyperaware of their professors' teaching methods, they will begin to see what adjustments they need to make in order to learn more effectively. Discuss the insights your students gained this week as a class, because there will be some common characteristics that students will describe about the ideal/clear professor. However, there will be variations on what your students prefer based on their VARK preferences.

- **Do a mini lecture and ask students to take notes.** Before you go too far into the chapter, do a mini lecture, perhaps about study skills or maybe just something fun with a lot of facts. Ask students to take notes. Pepper your lecture with words like advantages, important, causes, findings, purpose, reason, and conclusions. Use numbering such as first, second, third. After about 10 minutes, ask students to compare notes with the student next to them, and notice the differences, if any, in their notes. Alternatively, show your class a 10 minute segment of a lecture from YouTube (consider using the first 10 minutes of Randy Pausch Last Lecture: Achieving Your Childhood Dreams, found by searching Randy Pausch on YouTube). This should lead into a discussion about how people may take notes differently, but also highlight the fact that signal words are used to help emphasize points. A similar "formal" exercise like this appears in the chapter as Exercise 7.4.

- **Remember that ESL Students may require additional attention from you.** Make sure you also go over the listening tips for students who are not native speakers of English. You may have to reserve some time on the side for extra work with these students. It can be a sensitive situation if they are only one or two in the class. Instead of singling out your international students in class, invite them to your office or to meet you in the school cafeteria for lunch. Tell them that it's important to you that all of your students have the best opportunity to learn in your class, and ask these students if they have questions. If they don't have any questions at this point in the term, reiterate your willingness to help if the need arises. It's important that you respect the boundaries of your international students. Some may not require additional help, while others may simply be shy about asking for it. Often, they can be highly motivated students.

- **Developmental Students and Returning Adult Learners:** Developmental students can be very passive learners. Make a point of calling on all students and help them to understand that college is a safe place to take a risk. Encourage all students to take notes on the material they have read and ask them to bring the notes into class and take the time to check their notes. Returning adult learners sometimes experience difficulties with balancing life with school. Take the time to check in with your students before or after class to see how they are doing. Remind your students who have young children about the *FOCUS* on Kids worksheets available in CourseMate. This chapter's worksheet is on listening.

- **Going beyond the book.** As was mentioned earlier, there are literally thousands of resources available for students to learn the skills of engagement, listening, and note-taking. The missing link for many is connecting those skills to something that is meaningful and timely. Have your students find out if there are note-taking or study skills workshops offered on your campus. If so, find out the times and require students to go. If it is a workshop showing students how to take notes from a text, make sure students use a reading from a text book in a course they are currently taking. In fact, whatever activities you use in this chapter, require students to use real, live material that they apply to courses they are currently taking.

© 2012 Cengage Learning. All Rights Reserved. May not be scanned, copied or duplicated, or posted to a publicly accessible website, in whole or in part.

4. How should I use the *FOCUS* Challenge Case?

Rachel loves children and has enrolled in two evening classes working towards an associate's degree in early childhood development. Despite looking forward to opening her home-based daycare center, Rachel is struggling in her first class, Child Development I. Her instructor is young and has an accent. Rachel is struggling to pay attention and take notes, her mind wanders and she blames the instructor's accent for the difficulty she is experiencing. Before class she struggles with reading and taking notes because her young children demand much of her time. Rachel does not know what to do, she is embarrassed to ask questions in class and she does not want the instructor to think she is struggling so early in the course. It is too late to drop the course and she needs the credits for her degree.

Be aware that this situation is common among first-year students. Often they are faced with instructors who have little teaching experience, are not native English speakers, or seem unavailable to students. There are many ways to use this Challenge Case in your class:

- **Direct It!** Assign a "scene director" for the Challenge Case. After students review the Challenge Case, assign a student to role-play Rachel and her instructor, Ms. Kindler. The director can stop the scene at any point and redirect the "actors" as well as get input from the "critics"—the other students in class!
  - o Scene 1: Direct Rachel to ask questions in class. What questions should she ask?
  - o Scene 2: Direct Rachel to meet with Ms. Kindler during her office hours. How should Rachel discuss her concentration problems? What advice could her instructor give her?
- Ask your students to reflect on suggestions they might give Rachel's instructor, if they could.
- What do the pictures around the Challenge Case tell your students about Rachel?
- After they identify ways her instructor could be more engaging in class, ask them how Rachel could become more engaged. Remind students that it is Rachel's responsibility (and theirs, as well) to become engaged in the classroom, not her instructor's job to be more engaging (although many conscientious faculty work continually on developing new and better teaching skills).
- After this exercise, take a few minutes with the class to discuss one or two things Rachel can do to make the situation better.
- What resources are available to students like Rachel at your school?
- Ask them if they would follow the advice they give Rachel themselves. If they wouldn't, ask them why.

5. What important features does this chapter include?

Again, you will see some of the really important recurring features in this book. While you and your students are becoming very familiar with these features, now would be a good time to change things up a bit. One way to do this is to ask students to complete their favorite feature. Have them present their feature to the class and explain what criteria they used in their selection.

Readiness and Reality Checks

As mentioned in earlier chapters, it's important for students to think about *what they don't know about* what they are about to learn to help them *FOCUS* on learning new things. However, this chapter can be a bit tricky for students. Many students *think* they know how to take notes and listen in class. But what might be missing are the techniques of doing *both* well at the same time. It will be interesting for students to check their "reality" with their readiness for this chapter. Start class off with the following activity: enlarge the Readiness and Reality Checks and paste them on butcher block paper, which you tape to the wall. When students arrive, give them sticky notes. Ask them to anonymously rate each item, and then place all of their sticky notes on the butcher block paper (or simply put their marks on the butcher block paper itself). Look for patterns in the class. This could be a fun way to integrate the concept of being prepared for class in a non-threatening environment.

How Full Is Your Plate?

Ask your students if they would rather have a surgeon who was fast or one who was thorough? Slow and steady wins the race. This feature asks students to slow down, a concept not often discussed today. Speed is exciting, but take a look at the homework your students are turning in. Was it done quickly or was time taken to turn in a quality product? Remind your students to take the time to slow down and concentrate on increasing the quality of their lives.

Control: Your Learning

Students need to understand that while they may not feel as if they are in the driver's seat as a student; they do have some control over how much they learn. A good back seat driver lets the driver know when it's dangerous or they are not comfortable while not insulting the driver. Students should be assertive enough to explain to a teacher when they do not understand without offending him or her. If they can understand exactly why they are having trouble, they have a better chance of explaining this to the instructor, or simply change what they need to do to optimize their learning. The Lecture Style Analysis Sheet/Co-Worker Analysis Worksheet is a great way for students to zero in on exactly what is happening in each of their classes and provide some needed insight.

Self-Assessments

Exercise 7.1 (How Well Do You Listen?) asks students to respond to questions about how well they listen in a variety of circumstances. At the end of the assessment the students add up their scores and can see where their scores fall within three ranges that differentiate among excellent, good, and listeners who need to change. This is a great opportunity for some peer teaching. Ask your excellent listeners to "teach" the class. They may identify certain behaviors for their peers that enable them to listen "hard."

VARK Activity

This activity is designed to help students make connections between their preferred VARK learning modality and an actual assignment. Taking good notes really does involve all of the modalities so think about assigning students to do something that they would not normally choose—this might be the time to develop a skill a little more rather than use their preference.

Careers Outlook

The career focus in the chapter is early childhood education and we meet Home Day Care owner, Tori Craig. Craig explains that working with eight to ten children every day requires organizational skills. She suggests to students that getting a degree in early childhood development is critical, and that taking some business classes is helpful in running the business. Do you have students interested in this career? What personal skills would be important for this job? Nationally the workforce demand is good for this profession.

6. Which in-text exercises should I use?

There are four exercises built into this chapter. Each is unique and a very engaging for students. Connect these activities, if you can, to courses students are taking and real-life situations.

EXERCISE 7.1 HOW WELL DO YOU LISTEN?

Why do this activity?
There are a number of reasons why this is a good activity for students. Students may never have even thought about how they listen. Here, they can quickly identify areas where they need improvement. They also get immediate feedback on areas where they excel. In addition, it reinforces for students that they have a great amount of control over their own success in college. This activity requires students to respond to questions and results in a score that differentiates excellent listeners, good listeners, and listeners who need to improve their skills.

What are the challenges and what can you expect?
The only real challenge will be that students may not want to admit to the some of the things that they don't do. If their scores are low, they may be embarrassed to admit it. You have to create a climate where students can readily admit what they need to improve upon. Providing an enlarged copy of the diagnostic could help here. Again, pass out sticky notes to your class. Ask them to anonymously place their answers on the butcher block paper. Pay special attention as your students use their sticky notes. This will allow you to identify students who have low scores without alerting their peers. This can also be done on a whiteboard by having students mark "X's."

How much time will it take?
15-20 minutes

How should I debrief?
A good way to debrief is to have students line up on a continuum. Ask those on the lower end why they think they are not good listeners, and then ask for someone on the high end to give that person one specific tip that works for them. Continue to do this with all students. Another option is to have students send you an e-mail about what they discovered about their listening skills.

EXERCISE 7.2 "FOCUSED" MULTITASKING

Why do this activity?
This activity is designed to help students see how focusing one's attention and using all of one's VARK preferences at once can yield different results. This activity also highlights the different note-taking systems and allows students to try something they may not have used before.

What are the challenges and what can I expect?
There are no real challenges for this activity. Also consider using a YouTube clip of a lecture for this activity.

How much time will it take?
20-30 minutes

How should I debrief?
Give each group a quiz based on the lecture. Have students compare their scores and see which note-taking group did the best. What did students think about while listening/viewing the lecture? Were they able to "focus?" Why or why not?

EXERCISE 7.3 HOW MUCH DOES ASKING QUESTIONS HELP?

Why do this activity?
This is a great activity to prove to students why it's important to ask questions in class. In Rachel's case, she was hesitant to ask questions for fear of looking as if she didn't know what was going on. This activity shows students that asking questions clarifies information and in the process you are imprinting and remembering more than if you were passively listening.

What are the challenges and what can you expect?
Students should really enjoy this activity and laugh a lot when the drawings don't look at all like the one that the student lecturer is trying to describe. One challenge is that this can be time consuming if students have drawings that are very complicated and a time limit is not assigned. Here are two sample drawings you can use with your class.

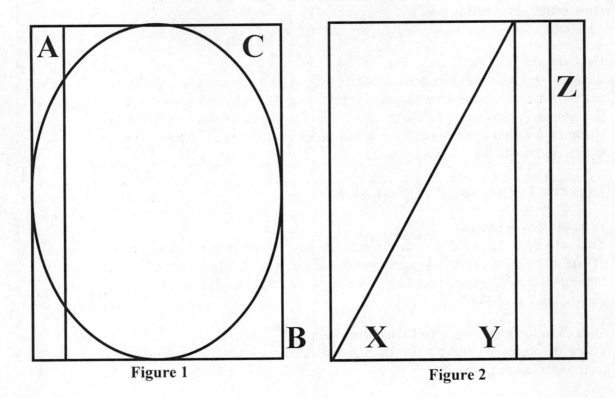

Figure 1   Figure 2

How much time will it take?
25-30 minutes

How should I debrief?
Have students fill in the chart with the rounds as well as the elapsed time, what they thought was correct, and what actually was. In some ways the chart will "debrief" for the class, but you should ask for a few students to recap what they learned by doing the activity. Asking questions in lecture classes takes more time, but it typically gets much better results.

EXERCISE 7.4 NOTE-TAKING 4-M

Why do this activity?
Effective note-taking is critical to college success. Allowing students to compare their notes with others can only help students to see where they might need to improve. Consider letting students try this technique for a real test in your class. Let pairs of students work together for the "best possible" notes to use in a real situation.

What are the challenges and what can you expect?
You will find that some students take copious notes because they don't know how to distinguish between essential and non-essential material. If two or three students with the same style are put together, they won't learn very much from each other. These students

may think quantity is better than quality. Try grouping students based on their types, or level of skill they have demonstrated in some other note-taking activity. Students should answer the "M" questions: what do students find that matches in their notes, what is missing, what does the lecture mean (the main points), and then measure how much they learned by using a "Visible Quiz."

How much time will it take?
10-15 minutes

How should I debrief?
You have a few options here. First, you might create a few sets of notes. Purposefully create some good and some bad examples. Or think about saving notes from the semester before to save you from creating your own, but make sure it's the same lecture. Ask students to identify which are more helpful notes. Why? Which "M's" played a part in the good or weak notes? Remember quantity does not necessarily mean quality.

7. Which additional exercises might enrich students' learning?

Taking Notes the Colorful Way
Class activity
Materials needed: Three different colors of magic markers, an article from the newspaper (choose something current and interesting)
Time: 30-50 minutes, depending on the size of the group
Goal: To help students identify the main parts of a story
Place students in small groups of two or three. Give each student colored markers and the story. Have one additional copy of the story for the group. Have each student read the article and individually using three different colors; mark the headings, main ideas and details of the story. Next, students in the group compare colors and work together to produce one colored coded story that they all agree on. (If you don't want to use colors, students can circle some parts, underline others, and star the last).

Listening with a Purpose
(Staley, C. [2003] *50 Ways to Leave Your Lecture* [p.112])
Class activity
Materials needed: none
Time: lecture plus 20-40 minutes
Goal: To help students listen attentively to lectures and respond to course material

Team	Role	Assignment - After the lecture is finished
1	Questioners	Ask two questions about the material.
2	Nay-Sayers	Comment on two points with which the group disagrees.
3	Yea-Sayers	Comment on two points with which the group agrees.
4	Explainers	Give two specific examples that explain the lecture.

Before the lecture, give the teams their assignments. After the lecture, allow the teams to confer. Proceed from group to group, asking each team to do what you have requested. After all teams have finished, discuss listening skills with the entire group. (Variation: additional roles many be created for variety or to demonstrate a particular principle.)

<u>Web Connections—Finding Help Online</u>
Out of class activity
Materials needed: A computer
Time: 30-50 minutes
Goal: To help students identify sources online that will help them learn to be better note takers
Have students search and find at least five different web addresses for note-taking. List the web addresses and have students choose the best source and explain why. Collect the top choices for students (they can send you their choices electronically) and create an online note-taking supplement for the class.

8. What other activities can I incorporate to make the chapter my own?

We all tend to have our biases on our favorite way to attend, be engaged, and take notes. Share your story with the class. You might further put your own spin on this chapter, depending on how your class is organized. If you are lucky enough to be teaching this class as part of a learning community, you will have multiple opportunities to use real class information to try our some of the note-taking techniques.

Included here, all in one place, are Activity Options taken from the Annotated Instructor's Edition.

ACTIVITY OPTION (p. 160): In addition to being cheated out of learning, the issue with interrupting class is really about a student's right to learn. When one student disrupts the class, they have robbed others of their right to learn and in a sense stolen their money. Sometimes students won't speak up about others who are unruly, but you can be sure that you have students in class who are upset if their learning is frequently disrupted. You might even ask students how they would feel if someone was constantly talking to their neighbor. To test this out, before class, ask two students to stage talking in class and then debrief. How did classmates feel about the disruption?

ACTIVITY OPTION (p. 162): Divide the class into groups and give each group a different topic to speak on. These may include the topics presented in this chapter. Have each group select a spokesperson and have the group decide on the gestures the spokesperson is to use. Have students decide which speaker was most effective and why.

ACTIVITY OPTION (p. 164): Assign students to listen to the same lecture. You may have some on campus that you can download for the class in podcast format, a YouTube lecture or ask students to attend the same lecture. Have students watch for gestures and speech patterns to figure out what were the most important points. Have students return to class to report what they thought was most important. As an alternative, you can give a lecture or videotape someone to do this as an in-class activity.

ACTIVITY OPTION (p. 166): For homework, have students observe their other classes for a week and come to class briefly describing the type of lecturers they have. They must include one example that illustrates the type. As a class compare the types and strategize about how students can successfully adapt to the style.

ACTIVITY OPTION (p. 169): This is a great opportunity to get students to line up based on their scores, ranging from low on one side of the room to high on the other. First, remind students that it's okay if they are not yet good listeners. The goal of this activity is to learn from each other. What can students who are not aural learners on the VARK do to compensate or translate into a learning preference they do have?

ACTIVITY OPTION (p. 174): Prepare a lecture on a simple topic that can be easily recorded in the Cornell system or as a mind map. Have students listen to the lecture and take down the important information in the Cornell system. Then, divide students into groups and give them a graphic organizer to fill in as a mind map for the lecture. Have the groups compare their maps.

ACTIVITY OPTION (p. 180): Two sample drawings you can use with Exercise 7.3 appear above. These drawings are also shown in the on-screen FOCUSPoints for this chapter.

9. What homework might I assign?

Give students lecture notes that you have prepared and have them use one of the note-taking techniques described in the chapter to take notes. Tell students that they must write the notes on one side of a 3 x 5 index card that they can use later for an in-class quiz. The goal is to help students see the value in taking concise notes.

Journal Entries
One: Have students write a one page journal entry, or send you an e-mail describing a note-taking strategy that works best for them and why. Tell students that it does not have to be exactly like the approaches suggested, but would be even better with a combination of strategies that works best for them.

Two: Have students write a one page journal entry, or send you an e-mail reflecting on a situation where they felt there was a disconnect between them and their instructor. Did they do anything about it? If so, what? What was the result of doing or not doing anything? If they could do things differently now, what would they do?

Three: Use the Insight → Action prompt as journal or blog assignment.

10. What have I learned in teaching this chapter that I will incorporate next time?

CHAPTER 8: DEVELOPING YOUR MEMORY

1. Why is this chapter important?

In the last chapter we talked about the fact that you can't open a college success book without seeing sections, chapters, and whole books on how to be involved in class, pay attention, and take notes. The same can be said for learning how to successfully develop memory skills. No matter what and how they study in college, students will be required to memorize and recall information. While some people just seem to be naturally good at it, others are not. But, the good news is that all students can learn to make the most of their memories.

While we often talk about memory-enhancing techniques, most students have never been taught them specifically. If you survey your class, most likely students have done a ton of studying, but most would be hard pressed to tell you exactly what technique they use, other than simple strategies like re-reading or highlighting. Sometimes students will say, "I can't understand why I did so poorly on my literature exam; I re-read the short stories six times!" (But how much did they process and commit to memory?) Or "I wore out my yellow highlighter studying for my calculus test!" If you check their textbooks, nearly all of every page is highlighted because they don't know what's important. When studying for a calculus test, re-reading isn't a good way to master the material; working problems sets until you understand the principles and processes is. So, what are some of the techniques this chapter suggests that can actually work wonders?

First, in this chapter students will learn some of the basic research and information about memory. Memory and cognition are actually complex research topics, but this chapter makes this information accessible to students, and then focuses on practical strategies for students to try. They will learn about the "Three R's of Remembering: Record, Retain and Retrieve." The image of a digital camera is used to help students visualize the camera and how it works to remember these terms. Once students have mastered this, they go on to learn different ways to master their memory. The broad categories that students learn about include how to make information stick, how to make it meaningful, how to make it mnemonic, how to manipulate it, and how to make material funny. Students should be encouraged to try each of the techniques and find a few that really work for them.

2. What are this chapter's learning objectives?

➢ Why memory is a process, not a thing
➢ How memory works like a digital camera
➢ How to improve memory using 20 different techniques
➢ How memory can fail you

© 2012 Cengage Learning. All Rights Reserved. May not be scanned, copied or duplicated, or posted to a publicly accessible website, in whole or in part.

3. How should I launch this chapter?

Think about launching this chapter by asking students how they memorize information for a test. Ask students to start to list the different ways they approach material and write them on the board. When there are no more examples coming from the class, ask students to see if these techniques cluster together in any way. You might begin to see examples of mnemonic devices, silly sentences, chunking, manipulating materials, or other ways that can be grouped together. Help students to label these groups of techniques, and let students know that you are going to learn more about each of these approaches. It's likely that students will hit on at least several of the broad categories introduced in the chapter.

- **Ask students to take a few minutes to think of a time when they went into a test feeling prepared.** Why? What did they do to prepare and how did they do it? Ask students to describe how they felt? Confident? In control? Relaxed? Now ask students to explain what they did. Did they work alone? Did they work with a group of friends who quizzed each other? What specific techniques did they use?

- **Ask students to recount a time when they went into a test unprepared, because they didn't study enough, or were just not sure they were prepared.** It's generally clear to students when they know that the reason they did not feel prepared going into a test was because they simply did not study enough. What is harder to pinpoint is the feeling of uncertainty. Sometimes students do study a lot, but they are just not studying in an efficient way, or they study using lower level thinking skills (to recall facts, etc.) when the exam asks them to apply information instead. Some of the study techniques in this chapter should help. For example, the "Curiosity" mini-article, Act on Your Memory! contains some excellent strategies used by actors to memorize their lines.

- **Developmental Students and Returning Adult Learners:** Developmental learners often struggle with memorizing information. Organization and retention can also be problematic. Remind all students that not all techniques work for everyone, and that it is important to try new ways to organize and remember information. Returning adult learners often have multiple things they are trying to remember. Encourage them as well to practice some of the techniques covered in this chapter. All students will benefit from Kevin Baxter's story in the *FOCUS Challenge Case*, no matter what age they are.

- **Going beyond the book.** Studying and remembering information is really a multi-part process. First, you have to be studying what is really important. Students can do a bang-up job of remembering a list of facts or times and dates, but if it's really not important for the test, it is not going to help. Facts and dates may not be all that important on an essay test. Do they really comprehend the information they're memorizing? It's important to know what needs to be learned, and what a test will be like. Will there be multiple-choice questions? Will the test include essay questions? Encourage students to ask their professors about suggestions that they may have on how to approach the material for the test. Does the professor have any sample tests that can be looked over? Do they know any students who had the professor the previous semester? The more one knows about how they will be tested, the more focused their study techniques can become.

4. How should I use the *FOCUS* Challenge Case?

Kevin is like a growing number of students who are now in college. These students are either returning to college to finish a degree they started a long time ago or older students who have always longed to get a degree and are just starting. Maybe they are in a job with no future, or one that they don't enjoy. Many of the jobs that individuals held twenty years ago did not require a college degree, but now they require at least an associate's degree. Students like Kevin, bright and capable, find themselves at a crossroads in their lives. Do I give up my full time job and security to go back to school? When you think about it, at 40 with longevity predictions well into one's 80s, Kevin has many years left to do something he loves. But, Kevin begins to question his ability. It's clearly not as if he isn't trying. He needs to work smarter, not harder. There are many ways to use this Challenge Case in class:

- **Direct It!** Assign a "scene director" for the Challenge Case. After students review the Challenge Case, assign a student to role-play Kevin and another student to role-play Kevin's advisor. The director can stop the scene at any point and redirect the "actors" as well as get input from the "critics"—the other students in class!
    - o Scene 1: Direct Kevin to meet with his advisor. What would/should Kevin say to his advisor, what encouragement could his advisor give him?
    - o Scene 2: Ask the students to "write" Scene 2. Who would they suggest Kevin speak with? Is there a learning lab or other learning assistance program available on your campus? Suggest students review what they have learned about your campus to create Scene 2.
- Have the class discuss one or two things Kevin can do to be more effective studying.
- What advice would they give him?
- What do your students have in common with Kevin?
- How could Kevin improve his memory?
- What study techniques might be helpful for Kevin?
- What resources are available for Kevin on your campus?

5. What important features does this chapter include?

Again, you will see some of the really important recurring themes in this book. By now you are familiar with these. A few points will be discussed about each.

Readiness and Reality Checks

By the time students are in college, they have had more than their share of opportunities for remembering things. Most likely they have not thought very much about what they have done, or how they have studied. They just know that they have been faced with many memorization challenges—for many students strict memorization was what exams consisted of. The Readiness Check may be eye-opening for some students. And because many students either don't find high school challenging or bypass opportunities to learn at their best in that environment, they may assume they have this topic nailed. Of course, it will be interesting for students to check their Reality Check results at the end of this chapter.

Curiosity: Act on Your Memory!

Most likely, students in your class watch their fair share of television and movies. They may well be interested in how actors and actresses learn their lines. It's not just about saying their lines or simply learning them, but successful actors and actresses learn their lines by techniques such as chunking, setting goals (what am I trying to accomplish in the storyline as I deliver the lines?), moving around while learning, and concentrating on the meaning of the words. Hopefully, the curiosity surrounding the success of their favorite stars will motivate students to study their approach. You might want to start this discussion off by asking students how they learn song lyrics without even trying. Is repetition at work? Do they associate particular songs with important events attached to them, like first dates?

VARK Activity

This activity is designed to help students make connections between their preferred VARK learning modality and an actual assignment. This activity is really helpful for students to try a way of remembering something based on the way they learn best. Have each student present to the class one of the activity options (their choice). In addition to presenting the activity, have students explain why they chose a particular activity, how it's a good match for their VARK learning preferences and what they learned about themselves while doing the activity. This is also described in an Activity Option.

Self-Assessments

There are two self-assessments for this chapter, "Subjective Memory Test" and "Test Your Memory." The "Subjective Memory Test" self-assessment has two sections, one (A) for general memory tasks and another (B) for academic memory tasks. Students are asked if their scores for parts A and B differ, and if their scores dropped as they went down the list (since the list gets harder and harder). An Activity Option asks students to determine the reasons why they did better on one part than on the other. "Test Your Memory" is an objective assessment that asks students to memorize words and then test for recall.

Career Outlook

The career focus in this chapter is computer assisted drafting. We meet Carlos Gomez, a computer aided draftsman. Has anyone in the class considered a career as a computer aided draftsman? What about the job outlook for this career and job stability? What impact does this profession have on one's other goals in life? What careers are associated with this field?

How Full Is Your Plate?

It is fairly easy for individuals to commit to the idea of time management. The hard part seems to be to practicing those principals and actually using the tools. Challenge your students to get in the practice of reviewing their planners each night or morning before starting their day.

FOCUS TV: Memory

This episode provides a closer look at memory and introduces Kevin Baxter to your students. The field report introduces students to memory expert Dr. Susan Di Santi as she explains memory to the field reporter. This episode is available in CourseMate or via the Power Lecture CD's FOCUSPoints.

6. Which in-text exercises should I use?

There are two exercises built into this chapter. Each is unique and very engaging for students. Connect these activities, if you can, to real life courses and situations for the students. Included here are descriptions of why they have been included, how much time each one will probably take, and how you might debrief each one.

EXERCISE 8.1 SUBJECTIVE MEMORY TEST

Why do this activity?
This assessment helps students understand their own perception of how well their memory works. Many students want to improve their memory and generally students perform better on general memory tasks compared to academic memory tasks.

What are the challenges and what can you expect?
There are no perceived challenges for this activity. It is helpful to remind students that the lower their score the better.

How much time will it take?
This activity should take about 10-15 minutes including the time to debrief.

How should I debrief?
Ask students how they scored on Part A and Part B. Generally, students will perform better in general memory. Ask your students what are their top three difficult academic memory tasks and as a group brainstorm techniques students have used to improve in those areas. Do students believe there is one technique that will work in all academic memory situations? Ask students to review the list of Who, What and How questions that appear on page 189 to help them understand that there is no one-size-fits-all approach to memory.

EXERCISE 8.2 TEST YOUR MEMORY

Why do this activity?
This is a great activity to help students to see that there are varieties of memory techniques that one can use to study the same list of words.

What are the challenges and what can you expect?
There are really not many challenges for this activity. The list of words is not too long, and, in fact, it can be a good confidence builder for students who never thought they were very good at memorizing information. Students will be able to see that a few simple techniques can really improve one's ability to remember information.

How much time will it take?
This activity should take about 30 minutes; depending on how much time you wish to devote to debriefing.

How should I debrief?
One of the really valuable parts of this activity is for students to see that there is more than one way to approach remembering information. Students should share their techniques with the class. See if there are a few common approaches to learning this material. List the different approaches. Have students indicate their learning type to see if there is any connection between types and approaches to learning the lists.

---

7. Which additional exercises might enrich students' learning?

<u>I Want To Be an Artist</u>
Class activity
Materials needed: Newsprint, markers, and a list of 20 words (randomly chosen from a newspaper)
Time: 30-50 minutes, depending on the size of the group
Goal: To help students create a visual to remember information
Place students in small groups of 3-4. Give each student colored markers and paper. Groups should develop a picture (visual) that helps them to remember all of the words they have been provided.

<u>Silly Sentences</u>
Class activity
Materials needed: the same 20 words used in the activity above (or 20 others if you wish), newsprint, and markers
Time: 20-40 minutes
Goal: To help students create a visual to remember information
Students should work in groups (maybe in the same groups as in the activity above), to learn the list of words by coming up with some silly sentences to help them remember the lists. Have groups share their sentences with the class and have class members decide on which sentence would most help them remember the words.

<u>Compare and Contrast</u>
Out of class activity
Materials needed: A prepared lecture on the pros and cons of studying in groups or studying alone (or some similar lecture)
Time: 30-50 minutes
Goal: To help students differentiate and remember similar information
Deliver a short lecture to the class on the positives and negatives of studying in groups versus studying alone. As a class, develop a chart that helps students compare and contrast material presented. After the chart is completed, have students put the charts away. Give a quiz asking students to list the pros and cons. (You may decide if the quiz counts.) When students are finished completing the quiz, ask them to describe how they remembered the information.

8. What other activities can I incorporate to make the chapter my own?

If your students are part of a learning community, taking courses that are linked, check with the other instructors to see if there is any content that they suggest students learn for the next test. Use a number of the techniques suggested in this chapter to learn the material. If you are teaching returning adult learners you might ask them if there is something at work that they need to learn. Are they taking a certification exam? As much as possible, make learning the suggested approaches in this chapter personal and relevant by using real-life, right-now material.

Included here, all in one place, are Activity Options taken from the Annotated Instructor's Edition.

ACTIVITY OPTION (p. 193): For the next class, have students bring in a list of terms they need to memorize for another class. Often first-year students are taking biology or history, or even math formulas can work for this exercise. Have students present their challenges and, in small groups or as a whole class, brainstorm ways to chunk or categorize the information.

ACTIVITY OPTION (p. 194): Divide the students into groups based on learning preferences. Give each group a different short poem to memorize. Try to select poems that most people would not know. Ask the group to devise clues to help them remember the poem. Have one student in the group write down all the ways that were suggested for learning the poem and the ways they used. Call the groups together and have one person in each group recite the poem.

ACTIVITY OPTION (p. 196): Since students have probably done this activity in preparation for class, consider doing a visual activity in class. Put a variety of items out on your desk (about ten), and leave them there for two minutes. Put them back in a bag and then ask students to write down as many as they can. If you are using related objects, like the things from your briefcase, students are more likely to remember them, as opposed to unrelated items. You might even try two sets of items to make this point and then guide students to the conclusion that categorizing, relating, and grouping things can help them remember.

ACTIVITY OPTION (p. 196): Have students make a list of their classes and beneath that the types of tests given. Have students think of the five ways to "Make It Stick." Have students list which method or methods would be best to use to study for the next exam.

ACTIVITY OPTION (p. 197): Give students an article and tell them to read it for the next class session. During the next class, ask students to take out a piece of paper. Do not allow them to have the article out. Tell them to, honestly, write on the back if they read the article or not. Then have them turn the paper over. Begin discussing the article and have them take notes. Have the students who had read the article and had not read the article compare notes. Hopefully, those who had read the article understood the lecture better and took better notes.

ACTIVITY OPTION (p. 198): After reading, "Curiosity," have students list each class and the technique they would use it in and how.

ACTIVITY OPTION (p. 199): Have students draw out a loci system to memorize something presented in this book. Have them be prepared to share it next class.

ACTIVITY OPTION (p. 200): Break the class into four groups and have them memorize ¼ of the presidents of the United States or some other common list. (You might have to fill in the gaps for a few students.) Assign one group to use the spelling approach, another the loci, another the link or narrate, and the final group the peg system. Give groups about fifteen minutes to learn their lists, and then report back to the group the strategies they used and how successful they were.

ACTIVITY OPTION (p. 200): Pass out a short article to highlight. Have each student work individually. Then divide into groups and decide which person highlighted most effectively. Have each group present the best one to the class. Did the best paper from each group have anything in common? If so, make a list on the board of strategies to use when highlighting.

ACTIVITY OPTION (p. 201): Present this scenario to your students. Explain to them that they have three hours to learn a chapter. Have them write down what they would do to master the material. Make a list of the approaches on the board. Have students identify which approaches would be active, effective approaches and why. Would there be any that would be just a waste of time?

ACTIVITY OPTION (p. 201): Give students one week to prepare for "Show and Tell." Have students apply at least one of the techniques presented in the chapter to information they needed to learn for another class. They will need to write out what was the class, what they needed to learn, and what techniques they used. If they make flash cards, used a loci system, or created another memory tool, they need to bring it in to share with the class.

ACTIVITY OPTION (p. 203): Have students quickly come up with a mnemonic sentence to remember the seven memory faults. Give them five minutes to do so, and then have a few students volunteer to read their sentences to the class.

ACTIVITY OPTION (p. 205): Have each student present to the class one of the activity options in the VARK Activity (their choice). In addition to presenting the activity, have students explain why they chose a particular activity, how it's a good match for their VARK preferred modality, and what they learned about themselves while doing the activity.

ACTIVITY OPTION (p. 206): To conclude this chapter, students should communicate the most important memorization method they learned about in this chapter. Ask students to e-mail one classmate, or you, a short description of which strategy they selected and why. Put this all into one document and send it to the entire class as a list of best practices for students.

9. What homework might I assign?

Ask students to turn in study techniques for a test or quiz they will take. The goal here is to help students apply some of the techniques they have learned in this chapter to information they are currently learning.

Journal Entries
One: Have students write a one-page journal entry, or send you an e-mail reflecting on the most valuable technique they learned in this chapter. Do they think they can use it in all types of memorization? If so, why and if not, why not?

Two: Use the Insight → Action steps as journal or blog assignments.

10. What have I learned in teaching this chapter that I will incorporate next time?

_____
_____
_____
_____
_____
_____
_____
_____
_____
_____
_____
_____
_____
_____

CHAPTER 9: READING AND STUDYING

1. Why is this chapter important?

It goes without saying that reading and studying in college are critical to student success. You might think that students have been doing this all of their lives, so why should this be a problem? After all, these students have made it to college so they must have been doing some things effectively all along, right?

Consider things like this as you teach this chapter. First, many of today's students do read, some don't read very much, but research indicates that half or fewer say they don't enjoy reading, and few read for pleasure. Some have never been taught how to read effectively, how and what to highlight or take notes when they are reading. In addition to students using their own approach to reading and studying, which may work part of the time, students may begin to wonder why they have to learn about something they already know how to do. The question is: Will the study habits they've used in the past be sufficient for the rigor of college courses? Often the answer to that question is no.

While most students have done plenty of reading prior to college, they may not have been taught reading strategies since sixth grade. In addition, don't be surprised to find that a fair number of students have never read an entire book—not even a novel. Non-readers are probably not going to tell you this because they are embarrassed, so you might even comment that this is a fact because of movies, television, and the Internet. Hopefully, students will see that there are times when the media that they have used before to get by, the bits and bytes of information, may not work anymore. Developmental students and students with reading disabilities present other opportunities for teaching this chapter. Let students know that in this chapter they will learn techniques that will serve them for a lifetime, and that it's not too late to become an optimally successful reader.

Students will not only learn how to distinguish between the different kinds of reading, they will learn about the right ways to read, how to take notes when reading and specific techniques like SQ3R (study, questions, read, recite, and review). They will also learn about a concept called metacognition. Metacognition is thinking about how one thinks and learning about how one learns. This concept is not about how someone else thinks or learns but how one might think about their own thinking and learning. Students will learn what they do efficiently, and what they may need to improve. Students will learn techniques for taking notes such as writing in the margin and how *not to* make the entire page bright yellow when highlighting.

2. What are this chapter's learning objectives?

> Why reading is important
> How to engage in focused reading
> How to tackle reading assignments
> What metacognition is and how it can help students
> How to become an intentional learner and create a master study plan
> Why learning is greater than the sum of its parts

3. How should I launch this chapter?

Consider launching this chapter by asking students for a show of hands in response to the question "Who thinks of themselves as an efficient reader?" Quickly ask students to explain what they do. Then, ask for a show of hands for those who feel they are masters at studying. You will probably find a number of the same students raise their hands because of the strong connection between reading efficiently and studying. But don't be surprised if you find that there are fewer students who believe they are masters of studying. Why? Some students may enjoy reading novels and see that as "being a good reader," but the proof for reading and studying effectively is in the tests they take, and their grades on tests may not be as high as they'd like.

- **Ask students to take a few minutes to describe reading something they really enjoyed and why.** Help students to label the different kinds of reading that they do: flipping through a magazine and scanning the directions for uploading music for their iPod is very different from reading a text book. Help students realize that the way they approach reading the material that they will then have to study further is connected to how efficiently they will remember information for a test.

- **Ask students to describe a time when they felt that they studied efficiently.** What time of the day was it? Where were they? What were they wearing? Were they listening to music at the same time? How long did they study? Did they take breaks? How did they know they were studying efficiently? Did they feel that they studied efficiently because they got a good grade on a test or quiz, or because they felt as if they really understood the material? Ask students to share their experiences with each other. Do you find any common characteristics in the class?

- **Developmental Students and Returning Adult Learners:** Developmental learners tend to lose focus in reading assignments. Remind students to take a short break after reading when they begin to lose interest. Encourage your students to seek help especially if they are enrolled in other reading intensive courses. Returning adult learners face many challenges in the area of reading and studying. Remind all students to find a space and time for reading and studying that works for them to focus on the tasks at hand. Also remind students with young children about the *FOCUS* on Kids worksheet for this chapter available in CourseMate.

- **Going beyond the book.** If you are teaching this course as part of a learning community of linked classes (for example, first-year seminar, introduction to psychology, male-female communication, and freshman composition) hopefully you will have access to the readings and books that all of the students in your class will be reading at the same time. (*Hint*: if you have any way that you can convince someone to connect your student success courses with another course, do it! Even these small linked courses become communities of learners, or learning communities, and without doing things much differently, research shows that learning is enhanced.) If your campus uses a common reading—a novel that

© 2012 Cengage Learning. All Rights Reserved. May not be scanned, copied or duplicated, or posted to a publicly accessible website, in whole or in part

brings in critical social issues, for example—for all entering students, use this book or even parts of it to apply reading and studying strategies. You might even consider choosing one of the current best sellers and form a book club to discuss the common reading once a week over coffee or lunch. This social connection to reading may be just what non-readers, like Katie from the *FOCUS* Challenge Case, can benefit from.

4. How should I use the *FOCUS* Challenge Case?

Katie Alexander is probably a student that an instructor would enjoy having in class. She is energetic and outgoing. It's not until the first test or quiz that you begin to wonder why Katie didn't do well. Is it because she isn't smart? Mostly likely it's because Katie doesn't know how to approach the material. She is overwhelmed. At her first college she was diagnosed with dyslexia. Katie depended on watching movies for the books she had to read in high school and can't rely on that strategy anymore. She wants to do well, but she is drowning. Try these options for getting a conversation going in class about the Case Study:

- **Direct It!** Assign a "scene director" for the Challenge Case. After students review the Challenge Case, assign a student to role-play Katie and another student to role-play Professor Harris-Black. The director can stop the scene at any point and redirect the "actors" as well as get input from the "critics"—the other students in class!
  - o Scene 1: Professor Harris-Black has asked Katie to stop by her office. Katie has failed the midterm. What questions should Katie ask her professor? What could her professor suggest to Katie?
  - o Scene 2: In this scene, ask someone to role-play Amanda. Direct Amanda to give some serious advice to Katie about her priorities and the services available on your campus that could help Katie be successful.
- Have the class discuss one or two things Katie can do to be more effective at reading and studying.
- Looking at Katie's receipts, calendar and method of studying, are Katie's priorities straight?
- Would Katie benefit from recorded textbooks?
- How could/should she use the services of Disability Support?

Students like Katie are fairly common among today's students. They are often kinesthetic learners who want structured, detailed material they can grab hold of. Abstract information doesn't sink in, and coupled with poor reading skills, the combination can be debilitating. Katie may benefit from working with a reading tutor, one-on-one, a specialist who can teach her specific strategies that will work for her. But inarguably, improving her reading and utilizing any accommodations she is eligible for will be essential to her college success.

5. What important features does this chapter include?

The recurring themes in the book can guide how you approach this chapter. Because students should be familiar with these, you might find out which features they like the most and tailor your class to what they like. Think about asking the class to break into small groups comprised of those who like the same feature. Can they lead a discussion on part of the feature they like the most?

Readiness and Reality Checks

For this Readiness Check, check to see how students responded. Most likely students will report that they do think reading and studying will affect their college success. What might be of interest is to see how much control students think they have over reading and studying. Students may just see themselves as "good or poor" readers and studiers, based on past experience. What they might not realize is that everyone will benefit from learning the techniques in this chapter, no matter where they start in terms of their skills. As always, it will be interesting for students to check their reality with their readiness for focusing on this chapter.

Stressed Out?

This section helps students to understand the impact of stress and how stress can lead to other health issues. Encourage students to track their stress symptoms and discuss ways they can reduce their stress levels.

Self-Assessments

There are two exercises in this chapter that are self-assessments. The first is in the section *Read Right!* on page 211. It is a prompt on study habits and asks students to check off issues such as boredom, fatigue, surroundings, etc. that might present reading challenges. Because reading has become an issue of national concern with more people engaging in alternative activities like movies and the Internet, the chapter points out that reading is a skill we must not lose as a culture and why.

The second is contained in Exercise 9.6: Do You Know How to Study? This assessment looks at metacognition and how students rate themselves.

Curiosity: Reading When English Is Your Second Language

This article is of value to both native speakers of English and those whose first language is another. English is not the easiest language to learn. The readings in this part of the chapter contain suggestions for ESL students, but are fun and interesting to everyone. Ask a volunteer to read the humorous poem "Hints on Pronunciation for Foreigners" aloud, and listen to whoever reads it stumble unintentionally! It's much more challenging than anyone could imagine! You might choose to meet separately with your ESL students to talk further about this mini-article, as well as encourage empathy in native English speakers by pointing out how challenging it might be for them to attend college in Korea or Russia or some other country with a language very different from English.

Careers Outlook

The career focus in this chapter is hospitality. In this chapter, we meet Jeff Pozzuto, Concierge. What about the job outlook for this career and job stability? Fortunately, the outlook is good. What other benefits are there to this job? If some of your students are interested in the hospitality field, encourage them to visit your career center or placement office to get more information.

FOCUS TV: Reading

This episode examines the different types of reading required for different settings. Dr. Gert Coleman discusses how reading text messages and e-mails is different than reading textbooks and novels. The importance of reading as a process and for comprehension are introduced in this segment. This episode is available in CourseMate or via the Power Lecture CD's FOCUSPoints.

6. Which in-text exercises should I use?

Included here are descriptions of why these in-text exercises appear in this chapter, how much time each one will probably take, and how you might debrief them. Each activity addresses a particular skill that students can develop.

EXERCISE 9.1 KEEPING A READING LOG

Why do this activity?
This activity introduces students to the concept of reading for pleasure. By doing this activity students learn that reading can be enjoyable and should discover the satisfaction that comes from reading an entire book of their own choosing.

What are the challenges and what can you expect?
Students may need to be encouraged to continue reading, especially if your class has moved on to another chapter. Consider having a reading check-in every week for a month to check up on your students' reading progress. For students who utilize recorded texts, ask them to obtain an unabridged recorded book to listen to for pleasure. Some students might actually want to have the print copy as well to follow along as they listen.

How much time will it take?
This activity could take as long as a month depending on the length of the book students select and how fast they read. Set a deadline for turning in the letters and consider having a weekly update.

How should I debrief?
At your weekly check-in, take 5 minutes to ask everyone what they are reading, how it is going, how much are they reading, etc. Also, ask that students bring their log in weekly for your review. In addition to turning in the letter, ask that students turn in their log at the end of the month.

EXERCISE 9.2 MARGINAL NOTES

Why do this activity?
In this activity students are asked to go back though the section on reading in this chapter. If they used a highlighter or underlined words, they are to make notes on a separate piece of paper or on sticky notes they attach, or write in the margins why they chose to mark these particular items.

What are the challenges and what can you expect?
One of the biggest challenges is that sometimes students mark entire paragraphs. Hopefully when students they try to explain why they did this, it will make sense to them that this technique is not highly effective.

How much time will it take?
This activity should take about 30-40 minutes depending on how much time you debrief.

How should I debrief?
What you probably want to know is what students learned about themselves during this activity. This metacognitive exercise will help them take a look at their technique and self-assess as to whether or not it's effective. If you can find an example of a student who is an effective "highlighter" or "under-liner," ask him or her to share the examples with the class. You can also show them your copy of this section of the text and what you've marked as important and why as a model.

EXERCISE 9.3 WORD HUNT

Why do this activity?
This activity helps students get into the habit of looking up words that are unknown to them. Students are asked to highlight the additional words in this chapter that they need to look up.

What are the challenges and what can you expect?
Some students might be reluctant to share their list with other students. The list could also be turned in to you for comparison purposes.

How much time will it take?
Students can highlight words outside of class and bring their list to class. This activity should take no more than 10-15 minutes to process.

How should I debrief?
As with any activity, start by asking students if they were surprised by anything. How many of your students regularly look up words that they do now know? If students continued to do this, what would be the benefits?

EXERCISE 9.4 TWO-WAY INFERENCES

Why do this activity?
This exercise and the accompanying text help students to understand inferences.

What are the challenges and what can you expect?
Developmental students may have difficulties with understanding inferences. Consider having a reading specialist visit the class and explain some strategies to use when making inferences. You could assign this activity outside of class or have access to a quotation dictionary or online quotation website such as www.quotationspage.com as well as magazines for pictures or a commercial photography site such as www.shutterstock.com.

How much time will it take?
Depending on whether the activity is done in class or at home, students should be able to complete this activity in 20-30 minutes including time for reporting out.

How should I debrief?
Ask students to share their picture chosen for the quote and their quote for the provided picture. How did they come upon the picture and the quote? Is the quote written in the active or passive voice? How does the concept pictured relate to the real meaning of the quote?

EXERCISE 9.5 PARAGRAPH ANALYSIS

Why do this activity?
This exercise helps students to learn to read for the main idea. At the end of this activity students will have improved their skills at discerning the topic of the passage, understand the main idea, be able to list supporting evidence and any inferences that are detected.

What are the challenges and what can you expect?
Developmental readers may be challenged at first. If your class is all developmental learners, consider doing the first paragraph as a class, together. Then assign Paragraph B and C to two groups to do together.

How much time will it take?
Depending on the reading ability and speed of your class, this exercise could take between 20 and 40 minutes to complete and debrief.

How should I debrief?
Begin by asking your class if it helps to read the questions before they read the passages. Did this get easier as they practiced reading for the main idea? Were they able to detect inferences as they read?

EXERCISE 9.6 DO YOU KNOW HOW TO STUDY

Why do this activity?
This is a relatively quick self-assessment of metacognition and helps to frame the discussion and learning around this topic.

What are the challenges and what can you expect?
There are no real challenges to this assessment. It might be helpful to remind students this is a "self-assessment" and there are no right or wrong answers. Low scores only indicate an opportunity to improve.

How much time will it take?
Taking the assessment should not take longer than 10 minutes. Plan on an additional 5-10 minutes to debrief.

How should I debrief?
Are students surprised by their scores? Ask volunteers who have scored between 40 and 50 points to share some real-life examples of these statements. Ask for a show of hands if students have areas which need improvement.

EXERCISE 9.7 "DISCIPLINED" STUDYING

Why do this activity?
This activity is designed to help students make connections between the discipline and the study method used. Students look at three different texts: math, psychology and music and indicate how they would go about studying the text.

What are the challenges and what can I expect?
There are no real challenges in this activity. You might suggest that students present how they would approach studying these texts to the class so that they learn from each other.

How much time will it take?
This activity can be done outside of class: the only time it takes is the actual debriefing in class and you can take whatever time you need especially if you have students present to the class.

How should I debrief?
If students present to the class, have them explain why they chose a particular method of studying and what they learned about themselves while doing the activity. Also ask students who have math, psychology and music classes to talk about how they are studying their texts.

7. Which additional exercises might enrich students' learning?

Crossword Race
(from Staley, C. (2003) page 95.)

Class activity
Materials needed: A crossword puzzle that you create, using terms from the text, generated at http://puzzlemaker.school.discovery.com/CrissCrossSetupFrom.html
Time: 30 minutes or so, depending on the size of the group
Goal: To motivate students to read the text, learn course material, and work collaboratively
Generate a puzzle using course content at the above web site or another one you find. You may allow students to work on the solution in pairs or small groups, perhaps as a timed competition.

Marking Your Mark
Homework and class activity
Materials needed: Four highlighters, any article of 4-5 pages of interest and relevance to the class (provide copies for each student along with four extra copies)
Time: 30 minutes
Goal: To help students learn how to highlight important information in a reading
For homework, assign students the article you have chosen and ask them to read it, highlight what they think is important, and then make a summary of the reading in outline form, only using the words that they highlighted. When students return to the next class, put them into four groups. Tell students to choose the best outline in the group and decide why they chose that particular one. As a group, have students highlight a blank copy that you provide. In class, compare the four highlighted articles. Are there similarities or differences? Discuss what students learned doing this activity.

Words of Success
Homework and class activity
Materials needed: The local newspaper and a quiz
Time: 30-50 minutes
Goal: To help students choose the main points of readings and develop study cards
Assign students to read one section of the newspaper as a class assignment. For example, you might choose to assign the local news, world news, sports, entertainment, or the home and garden section. If the section is long, assign a set number of pages. Allow students to write down 20 words in any way that they want (in a mapping format, clustered together, etc.) and bring the words to the next class in preparation for a quiz. Give them a quiz on the reading with some specific facts that they must recall. Did students choose many of the same words? Is there any connection between the words that students chose and how well they did on the test?

8. What other activities can I incorporate to make the chapter my own?

If your students are in a learning community with linked classes, check with the other instructors to see if there is any reading material that you could use to when teaching students about reading and studying techniques. If not and students are in a variety of different courses, ask students to bring in or do their homework assignments on material that will serve a purpose for them. Improved reading and study techniques may well translate into great grades.

Included here, all in one place, are Activity Options taken from the Annotated Instructor's Edition.

ACTIVITY OPTION (p. 212): Consider meeting your students in the cafeteria for lunch every few weeks to discuss a book. If your campus has a Common Book program (where all entering students read the same book), you could dissect chapters together over lunch. Or, choose any book that students want to read and read it together. Think about something small—a book that might be appealing to "reluctant readers."

ACTIVITY OPTION (p. 212): As a class, choose the top five from the list of fifteen common reading issues listed. Which can be changed? Get a discussion going with the goal that each issue can be improved. It is about one's own control and attitude about the reading challenge.

ACTIVITY OPTION (p. 213): Focusing on what is read is vital for good comprehension. Ask students to list three times when they really do pay attention to the material. Ask students to fill in the blank, "I really pay attention when I read _____." Make a list on the board and have students explain why they paid attention at that time. Explain that college is the ticket to many aspects of a quality life. Paying attention to learning is critical to success.

ACTIVITY OPTION (p. 213): Have students suggest some codes that can be used when marking a text and list them on the board such as ? for questions, * for agree with, - for disagree.

ACTIVITY OPTION (p. 214): This activity can be assigned for homework or done in class. Give students a two- or three-page article or current newspaper story to read. Tell them to read the article only once, writing their comments, questions, and reactions as suggested in this chapter. Have students pair up and show each other what they highlighted and what kinds of notes they put in the margins. Was their approach different from their partner's? If so, what differed and why? Have them share their responses with the class.

ACTIVITY OPTION (p. 214): Even simple, everyday reading requires cultural literacy. Ask students to bring a cartoon or joke to class that requires cultural literacy to understand. The amount of information out there increases exponentially every day, especially with the advent of the Internet, so one can't know everything. But the more one reads the more likely one is to be culturally literate.

ACTIVITY OPTION (p. 215): Apply the SQ3R method to the next chapter you will be covering in this textbook. Have students read the title, headings, and first and second sentences of each paragraph. Then have them write a one-paragraph summary of the chapter.

ACTIVITY OPTION (p. 216): Have students divide up into their dominant learning style. Have a leader in each group gather a list of strategies the members of that group use for reading and studying. Copy the list for each member of the group. To expand their strategies, encourage the members to try strategies that others with their same learning style find helpful.

ACTIVITY OPTION (p. 217): Have your students participate in a community outreach activity. If the college has a child care center, perhaps your class could visit the center and read stories to groups of children.

ACTIVITY OPTION (p. 221): Divide students into groups. Make copies of several comic strips for each group. Have each group try to figure out the author's message for each strip. Have students compare their results. Or bring in a comic without a caption to class and ask students to write in their own joke.

ACTIVITY OPTION (p. 234): This is a good opportunity for reflection. Ask students to summarize their responses to the Reality Check and send it to you via e-mail.

9. What homework might I assign?

Ask students to show you how they highlighted their text for an upcoming test in another class by bringing the textbook for that class to your class. Take a quick look to see if they highlighted too little or too much, and if they captured the main points. Remind students that it's best to highlight the second time they do the reading.

Journal Entries
Have students write a one-page journal entry, or send you an e-mail describing a reading that was very difficult for them this past week. If they read nothing that was difficult, ask them to describe something they read, and explain the strategy they used to read it and comprehend it.

10. What have I learned in teaching this chapter that I will incorporate next time?

_____

_____

_____

_____

_____

_____

_____

_____

_____

_____

_____

_____

_____

_____

_____

_____

_____

_____

_____

_____

_____

_____

_____

_____

_____

_____

_____

_____

_____

_____

CHAPTER 10: TAKING TESTS

1. Why is this chapter important?

Wouldn't it be great if students could go through college without ever having to take a test? Think of all the hours *you'd* save by not having to grade stacks of exams? But test taking in college is a necessary evil, and some students appear to be better at it than others. There is hope, though. In this chapter students will learn about how to control test anxiety; what do to before, during, and after a test; as well as why it is important to avoid a growing concern among faculty nationally—cheating! If students follow the wealth of advice provided in this chapter, their attitudes toward tests may change for the better, and so may their performance.

Test anxiety can stem from many different sources. A fear of failure or a drive toward perfectionism can immobilize some students. They may feel pressure to maintain a scholarship or not disappoint someone. But one of the main reasons that students' anxiety mounts is because they simply don't prepare enough or prepare carefully enough. However, there are always ways to help students overcome the stress surrounding exams, and for these students, this is one of the most beneficial components of this chapter.

It's not surprising that the better you prepare for a test, the less anxiety you will have, generally speaking. Careful planning and knowing what will be covered on a test are keys to success. The more students know about their learning style and behaviors, and the more they use this knowledge when preparing for and taking tests, the more successful they will be. This chapter is key for student success. And, the more you can help students apply what they are learning in the chapter to tests they are taking now in all their courses, the better.

2. What are this chapter's learning objectives?

➤ Why students should change their thinking about tests
➤ What to do before, during, and after a test
➤ Why cramming doesn't always work
➤ What test anxiety is and what to do about it
➤ How to take different kinds of tests differently
➤ How cheating can hurt a student's chances for success

3. How should I launch this chapter?

One of the best ways to launch this chapter is to connect it to students' current lives. Chances are, they have just finished a test, or could be taking one very soon in one class or another. Start with a show of hands. How many students have taken at least one test so far this term? Two? Three or more? How many students would like to do better on the next test they take? Probably lots of hands will fly into the air. Assure students that if they make use of at least some of the techniques in this chapter, they will.

- **Line students up on a continuum with students who feel they always do well on tests at one end and those who feel they do not on the other end.** Have students think about their typical approach to test-taking—in high school, on standardized tests, or in their current courses, for example. Ask them to place themselves on either end of an imaginary continuum with one wall representing "Always do well" and the opposite wall representing "Always do more poorly than I'd hoped." Generally, you will find students spread across the continuum with most wanting to improve. Ask students why they placed themselves where they did. What are they doing right or wrong? Ask what they think they need to do to move themselves along the continuum in a positive direction.

- **Line students up on a continuum with students who study the night before a test (cram) on one end and those who begin to prepare at least a week in advance (or continually during the term) on the other end.** Ask students to share their experiences with each other. Are there common characteristics among students at both ends or in the middle? Are there ever times when cramming works? In fact, you might find some very successful students who wait unit the last minute to prepare. Have a discussion on why this might not work all of the time. Can anyone in the class share a last-minute cramming horror story?

- **Developmental Students and Returning Adult Learners:** Developmental learners may fear tests. They may spend hours preparing but have poor results. Often they procrastinate and spend the final hours cramming for a test. This can be discouraging! Reassure your students that the techniques in this chapter can make a difference. Returning adult learners may be faced with high stakes testing—such as admissions exams for selective academic programs like nursing or other required testing for their jobs. Reassure them that the techniques in this chapter are equally effective for standardized exams and classroom tests.

- **Going beyond the book.** Like most study skill techniques, there are literally thousands of resources available for individuals to learn test taking skills. Are there workshops on your campus? If so, see if you can time it so that your class can attend one in preparation for a test or quiz you are giving. If you check with the workshop leader, you might even ask them to come to your class. If the presenter can't come to your class, find out the times and require students to go. Whatever activities you use in this chapter, or beyond the book, make sure that students apply them to tests in courses they're currently taking.

4. How should I use the *FOCUS* Challenge Case?

There might be a Joe Cloud sitting in your class right now, and you may not even know it. Students like Joe from both large and small high schools may have been very successful prior to college. Joe is from an underrepresented population, and "all eyes are upon him," paying all his college expenses and watching his academic progress from afar. In his case, the performance pressure mounts until it reaches a dangerous level. His coping mechanisms have begun to fail. While some students may realize that they are struggling in a class and get help, others, like Joe, will just continue to do what they are doing, falling further behind, or simply stop attending a particular class. Perhaps they are too timid, or disclosing failure is not culturally acceptable, for example. Joe was beginning to experience panic attacks brought on by mounting anxiety. The more he tried to catch up in the class, the more ineffective he became. Have the class discuss one or two things Joe could have done before things got out of control. What advice would they have given him? Other ideas to start this discussion include:

- **Direct It!** Assign a "scene director" for the Challenge Case. After students review the Challenge Case, assign students to role-play Joe, Professor Cloud and Sam. The director can stop the scene at any point and redirect the "actors" as well as get input from the "critics"—the other students in class!
  - o Scene 1: Joe is in Mr. Crow's office. Mr. Crow hands the crumpled test back to Joe. Direct the actors to have a conversation about Joe's attitude and how he can change his behavior. What advice could Mr. Crow give Joe about keeping his midterm?
  - o Scene 2: In this scene, Sam confronts Joe about changing his patterns. What suggestions does Sam have for Joe? How does Joe react to these suggestions?
- Does rereading a math text help for an exam? Why or why not?
- Do you agree with Joe that once college is over, you will never have to take another test?

As you read this *FOCUS* Challenge Case, you cannot help but feel for Joe. Many of your students will empathize with him because they themselves are in similar situations or they have friends who are. What's important about debriefing this *FOCUS* Challenge Case is to bring up the subject of actual intervention. Without individual help from his instructor, the Counseling Center, the Office of Multicultural Affairs or some similar office on his campus, Joe may be doomed. He is in danger of becoming a retention statistic and returning home feeling himself to be a failure.

5. What important features does this chapter include?

If you assigned different students to different groups to prepare and discuss specific features of the chapter for chapter 10, change the assigned features for this chapter. If you haven't done this, try it this time. Ask students to work in small groups to present the features outlined here.

Readiness and Reality Checks

Most likely students will report that they do think test taking will affect their college success. What might be of interest is to see how much control students think they have over test taking. Students may just see themselves as "good or poor" test takers.

What they might not realize is that everyone will benefit from the techniques in this chapter, no matter where they start in terms of their skills.

Stressed out?

While it is true that some short-term stress can be beneficial, we all know that long-term stress can be harmful. What stressors are your students facing? Students in your class are probably facing different levels of stress—from family and relationship stress to economic stress to academic stress. Ask your students to keep a stress diary for a week. Have them record what stressors they faced, how high their stress level was, and what they did about it.

Control: Your Learning

In this section students are asked to control their learning and think about their toughest class or on the job experience. They are asked to identify a key challenge they face as it related to the chapter and to develop a step by step action plan with how to deal with it. There is a very specific example that Joe Cloud, the *FOCUS* Challenge Case student in the chapter, could develop. Make sure that you ask students to share their step-by-step plans with each other. Are there common approaches? There should be. What are they? Some of the key indicators will be things like making sure they understand exactly what is on the test or to reread some of the sections in this text. See what comes up in your class as common themes.

Self-Assessments

There are no formal assessments in this chapter; however much of the chapter is written such that students are constantly asked to assess what they do before, during, and after tests by placing a + ("Yes, I do this") or a ✓ ("I really should do this more") before each suggestion. There is one self-assessment that is in the form of an exercise, **10.1 Test Anxiety Survey**. Students fill out the survey and come up with a score. Students are asked to add up their scores and to see if their scores are in a healthy range. If not, there are some descriptions that follow including four different but related components of test anxiety.

Career Outlook

In this chapter, we meet Kelleigh Crystal, Teacher's Assistant. This profession is expected to increase in the coming years. Most schools will only hire assistants with and associate's degree or higher. Kelleigh worked as a nanny after graduating from college and learned that she loved working with children. Do you have students who are interested in working as a teacher's assistant or a teacher? Kelleigh writes that it is important to be patient and that individuals in this profession tend to take their work home with them at night. Ask your students to brainstorm other characteristics of this career, both positive and negative.

FOCUS TV: Test-taking

This episode examines the fear involved with taking tests and how students can overcome these fears. Rob Franek, vice-president and publisher of The Princeton Review, provides an overview of the mistakes students make when preparing for tests. This episode is available in CourseMate or via the Power Lecture CD's FOCUSPoints.

6. Which in-text exercises should I use?

Three activities are built into this chapter. Included here are descriptions of why these in-text exercises appear in this chapter, how much time each one will probably take, and how you might debrief them.

EXERCISE 10.1 TEST ANXIETY SURVEY

Why do this activity?
This activity will allow students to assess their levels of test anxiety in a safe space. Some students may be comfortable discussing their results in class, many will not. Consider doing this as a homework assignment and pair it with a journal or blog activity.

What are the challenges and what can I expect?
Other than the comfort levels of some students, there are not many challenges with this survey. For those students who score between 37 and 60, be prepared to provide them with possible options such as talking with a counselor, attending an anxiety reduction workshop, or getting help via another intervention.

How much time will it take?
This activity should be done outside of class; the only time it takes is the actual debriefing in class. For example, you may wish to conduct an in-class discussion, an online chat, or ask for an e-mail summary.

How should I debrief?
If you chose to debrief this in class, ask students to write down their score on an index card without their name. It could be helpful to some to see the range of scores on the board along with an average score. Then lead the class in a discussion of how stress has affected them during test-taking and suggestions they have for reducing the stress. This can help to frame the discussion of the four indicators of test anxiety.

EXERCISE 10.2 MULTIPLE-CHOICE TEST

Why do this activity?
This activity allows students to practice taking multiple-choice tests and identify the principles of test-taking they are using from the chapter. Applying these principles will help students to prepare for multiple-choice tests.

What are the challenges and what can I expect?
There are no real challenges in this activity.

How much time will it take?
This activity should take no more than 15 minutes to complete and debrief.

How should I debrief?
Ask students to identify the principles they used to choose the correct answer. Students will list different principles, ask them to discuss why they used that principle.

EXERCISE 10.3 UNDERSTANDING "VERB-AGE"

Why do this activity?
This activity helps students to "zero" in on the verb. Students are asked to respond to four questions with the only difference being the verb that is used in the question. This is an excellent demonstration of how to write to the question that is asked.

What are the challenges and what can I expect?
There are no real challenges in this activity. If you have developmental students who seem to struggle with the activity, remind all students to review the verb listing on pages 253 and 254.

How much time will it take?
This activity should be done outside of class; the only time it takes is the actual debriefing in class. For example, you may wish to conduct an in-class discussion, an online chat, or ask for an e-mail summary. Alternatively, students could post their answers on the course discussion board on your course management system.

How should I debrief?
Ask students about subjective exams and have them give one or two examples of exams they have had this semester and how this chapter will help them with future exams.

---

7. Which additional exercises might enrich students' learning?

Absolutely Right!
Class activity
Materials needed: A list of words (included here)
Time: 30 minutes, depending on the size of the group
Goal: To help students understand how certain words can be clues to the answers on tests

Give students the following lists of words (scramble them up) and see if they can group them into two categories. One category is *absolutes* that make a statement most always false. They can be positive or negative. The second category is *maybes*. When something is described using these terms, most likely it's true. See if students can describe what is similar for the words that they place in either group.

Absolutes

always	never	entirely	everyone	everybody
without a doubt	only	absolutely	100%	all
largest	biggest	smartest	no one	never
worst	least	every	no one	nobody

Maybes

sometimes	usually	a few	average	more
larger than	smarter than	frequently	better	most
occasionally	may	might	typically	commonly

Follow the Directions
Homework and Class activity
Materials needed: Any article of 4-5 pages of interest and relevance to the class
Time: 30 minutes
Goal: To help students learn how to respond to a specific question about an assignment or for essay questions
For homework, assign students the article you have chosen and ask them to read it. Give students one of the following words included here and ask them to write a short essay question about this article using the verb they were given. Ask students to answer the question and bring it to class. Share questions and discuss what students learned doing this activity.

compare	contrast	defend	define
explain	evaluate	hypothesize	identify
illustrate	justify	list	relate
summarize	outline	clarify	analyze

Grabbing for Success
Class activity
Materials needed: Two paper bags and strips of paper
Time: 30-50 minutes
Goal: To help students to identify test taking strategies
Assign students into two teams. Teams are to take 15 minutes to develop 15 true or false questions about this chapter. Each team places their questions into a different paper bag. Students on team A have to respond to questions that team B has prepared for them and vice versa. The instructor, you, have the right to throw out a question. (Yes, there are bad questions!) The winning team gets candy or bonus points.

8. What other activities can I incorporate to make the chapter my own?

FOCUS encourages students to tie information from the chapters to themselves personally and to real life, just- in-time activities. Consider having students make a list of the tests or quizzes that are coming up for them, and ask them to assign themselves specific study techniques, of their choice, for their tests. It's important for students to reflect on the activity so that they learn what works best for them and that improved test taking techniques will translate into better grades.

Included here, all in one place, are Activity Options taken from the Annotated Instructor's Edition.

ACTIVITY OPTION (p. 238): Generate a discussion with students about their level of interest in this chapter's material. Some students may believe that they are already good at taking tests. Some may have test anxiety and want to avoid the material. But if they don't care and are not good at test-taking, they are in big trouble. Ask students to jot down, anonymously, why they are or aren't interested in this chapter. Gather the responses and get a discussion going.

ACTIVITY OPTION (p. 239): Ask students to briefly write down how they prepare for tests. Then type out the following questions and pass them out. Have students answer them honestly. Are you a last-minute person? Do you always show up a little bit late? Do you cram too many things into a day? Do you prepare ahead of time for anything? Or do you just show up and take your chances in most areas of life? Have students think about their responses and write a short paragraph about how they respond to tasks in general.

ACTIVITY OPTION (p. 240): Put students in groups of three for about five minutes to discuss their best ideas about how to prepare for tests. After five minutes, come together as a class, and go around the room and ask each student to explain one technique. Students cannot repeat techniques. What may come out of the discussion is that different techniques work for different students, but that particular themes emerge that hold true for everyone.

ACTIVITY OPTION (p. 241): VARK the test. Let students' learning styles work for them by creating a test that includes all four learning style options. For example, include a section in which students create a diagram from text material (visual), a portion in which questions are given aloud (aural), a traditional true-false, multiple choice, and short-answer section (read/write), and a case study (kinesthetic).

ACTIVITY OPTION (p. 241): Assign each student a partner. Using sticky notes, have each pair organize the most important parts of the chapter for an open book test. Have different groups compare their organizing method. Make sure to have an open book test for this chapter, so they can see the effectiveness of their system.

ACTIVITY OPTION (p. 244): Divide students into four groups and ask each group to focus on the cognitive, emotional, behavioral, or physiological aspect of test anxiety. Ask the groups to come up with five suggestions on how to deal with this area of anxiety. Share the suggestions with the group.

ACTIVITY OPTION (p. 245): Divide students into groups. Have students make a list of positive self-talk they can refer to when negative, unproductive self-talk sets in. Have students share their lists with the class.

ACTIVITY OPTION (p. 245): Many college students have math anxiety. Invite a math instructor to class to discuss math anxiety and some ways to deal with it.

ACTIVITY OPTION (p. 248): Ask students to select three strategies from the list to keep in mind for their next test in another class and to report back their results after using them.

ACTIVITY OPTION (p. 249): Make a test that starts out with "Read the entire test before you begin." Then list fifteen simple questions. Make Question 14 read "After reading this question, just write your name on the paper. Do not answer any other questions." Pass the papers out. Give students about five minutes. Ask students what was the trick to the test. Explain to students that it is vital to read over the entire test before beginning. Instructors expect students to read, understand, and carefully follow directions when taking a test.

ACTIVITY OPTION (p. 251): Have students review the five strategies for taking true-false tests. Create a true-false test that includes absolutes, qualifiers, and negatives. Ask students to use a highlighter and highlight key words that they can use as clues when answering questions. After students complete the test, share the results.

ACTIVITY OPTION (p. 252): Consider bringing in a multiple-choice test you create with some tricky responses and have the class, as a group, go through some of the strategies listed.

ACTIVITY OPTION (p. 253): Have students review the list of strategies for taking multiple-choice tests. Create a multiple-choice test that demonstrates some of the clues from the list. Ask students to highlight key words that serve as clues, identify in the margin the strategy that was used, and share the results.

ACTIVITY OPTION (p. 257): Create a list of essay questions. Have students highlight the key verb in each question and explain how they would answer the question. They are not asked to answer the questions, just explain how they would answer them.

ACTIVITY OPTION (p. 257): Have students make a four-slide PowerPoint presentation to share their step-by-step plan for their most challenging class. Make sure that students identify which class they are talking about and what makes it challenging.

ACTIVITY OPTION (p. 263): For the final activity in the chapter, have students design a one-page tip sheet that contains suggestions for taking different types of tests that have personal relevance for them and e-mail it to you. Put all the tip sheets into one document and send it to the entire class.

9. What homework might I assign?

Because you want to be sure that students connect the techniques and approaches they are learning in this chapter to real tests and quizzes, make sure that their journal entries ask them to reflect about what they have learned, what they hope to gain, and what they have already applied to taking tests.

Journal Entries

One: Have students write a one-page journal entry, or send you an e-mail describing a recent test or quiz they took. What did they do to prepare (give specifics) and did they believe that it helped? Why or why not? Would they do anything differently next time? If so, what? What grade did they get on this test or quiz and were they satisfied? Why or why not?

Two: Have students write a two-page journal entry, or send you an e-mail describing what finals they will be taking. They should identify each class, and then describe the test that will be given. (If they don't know the format, see if they can ask their instructor. Tell them to inform the instructor that they need to know this information for a class assignment.) Have students make a time line that includes specific dates, and what they will do to prepare.

10. What have I learned in teaching this chapter that I will incorporate next time?

CHAPTER 11: BUILDING RELATIONSHIPS, VALUING DIVERSITY

1. Why is this chapter important?

Students will most likely be especially interested in this chapter. They will want to know more about something of key importance in their lives—their relationships with others. *You* might not even have thought much about the importance of relationships and their effects on college success. According to the National Center for Diseases Control (NCDC), one in three high school students in the U.S. is involved in an abusive relationship—emotional, physical, or sexual—a trend they have identified as a national health epidemic. (See this article on abusive relationships: http://www.gazette.com/articles/teens_47346___article.html/really_love.html) This chapter is more important to college success than one might even expect!

Some of the fundamental research on college persistence indicates that students must make both academic progress and connections to the institution and others to stay in college and succeed. The skills students will learn about in this chapter are about managing their emotions and getting along with others. So this chapter is not about academic skills like studying or reading, per se, but instead about the non-cognitive skills that affect college success. These non-cognitive skills that make up one's emotional intelligence (including knowing yourself, working well with others, handling stress, having empathy for other's situations, and being optimistic), for example, often have *more* impact on students' persistence and dream fulfillment than academic skills. Of course, some students come to college for the wrong reasons, such as their parents' insistence or the fact that they had nothing else that they could think of to do after high school. But, if you believe that basically we all want to do well in life and fulfill our dreams, then failing in college and not meeting your own and other's expectations can have a far-reaching impact on self regard. And low self-regard can have a variety of effects. For example, it may impact the way we deal with conflict.

In addition to learning about love and relationships and communication, this chapter flows from an emphasis on emotional intelligence into a discussion of diversity. If you don't really know yourself and how and why you act and think the way you do, you may not be able to understand someone else's perspective. For example, if a student in your class was raised to believe that individuals with particular backgrounds are less able than others, and that they don't understand why they think that way, diversity may be an illusive concept. An inability to understand yourself, and to be flexible and open-minded can be a barrier to appreciating diversity. The good news is that emotional intelligence can be taught and enhanced, and improvement will lead to more success in relationships, and greater appreciation for the diversity that surrounds us.

2. What are this chapter's learning objectives?

> ➢ What emotional intelligence is
> ➢ Whether EI can be improved
> ➢ How to improve communication with people you care about

- ➤ Why diversity enriches our lives
- ➤ What cultural intelligence is and why it's important
- ➤ How globalization changes our world

3. How should I launch this chapter?

This chapter is easy to launch because of students' natural curiosity about the content. Students are generally intrigued by the notion of emotional intelligence; many have never thought or heard about it before. And most students are either in a romantic relationship now, just ending one, or in the market for one, so chances are you won't need to do much to get students to rally around the beginning sections of the chapter. Note that the chapter starts with a more personal focus and moves to a broader focus on diversity and globalization. Research indicates that many of today's college students believe (inaccurately) that diversity is an issue we have "solved" as a society, or they have wearied from the emphasis on diversity in K-12, just as they have become tired of other academic emphases.

- **Use the *FOCUS* Challenge Case as a starting point to open up the chapter.** Because self awareness is really central to this chapter, students need to be taking a good hard look at how they react in various situations and why. But, identifying that they may not be responding in appropriate ways is not always easy. It's much easier to rationalize your own behavior and criticize someone else's behavior than it is to be self-critical. Use Kia as a way to open up dialogue. There may be students in your class who are doing something similar to sabotage their own success.

- **Ask students to identify ways in which the dimensions of emotional intelligence (EI) are connected to college success.** Or give students index cards with each of the EI skills written on them. Have students form groups and think about some behavior a student might display that works against being emotionally intelligent. See http://www.reuvenbaron.org/bar-on-model/essay.php?i=3 for a complete list of the five scales and fifteen subscales of emotional intelligence.

- **Developmental Students and Returning Adult Learners:** Developmental learners may need to develop ways to build their self-esteem and reduce negativity. In addition to this, they may be experiencing the P-C-P syndrome: parking lot-class-parking lot. Remind your students to connect with other teachers, students and staff. For both developmental and returning adult learners, spend some time discussing what mentors do and why they are important. Be prepared to help students find a mentor.

- **Going beyond the book.** Have students try a Google search using the words "college success and stress management" or "college success and adaptability." In fact, see if the class can generate a list of college success factors linked with vocabulary and concepts from the chapter and do some additional searching. You will see that there are many ways in which both you and your students can go beyond what is in this chapter. For students who are considering psychology as a major, you might suggest that they begin to explore the whole notion of emotional intelligence. For students who are considering communication studies as a major, the area of conflict management is filled with ways in which students will be able to see what they are learning and how it connects to majors and careers, as well as self development. For students who are particularly intrigued by diversity, they may be interested in finding campus groups that explore this topic. Excellent online resources can be found at www.tolerance.org/campus/index.jsp.

4. How should I use the *FOCUS* Challenge Case?

Kia Washington is a student who is at very high risk for dropping out. She begins her college career in a very stressful way. Her husband, James, has just been laid off after only six months on the job. Now she is also faced with possible unemployment and has enrolled in the community college nursing program. Although she had some stressful years at home before she got married, she managed to do very well academically in high school. Kia is not a good communicator. She prefers fighting to discussing her issues with James. She is not in a good place and sees her life as a "soap opera." Suggestions for using this case study include:

- **Direct It!** Assign a "scene director" for the Challenge Case. After students review the Challenge Case, assign students to role-play Kia and James. The director can stop the scene at any point and redirect the "actors" as well as get input from the "critics"—the other students in class!
    - o Scene 1: The title of this scene is "***End the Soap Opera Drama!***" Have students script an ending to this Challenge Case. How could Kia have handled the job loss conversation differently? How can Kia use the strength of inclusiveness and change her communication style with James?
    - o Scene 2: In this scene, Kia meets with her academic advisor. Assign a student the role of advisor. What advice could her advisor give?
- Ask students to discuss the "What Do *You* Think?" questions, and during the discussion give them an opportunity, perhaps before they even know much about emotional intelligence, to point out the evidence that Kia's IQ is probably much higher than her EQ.
- How can Kia improve communication in her family?
- Ask them how Kia may be sabotaging herself and her college success.

While it's possible to view the case as melodramatic, it is based on real first-year students with these exact issues, as are all the *FOCUS* Challenge Cases.

5. What important features does this chapter include?

Continue to use the recurring themes in this book. The Challenge → Reaction → Insight → Action steps are especially helpful to encourage students to think about how they might respond and what they would do in the all important aspects of relationships, diversity and globalization.

Readiness and Reality Checks

In this chapter, the Readiness Check responses for students could be somewhat different than in other chapters. As mentioned earlier, cognitive factors such as studying and test taking are concepts that students have heard about before. When it comes to learning about emotional intelligence, however, students may not know much about it, and they will be motivated to learn more. The comparisons between the Readiness and Reality Checks always provide a good opportunity for self—and group—reflection and class discussion.

Challenge → Reaction → Insight → Action steps

The Challenge → Reaction → Insight → Action steps in this chapter can and should be used to spark class discussion. The Challenge → Reaction steps ask students to read Kia's story and begin to think about her problems and possible solutions to get her back on track. The Insight → Action steps allow students to put into action what they have learned in this chapter and help to complete her story. In addition, students are asked to plan for change in regards to their own communication and relationships as well as approach to diversity.

Stressed Out?

In this activity, students are reminded that relationships are important, and when they are healthy and productive, our stress levels tend to be much lower. Have students list three relationships and analyze how they are going. If students indicate any relationships "Needs Work" have them indicate the ways they may be contributing to the stress and how they can improve the relationship.

Self-Assessments

This chapter has three self-assessments: **What's Your Conflict Style?**, **Your Views on Diversity** and **Diagnosing Your Cultural Intelligence**. These surveys are insights into conflict styles and students own views about diversity. These self-assessments can be used in reflective writing activities and class discussions.

Curiosity: Build Relationships, One Drop at a Time

In this chapter of *FOCUS*, curiosity is addressed early in the chapter when students read about building relationships "one drop at a time." They read a summary of the best-selling book, *How Full Is Your Bucket?*, and identify the analogy of adding or subtracting liquid from a bucket depending on how they respond either positively (adding to), or negatively (subtracting from) the bucket.

Career Outlook
In this chapter, we meet Jenny Dixon, Nurse. Jenny was drawn to the nursing profession because of her desire to help people as other nurses had in her family. Prioritizing and critical thinking skills are a must in this profession. As a profession, nursing has a very good future outlook and the pay is generally very competitive. Who in the class would be happy in this job? Why or why not?

FOCUS TV: Relationships
This episode takes a closer look at relationships and Emotional Intelligence. In addition to Dr. Constance Staley's interview with Kia Washington/Charmaine, Dr. Catherine Andersen, an EI expert at Gallaudet University, discusses the relationship between EQ and college success. This episode is available in CourseMate or via the Power Lecture CD's FOCUSPoints.

6. Which in-text exercises should I use?

As you have done in other chapters, have students connect these activities to real life situations. The descriptions of the activities follow, including how much time each one will probably take, and how you might debrief them.

EXERCISE 11.1 HOW WOULD YOU RESPOND?

Why do this activity?
This activity begins to introduce EQ to students with practical, real life examples. Asking students to consider how they would respond helps to begin the discussion on what constitutes an emotionally intelligent response.

What are the challenges and what can I expect?
There are no real challenges in this activity except that some students will state they need more information before choosing a reaction. Ask them to generalize, just to get the discussion going.

How much time will it take?
This activity and the debriefing should take no longer than 30 minutes.

How should I debrief?
Process each scenario and ask students how they responded. Do they agree that choice C is the most emotionally intelligent one? Why or why not?

EXERCISE 11.2 WHAT'S YOUR CONFLICT STYLE

Why do this activity?
This exercise allows students to rate their response on a conflict scale of 1 to 5, with 1 representing "strongly agree" and 5 representing "strongly disagree." Students can compare their responses with others in the class. Have students review figure 11.1 and

---

determine if they are Competers, Collaborators, Compromisers, Avoiders, or Accommodators.

What are the challenges and what can I expect?
It can be interesting to have students see where they fall on the concern for self and concern for others scale. Challenge students to remain flexible and work towards collaboration when possible.

How much time will it take?
This activity should not take more than 20 minutes to complete, debriefing could take longer depending on interest in the topic.

How should I debrief?
Ask students if they learned anything about themselves. Do you as the instructor agree with their self-assessments? Did they identify anything they want to work on?

EXERCISE 11.3 25 THINGS WE HAVE IN COMMON

Why do this activity?
This fun and quick activity looks at student's commonalities. It seems that we are programmed to look for differences. How hard or easy was it for your students to find things they have in common?

What are the challenges and what can I expect?
This activity is structured in a positive way that allows a discussion on diversity to follow. While no challenges are apparent in this activity, encourage students to mix it up and be in a group with students they don't typically work with.

How much time will it take?
The activity should take no longer than 5-10 minutes to complete. Depending on how you debrief the activity, plan on an additional 20-40 minutes.

How should I debrief?
Ask students to discuss their lists. Were they surprised to find some of the things they had in common with each other? Was this difficult or easy for some?

EXERCISE 11.4 YOUR VIEWS ON DIVERSITY

Why do this activity?
This activity looks at student's views on diversity. It can serve as a basis for a meaningful class discussion.

What are the challenges and what can I expect?
Some students will find discomfort in doing this activity, and that is not necessarily an unintended outcome. If your class does begin a heated discussion, remind them to be respectful and to listen to all opinions. Also know that some students will not change

their opinions regardless of the information they have been presented. Some may need time in college to process the new viewpoints to which they have been exposed.

How much time will it take?
The activity should take no longer than 5-10 minutes to complete. Depending on how you debrief the activity, plan on an additional 20-40 minutes.

How should I debrief?
Ask students to line up in a continuum with one direction representing the "Strongly Agree" and the other direction representing the "Strongly Disagree." Those in between the 1 and the 5 can find their place in the line. Ask each side to briefly state why they believe the way they do. How did they learn this? Is it always true? After the 1s and the 5s have spoken, ask if anyone would like to change positions. In addition to doing this, you could also ask those 1s and 5s to "temporarily" switch sides and justify the other position.

EXERCISE 11.5 FACING THE RACE ISSUE

Why do this activity?
This activity is designed to help students think about race and while it is a common identifier, it isn't an easy or accurate way to classify people.

What are the challenges and what can I expect?
Consider doing this as an on-screen activity as suggested in the teaching with technology annotation. See http://www.pbs.org/race/002_SortingPeople/002_00-home.htm

How much time will it take?
This activity should not take long to complete. The discussion after the activity could take 20-30 minutes.

How should I debrief?
You may debrief however you wish, based on the specific learning outcomes you wish to reinforce.

EXERCISE 11.6 WHAT'S THE DIFFERENCE?

Why do this activity?
This activity asks students to work with another student and list the ways in which they differ. The goal is to increase the appreciation of individual differences.

What are the challenges and what can I expect?
The Sensitive Situation annotation bears repeating here, first-year students do not always have well-cultivated empathy skills. Be prepared to intervene if necessary.

How much time will it take?
This activity should take about 20 minutes to complete and debrief.

How should I debrief?

Compare this with Exercise 11.3. Did students find it easier to find commonalities or differences? Suggest students review the website www.100people.org or show the brief video from the website "100 People Trailer."

EXERCISE 11.7 CIRCLES OF AWARENESS

Why do this activity?

This activity asks students to consider their cultural identity. How do student's see themselves and how can these categories can lead to learning about diversity, differences and behavior change? This activity can lead to powerful learning.

What are the challenges and what can I expect?

The Sensitive Situation annotation bears repeating here again: first-year students do not always have well-cultivated empathy skills. Remind students they will be sharing this with other students, if they don't want something revealed about themselves it is okay to leave it off of the activity.

How much time will it take?

This activity should take about 20 minutes to complete and debrief.

How should I debrief?

Ask students to circulate around the room and find three other students who have listed at least three of the same subgroups. Then find three students who have three different subgroups listed. Ask students to find out more about at least one subgroup they did not have on their list. Some suggestions are attend a club or organization on campus or in the community to learn more.

EXERCISE 11.8 DIAGNOSING YOUR CULTURAL INTELLIGENCE

Why do this activity?

This activity asks students to rate their agreement with statements about their cultural intelligence. Students can learn about their opportunities for improving CQ and about their strengths in CQ.

What are the challenges and what can I expect?

There are no real challenges with this activity. Developmental students may have some difficulties with the reading level of this assessment. One option is to read the statements aloud and ask that students then rate their agreement.

How much time will it take?

This activity should take about 15-20 minutes to complete and debrief.

How should I debrief?

Debrief this exercise by asking for a show of hands on areas of strength and opportunity for students. Brainstorm with the class on ways students could improve in each of these areas.

7. Which additional exercises might enrich students' learning?

An Emotionally Intelligent Friend
Class activity
Materials needed: Kia's Washington's *FOCUS* Challenge Case
Time: 30-50 minutes, depending on the size of the group
Goal: To help students identify the main parts of a story
Place students into five groups that correspond with the five components of emotional intelligence: intrapersonal (self awareness), interpersonal (relating to others), stress management, adaptability, and general mood. In these small groups, ask students to identify whether Kia displays strong emotional intelligence in the area they are assigned. If not, ask students to identify why Kia does not, giving a specific example of her behavior. Also, if they were her emotionally intelligent friend, what advice would they give her to help her improve? Share group responses with the class.

The Stars Don't Always Shine
Class activity
Materials needed: article from a recent People's Magazine
Time: lecture plus 30-40 minutes
Goal: To help students analyze the behavior of others in terms of emotional intelligence (EI) skills and conflict management
Make copies of a recent *People* magazine article about a Hollywood star who displays inappropriate behavior. Ask students to read this for homework, and come prepared to discuss the EI competencies and conflict management style of the star. To be sure that the students come prepared, tell students they must describe at least three of the five EI competencies using examples, and identify one of the five conflict management styles described in this chapter.

A Conversation with B.D. Wong On Diversity
Video and class discussion
Materials needed: access to the YouTube video, available at
www.youtube.com/watch?v=EC1f5phvCRA
Time: video length 8:12, plus 30 minutes for discussion
Goal: To provide a brief introduction to diversity from the perspective of actor B.D. Wong
After viewing the complete clip ask students to take notes from the video and attempt to answer the following questions:

1. Do you think the country is becoming more diverse? Why or why not?
2. Are you optimistic about diversity? Why or why not?
3. Are network television and media in general diverse (in terms of the ethnicities of actors, etc.)?
4. Are there still groups of people that are not accepted widely in America?
5. Do you agree with Wong that equality is a civil right?
6. What did you learn by watching this clip?

8. What other activities can I incorporate to make the chapter my own?

Depending on the composition of your class, you could approach this chapter a little differently. Although Kia is technically a non-traditional student going to college for the first time, her story may resonate with younger students as well. Many students experience relationship difficulties that get in the way of the learning that should be taking place in college. Emphasize her situation and ask students if they have friends who have experienced similar difficulties. In addition, if your class is very diverse, take full advantage of this if students are willing to share their perceptions of being part of an underrepresented population.

Included here, all in one place, are Activity Options taken from the Annotated Instructor's Edition.

ACTIVITY OPTION (p. 270): Ask students to work in small groups to describe behaviors of successful college students (i.e., studying ahead of time, being realistic about what you can and can't do, going to class, etc.) and see how these behaviors might fit into the five scales of emotional intelligence. Have the groups compare their findings.

ACTIVITY OPTION (p. 271): For homework, divide the class into three groups and assign each group the term *resilience, hardiness,* or *learned optimism.* Each group must come to the next class prepared to describe how their term connects to success in college. Students must define the term and provide examples or role plays that relate their term to college success.

ACTIVITY OPTION (p. 271): Ask students to describe the characteristics of the best leaders they've known or those in public leadership positions. Help them make connections between these characteristics and the five general scales of emotional intelligence: intrapersonal, interpersonal, stress management, and adaptability skills, and general mood, which underlies the other four areas.

ACTIVITY OPTION (p. 277): In groups, ask students to develop the top five characteristics of an ideal partner and rank them in order of importance. Ask students to develop this same list for what they might be looking for when they're in their seventies. Are the two lists the same? Do rankings change? Is what they chose as top characteristics in their college years the same as what they predict they would choose later in life? Discuss this as a class.

ACTIVITY OPTION (p. 278): Divide the class into six groups and give each group a card with one of the examples: trapper, blamer, mindreader, gunnysacker, hit and run fighter, or Benedict Arnold. Groups should not show each other their card. Have two to three students from each group volunteer to role-play their example, while the other groups guess which "crazymaking" behavior they are portraying.

ACTIVITY OPTION (p. 287): Create a Human Continuum as a way to launch a discussion about diversity in class. Create an imaginary line along the front of the room, for example, and label each opposite pole. You can use descriptors such as majority/minority, 100% American/foreign, and so on. Then ask students to place themselves along the line. You may be surprised at how students place themselves on this continuum. For example, students who are light-skinned may place themselves closer to a label for students of color than someone who has darker skin. Defining the meanings of the two poles held for students can lead to a rich discussion.

ACTIVITY OPTION (p. 295): For the final activity have students design a PowerPoint presentation (four slides) in groups on either the role of emotional intelligence, love, or conflict in the lives of college students and their success. Presentations should include a definition, describe possible challenges concerning the issue, its impact on college success, and suggestions on how to manage the challenge.

9. What homework might I assign?

Ask all students to observe a current popular television show and describe the conflict management style of the main character. Describe this in class. The goal is to help students be able to recognize conflict management styles.

Journal Entries
One: Have students write a one-page journal entry, or send you an e-mail describing one EI skill they think that they want to improve. Students must identify why they think they need to develop the skill using an example, and what they will do to improve it.

Two: Have students write a one-page journal entry, or send you an e-mail reflecting on a time when they showed good conflict management skills and a time when they did not. Ask students to label each of these styles using the five examples in the chapter. For the negative example, ask students to describe what they wish they had done.

Three: Use the Insight → Action prompts as journal or blog assignments.

10. What have I learned in teaching this chapter that I will incorporate next time?

_____

_____

_____

_____

_____

_____

_____

_____

_____

CHAPTER 12: CHOOSING A COLLEGE MAJOR AND A CAREER

1. Why is this chapter important?

Did you think, even for a minute, about the title of this chapter when you first read it? How about the addition of the word career? Do you think first-year students know much about how to build a career? Typically, students think about majors and jobs, and loosely use the word career. In this chapter students will not only be asked about what major they might choose and what jobs are associated with that major, but they are introduced to information about how to build a career related to a particular field. Students are encouraged to think about how the disciplines connect and how taking a course in one area connects to another. For many students things just don't connect. "Why should I have to take a course in interpersonal communication if I am going to work as a computer network analyst?" a student might ask, for example. This chapter will help students to self-assess, dig deeper, and look at connections between who they are, what they want to do in life, and which courses they will take. What better way to begin to find closure in the course than to tie things all together?

Understanding how things connect is a central theme in this chapter. When students first read about majors and careers, they are not thinking about courses and connections. The "College in a Box" concept is very concrete and visual for students and will spark a great debate on how the disciplines connect. This concept of how they connect is done so well in "The Circle of Learning" diagram that you don't want to overlook the opportunity to discuss it in class. Once the connections make sense to students, it's a lot easier to look at why they should stick it out in their most challenging, but sometimes least interesting, classes, and what really is involved in developing a career.

Careers just don't happen. Careers are developed over time. All too often college students want to jump out of the gate and earn the same amount of money that has taken their parents years of accomplishment and diligence to reach. As you read in the text, Mel Levine says that many young adults are not finding a good fit between who they are and what they are doing, so in his words they see themselves going nowhere. His observations may sound ominous, but all the more reason for students to volunteer, do internships, and gain experience. Make sure that students take these opportunities seriously. Having experience doing something can either confirm that this is what students ultimately want to do or have them experience an "ah-ha" moment when they realize that this career may not be for them. In fact, this entire chapter can be an "ah-ha" moment for students when things finally begin to fall into place and their college experience starts making sense.

2. What are this chapter's learning objectives?

- ➢ Why "College in a Box" isn't an accurate view of coursework
- ➢ How the disciplines connect in the Circle of Learning
- ➢ How to choose a major and a career
- ➢ What a SWOT analysis is
- ➢ How to launch a career

3. How should I launch this chapter?

Several, if not many, of your students may be thinking along the same lines as Ethan by now. Somehow, many students think things will quickly and naturally fall into place when they get to college, even during their first term. They expect to be drawn into a discipline, have clear insight into the "right" career for them, and when that doesn't happen, they begin to doubt themselves and their decision to attend college in the first place. Many, like Ethan, will drop out. Some will return, but perhaps only after their lives are even more complex, with a family, for example. Some wandering is to be expected when it comes to making choices that will affect the rest of your life. Think back: did you know when you were 18 or 19 that you'd have taken the career path you've taken? Here are some ideas for launching this chapter.

- **Use the *FOCUS* Challenge Case as a starting point to open up the chapter.** This *FOCUS* Challenge Case is a terrific one to open up the chapter. Significant research indicates that when students know what they really want to do and get into a major that is a good fit for them, the likelihood of graduating is fairly high. On the other hand, some students may just be following in mom or dad's footsteps or pursuing a major that they think will lead to a job that really pays well. Students need to discuss that Ethan's parents may have "enabled" him and without even realizing it, made things even more difficult for him. It's not uncommon to be in a searching mode in your first or first several terms. Use Ethan as an example of someone who is unclear and perhaps even impatient about figuring it all out—and talk about what "figuring it all out" means during your first term of college. Is it even possible?

- **Ask students to pair up and share with each other what they think they will major in.** Students enjoy both talking about what they do and don't know about different majors. It's kind of freeing to talk with someone who is not judging the rights and wrongs of the major. For some students it might be the first time that they even talked about certain possibilities. Come together as a class and share what you have learned. The bottom line is that you want students to really do some self-exploration in this chapter and to be open-minded about what it is they really want to do with their lives.

- **Developmental Students and Returning Adult Learners:** Some of your developmental learners may have no idea what to do for a career or may have a very unrealistic view of what it takes to get to the career they have chosen. Returning adult students may have chosen a career path for its shorter length or higher career earning potential. While these may be important factors, they could set themselves up for career dissatisfaction. This chapter is a wonderful opportunity for all students to take an in-depth look at themselves related to potential majors and careers.

- **Going beyond the book.** There are more resources available than you can imagine when it comes to choosing majors and careers. First, you might begin exploring your own campus. Depending on the size of your institution, there might be a fully staffed career center with individuals who help with résumé writing and career searching or just one or two individuals who help in this area. Regardless, it's a place to begin, and you want to be sure students know where it is and what resources it offers. One additional source that is a must for this chapter is www.careerbuilder.com. Not only can students look at jobs in a particular area, but they can look at upcoming local career fairs and the job outlook on this comprehensive website.

4. How should I use the *FOCUS* Challenge Case?

As mentioned earlier, Ethan Cole is not a rare student. In fact, if you think about it, 20 to 25 years ago, students like Ethan would not even be considering college. Dyslexics rarely went on to college, and ADD or ADHD were not diagnosed frequently. If truth be told, there are still professors teaching who are simply not interested in hearing about the "whys" of students' learning challenges. Either students make it, or they are out! If students like Ethan who struggle a bit and haven't discovered how to focus their passion meet up with a professor with this perspective, they can become totally discouraged and drop out without much deliberation. This *FOCUS* Challenge Case is filled with opportunities for discussion and the questions in "What Do *You* Think?" are a good lead-in. Consider using this section as a jumping off point. Other options for this Challenge Case include:

- **Direct It!** Assign a "scene director" for the Challenge Case. After students review the Challenge Case, assign students to role-play Ethan and his Study Skills instructor, Ms. Morgan. The director can stop the scene at any point and redirect the "actors" as well as get input from the "critics"—the other students in class!

  - Scene 1: At this point in the term, students have learned a great deal about campus resources, learning styles, and multiple intelligences. Direct a scene with Ms. Morgan and Ethan. What information would Ms. Morgan share with Ethan? What courses might she suggest? What resources would be helpful to Ethan?
- Before discussing the Challenge Case, ask students to review the pictures around the case and summarize Ethan's story.
- What resources on your campus would students recommend for Ethan?
- What type of courses should Ethan consider next?

5. What important features does this chapter include?

Of course, by now you and your students have literally memorized the "habit-forming" (hopefully!) features of the text. You may split up the features, so that some students who enjoy the Readiness Checks and Reality Checks focus on those, while others who really think the VARK Activity is the most interesting may discuss that feature. Let them follow their interests and lead the class. The Challenge → Reaction and Insight → Action steps are especially helpful to encourage students to think about how they might respond and how they connect to careers and majors. This chapter, overall, contains some of the most unique, innovative, and individually helpful material in the text.

Readiness and Reality Checks
Students should be fairly responsive when filling out the Readiness Check. Most students are interested in what they are planning to major in. And, interest in questions, such as how much they think this chapter will affect their career, should be very high. In fact, what might happen is that the comparisons between the Readiness Check and the Reality Check might point out that students are particularly interested in this chapter because of its practical value and their own insecurity about making what they may see as the "wrong" decision.

Challenge → Reaction → Insight → Action steps
The Challenge → Reaction → Insight → Action steps continue to be good opportunities for class discussions, student reflective papers, or class activities.

Control: Your Learning
In this "Control" activity, students are asked to identify whether or not their toughest course is a general education course or one in their intended major. If it's a general education class, they list the ways this course can help them in their career or help them become a truly well-educated person. Often students complain about general education courses and report having little interest in their content. "What does a course on art appreciation have to do with my future? I'm not going to be an artist. I'm not planning to visit art galleries every weekend." Talk with your students about how that course or any other they bring up will help them live fuller, richer lives. If the course is in their intended major, they respond to why it is so challenging. Are they keeping up with the work? Finally, students are told to send the instructor of this class an e-mail, indicating what they are trying to do to improve in the course, giving specific examples. If a particular course comes up as many students' toughest class frequently in your class discussions, you may wish to alert your colleague to the possibility of a student e-mailing them, so that they are given advance warning. Or you may wish to have your students e-mail their "Control Your Learning" plans to you. Alternatively, students can apply the learning to an on the job task and describe the knowledge needed from five academic disciplines.

How Full Is Your Plate?
This is a great assignment to help students determine their biggest accomplishments each day as well as the distracting obstacles in their lives. Ask students to journal this information and be prepared to share in class.

Career Outlook
The career focus in this chapter is on entrepreneurs. In this chapter, we meet Matt McClain, an entrepreneur who started his own production company. Matt spent six

years working in television and decided to go out on his own. He was involved in writing and directing the *FOCUS* TV episodes for this book. Do your students enjoy freedom? Are they brave, determined and confident? If so, a career as an entrepreneur may be for them. Does your college offer a program in entrepreneurship? If so, consider having an instructor and/or program students come to your class to talk about this program.

FOCUS TV
This episode features Ethan Cole/Josh from the FOCUS Challenge Case. Also featured is a humorous segment on asking students what they wanted to be growing up and what their major is today. This segment helps students to understand the *College in a Box concept, The Circle of Learning, and SWOT Analysis.*

6. Which in-text exercises should I use?

Have students connect these activities to real life situations especially their own majors and careers. Included here are reasons why you should do these, the challenges to expect, and how to debrief the exercises.

EXERCISE 12.1 WHAT ARE YOUR JOB PREFERENCES?

Why do this activity?
This fun and quick activity looks at student's job preferences and brainstorming careers that match their first choices.

What are the challenges and what can you expect?
There really are no challenges for this activity. This activity works well in class or as an assignment. If you are doing it in class it is helpful, but not necessary, to have career resource materials available such as *Occupational Outlook Handbook.*

How much time will it take?
This activity should take about 10 minutes to complete. If debriefed in class, allow about 20-30 minutes for report out.

How should I debrief?
If debriefed in class, ask students to summarize their preferences. For example, do you prefer to work alone or with people? Then ask them to discuss the career fields that they came up with. Are their similarities in your class? Were any students surprised by their choices?

EXERCISE 12.2 GET A JOB

Why do this activity?
This is really a terrific activity for students to identify the kinds of skills that college students need to develop to be marketable in the 21st century. In addition, it helps

---

students to see that they actually have a job in college—being a college student! The job may not pay well, in fact you have to pay for it, but students will see that their job in college really is to think and to learn.

What are the challenges and what can you expect?
There really are no challenges for this activity. When working in groups students fairly quickly come up with the job description of a college student.

How much time will it take?
This activity could take up to half an hour of in-class time.

How should I debrief?
After sharing job descriptions with the group, consider asking students to send you an e-mail, or write a brief essay if they think they are better qualified to apply for this *job* now than they were at the beginning of the semester. Make sure they tell you why or why not.

7. Which additional exercises might enrich students' learning?

<u>How to Build a Student for the 21st Century</u>
Homework activity
Materials needed: Students must find and print the *Time* article "How to Bring Our Schools Out of the 20th Century" from the December 18th, 2006 edition
Time: Full class time (at least one hour)
Goal: To help students identify the need to understand multiple disciplines to be successful in the 21st century
Divide the class into two groups. Assign all students to read this article. One group has to come to class to discuss the interdisciplinary aspects needed to create MySpace and the other group does that same describing YouTube. In addition, ask each student to identify two things that surprised them about this article and why.

<u>Building Resources</u>
Class activity
Materials needed: The Internet and an LCD projector
Time: Homework assignment, plus 30-40 minutes in class
Goal: To help students build a repertoire of websites for careers resources
For homework, ask students to identify four to five job search websites other than www.careerbuilder.com or www.monster.com. Using the websites that they bring to class, assess the effectiveness of each. Why is this source good? What features does the website provide? What evidence do they have that this is a credible site? If they find a job on a website, what is the next thing they should do? Ask them to choose a job that they find online, and go to the company's website. What about the website might make them believe this it is credible (the last time it was updated, check the address to see if this is a valid company)? What might a student check on before they go on an interview for a job that is posted without a website listed or one that they can't check out prior to going for an interview?

8. What other activities can I incorporate to make the chapter my own?

If you have mostly traditional students in your class, there will be much exploring and discussing majors and careers from a learning perspective. If some or all of your students are returning adult learners or a mix of both, you might ask older students to contribute their own career experiences. Why did they come back to school? Do they want to change careers? Why or why not? In you don't have returning adult learners in the class, ask the students to e-mail a family member and ask them about how they chose their career and if they had it to do over, if they would be in the same job.

Included here, all in one place, are Activity Options taken from the Annotated Instructor's Edition.

ACTIVITY OPTION (p. 300): Students should take a few minutes to share their responses to the "What Do *You* Think?" questions. Divide the class into four groups and give each group a question to discuss. After 5 to 10 minutes, ask one member of each group to present their response to the class.

ACTIVITY OPTION (p. 302): In Figure 12.1 students saw a typical schedule. Have students list their own schedules in a similar format and then place their courses on the Circle of Learning. Can they describe connections between two or more of the classes they're taking this term?

ACTIVITY OPTION (p. 305): The ten questions here can be turned into a project. First, find out which majors most students are interested in. Group students together and have each group interview for one major. Make sure that all majors of interest in the class are covered. In the same groups, have students develop a fact sheet about the major to be presented in class and distributed to all students.

ACTIVITY OPTION (p. 305): Ask students to interview a person who is very successful in a career. What does the person do, what specific jobs has the person held previously, and for how long? Students can do this as an outside assignment and bring their findings to class. Were there many instant success stories? Probably not.

ACTIVITY OPTION (p. 306): Ask your students to find two jobs: one they could get today and one that they could only get after they graduate with a degree. Then compare the two. The revelation may increase some students' motivation to apply themselves in college.

ACTIVITY OPTION (p. 307): To help students evaluate their career profile, have students make a SWOT Analysis following the model in Figure 12.3.

ACTIVITY OPTION (p. 310): Using Figure 12.6 as a model, ask students to profile their own academic anatomies. Then tie their responses back to their VARK Preference. Is there a correlation? Are kinesthetic learners more likely to choose their hands or whole bodies? Have students discuss their profiles.

ACTIVITY OPTION (p. 312): After students have completed their "Academic Anatomy," have them divide in groups by learning preference and discuss what careers they feel they will be best suited for based on their learning preferences. Also have students explain how their learning preferences will be used in each career.

ACTIVITY OPTION (p. 313): Assign students a real or fictitious possible job opportunity to research, and ask them to come to class prepared for a mock interview. Time permitting, let as many students participate in the mock interview as possible. The rest of the class should decide who they would hire and why.

9. What homework might I assign?

Assign all students in the class to choose a career, either their intended or another, and list the top six general studies classes they should take for this major and why. Students should come back to the next class prepared to discuss this. The goal is to help students understand the many connections between and among general studies courses and careers. Or write the names of different careers on slips of paper, one per slip. Ask students to draw a slip randomly to be "assigned" a career and work in pairs to find the best job offer they can find for that profession using online resources.

Journal Entries
One: Have students write a one-page journal entry or send you an e-mail describing whether this chapter made them change their mind about what major and career they will pursue or if they are still going to follow the same one they had originally decided upon. If students are still undecided they should write about that. In all cases, students must explain and give examples of what they learned in this chapter and how it influenced where they stand now.

Two: Have students write a one-page journal entry or send you an e-mail reflecting on a time when they were in a class in which they saw no purpose to something they were studying. Ask students how they might see this course fitting into the Circle of Learning concept now that they have read this chapter.

Three: Use the Insight $\rightarrow$ Action steps as journal or blog assignments.

10. What have I learned in teaching this chapter that I will incorporate next time?

_____

_____

_____

_____

_____

_____

_____

_____

_____

_____

_____

_____

_____

_____

_____

_____

_____

_____

_____

_____

_____

_____

_____

_____

_____

_____

_____

_____

_____

_____

_____

_____

_____

CHAPTER 13: CREATING YOUR FUTURE

1. Why is this chapter important?

Human development can summarized by Portia Nelson's poem, "Autobiography in Five Short Chapters." The poem (available at www.mhsanctuary.com/healing/auto.htm) details an individual's development in five very short chapters. In chapter 1, the individual falls in a deep hole in the sidewalk and they know it is not their fault. In chapter 2, they walk down the same street and fall in the same hole. Frustrated they are in the same place; they finally manage to get out. Chapter 3 finds them in the same hole but with the realization that it might be their fault. Chapter 4 is about seeing the hole in the street and finally having the knowledge and life experience to walk around it, while chapter 5 reveals a new path and finding a new street to walk down. Whether it is the end of a chapter, the end of a book, or the end of the course—endings are really about new beginnings.

This chapter represents the culmination of your work and your student's work toward creating the future they want for themselves. It is important to take some time to celebrate how far your students (and you) have come in this journey. In his book, *Creating Your Future: Five Steps to the Life of Your Dreams*, David Ellis suggests five steps on the path to creating the life people want:

1. Commit to creating your future
2. Create a vision of your future
3. Construct a plan to fulfill your vision
4. Carry out your plan
5. Celebrate what you've done and continue creating your future

The final chapter is really about those five steps. It is important for your students to think about the steps they need to take to get to the future they desire. The end of the first semester of college is not too early to begin this planning.

Some of your students may be in a certificate program, which means they don't have as much time to plan their next academic steps. They may already have an academic plan laid out and have a firm idea of their next career move. Others may not understand educational career paths, and this chapter will help students gain this understanding. Regardless of the type of student in your class, everyone can benefit from the résumé assistance.

2. What are this chapter's learning objectives?

> ➤ How to launch a career
> ➤ How to write a résumé and interview successfully
> ➤ What to consider when continuing education
> ➤ How to put the learning from college to good use

3. How should I launch this chapter?

This chapter is designed for students to create a plan for their future. Take advantage of all the activities and exercises in this chapter as they provide students with an opportunity to make their plan more concrete. Additionally, if time permits and you have the resources on your campus, consider having students attend a career or transfer fair. Exposing them to these resources early will help them to solidify their planning. Here are some other suggestions for getting this chapter started—and concluding your course!

- **Use the *FOCUS* Challenge Case as a starting point to open up the chapter.** Many students know someone like Anthony Lopez or have a similar story to Anthony's. Using this Challenge Case can be a great way of opening this chapter.

- **Developmental Students and Returning Adult Learners:** Developmental learners may fear risk-taking. If appropriate, tell a story about yourself when you were afraid to take a risk but did it anyway. Discuss with them how it turned out. Was it successful? If it was a failure, what did you learn from it? Returning adult learners may miss the value of this chapter. They may not realize that regardless of their age, it is still important to plan for the future. According to David Ellis, "Most people spend more time planning their next vacation than they do planning the rest of their lives." Very few individuals can argue about the importance of building a quality résumé, learning how to network, and gaining better interview skills.

- **Going beyond the book.** If you did not use the Portia Nelson poem activity in chapter 2 (**Life By The Book**), consider doing it now. Or if you did it in chapter 2, are your students in a different chapter now? Have they learned to avoid the street with the hole in the sidewalk?

  Show the video "Miracles Happen" (available at www.youtube.com/watch?v=s-WscYZuPtE) to get this chapter started. Process the video by asking students what "impossible" thing they thought was out of reach now seems possible. What "miracles" will they create in their future?

  If your campus has a career center, arrange for someone to come to your class to assist with mock interviews and résumé critiques. If your institution has a fashion program, consider asking a faculty member to come to your class to talk about dressing for the interview. Lastly, if your campus has a culinary program arrange to have a demonstration of appropriate interview dining etiquette. There are many possibilities for campus partnerships with this last chapter!

4. How should I use the *FOCUS* Challenge Case?

Anthony Lopez is enrolled at his community college in a social services program. He wants to help others who may be facing challenges he once faced. Chances are good you have a student like Anthony in your class or you have had one like him before. When

Anthony met former gang leader Nicky Russo, his life began to turn around. Leaving a life of drugs and crime, Anthony earned his GED and enrolled in an associate's degree program in social services.

As this chapter in his life begins to open, so do the possibilities for what comes next. Anthony is unsure if he wants to transfer on to a four-year school for a bachelor's degree. He is also wondering about graduate school and the myriad of options that are available to him. Many college students, especially first-year students, are unclear about the educational ladder. The concept of an associate's degree preparing a student for transfer, or a bachelor's degree preparing someone for a career or graduate school seems daunting to them. The question of what the future hold for Anthony (or your students) can begin to be answered with some planning. Excellent options for using this Challenge Case include:

- **Direct It!** Assign a "scene director" for the Challenge Case. Assign a student to role-play Anthony and another student to role-play Gina. The Director can stop the scene at any point and redirect the "actors" as well as get input from the "critics"—the other students in class!

  - o Scene 1: Direct Anthony to have a discussion with his sister about his educational goals, his concerns for Gina and his desire to have her off of the streets and in school.
- Examine the pros and cons of continuing beyond the associate's degree.

Refer back to Anthony throughout this chapter and ask your students to complete his story at the end of the chapter. The future begins today!

5. What important features does this chapter include?

All of the features in this chapter are designed to assist students with creating their future. Get creative and add activities that are meaningful for your class and don't forget to celebrate your and your student's accomplishments.

Readiness and Reality Checks
As discussed in earlier chapters, it's important for students to think about what they don't know about what they are about to learn to help them *FOCUS* on learning new things. Students should be interested in this chapter for several reasons. One, its about their future and regardless of whether your students are 18 or 58, most people like to think about how things can be. Second, students are interested in creating a quality résumé and doing well on an interview. These checks can also be the basis for a good class conversation.

Challenge → Reaction → Insight → Action steps
As mentioned earlier, have students complete the *FOCUS* Challenge Case and Reaction questions. This will help to stage the discussion around educational

planning. Similarly, bring closure to your class by having them complete Anthony's case study by coming up with possible outcomes. In the Action prompt, have students write about or discuss how the chapter has changed how they will approach the future. Are they hopeful about the future or do they still see roadblocks ahead?

Curiosity: FOCUS Your I's!

In this chapter of *FOCUS*, "Curiosity" provides a number of examples and thought-provoking bits of information about what students need in order to transition into the workforce after college. The need to focus on four "I's" are described: inner direction, interpretation, instrumentation, and interactions (the four "I's" of career-life readiness).

How Full Is Your Plate?

Time management and multitasking are very important skills for students and employees. Ask students to decide on three things that must be accomplished each day. At the end of the day reflect back on how successful they were in getting these things accomplished. Learning to prioritize will pay off as a student and in the workforce.

Career Outlook

The career focus in this chapter is on social work. In this chapter we meet Laela Perkins, Social Worker. Laela made a career decision and then decided it was not fulfilling to her, so she did some research and decided to get a degree in social work. She recognized that the need to make certain changes in society were very important to her. Laela suggests getting some experience before going back to school to get your master's degree. The experience helped her once she was back in school. The future workforce demand for this program is good, and a bachelor's degree is the minimum requirement to become a social worker.

6. Which in-text exercises should I use?

There are four exercises built into this chapter. All the activities are practical ways to help students think about their future. Below are reasons why you should do these, the challenges to expect, and how to debrief them.

EXERCISE 13.1 CAREER AUCTION

Why do this activity?
This fun activity helps students decide what is important to them in a career. By "bidding" on characteristics of careers, they can decide what they want in a career. For some, being your own boss may be far more important than being a top earner in their field.

What are the challenges and what can you expect?
Before beginning the auction, ask students to review all 10 items and remind them they cannot spend all of their money on one item.

How much time will it take?
This activity should take about 30 minutes including time to debrief.

How should I debrief?
Ask students about their winning items. Why did they decide to go after that item? If they were to prioritize the entire list, what would be ranked first, what would be last and why?

EXERCISE 13.2 GROUP RÉSUMÉ

Why do this activity?
There are a number of reasons why this is a good activity for students. By doing a group résumé students will be able to see the "collective wisdom" of the group. Throughout *FOCUS*, the importance of interpersonal skills and working collaboratively has been stressed in the text itself and the online "Team Career Activities." Not only does this group activity help students to see all the academic expertise in the class, it also provides an opportunity for students to think of skills that they've never even thought of when one of the group members lists it.

What are the challenges and what can you expect?
There really are no challenges for this activity, expect for the fact that you may want to limit students to about 15 minutes or so to do the actual task since you do want to give students the opportunity to present their group résumés to the class.

How much time will it take?
As stated above, you might want to limit students to 15 minutes.

How should I debrief?
Students are instructed to hang their newsprint on the walls to create a gallery and present their group résumés to the class. Students enjoy this aspect of the activity so make sure you leave time at the end of the class to do this.

EXERCISE 13.3 COVER LETTER CRITIQUE

Why do this activity?
This exercise is designed to get students thinking about the cover letter and how important a well-written cover letter is in a job search. This activity can be done as described in the Activity Option on page 329, or it can be assigned individually. This exercise also makes a good homework assignment for students.

What are the challenges and what can you expect?
Developmental students who are weaker in proofreading and writing may struggle a bit with finding the errors in the cover letter. If you do this in a group setting, make sure the groups represent all skill levels in the class.

How much time will it take?
This activity, if done in class, should take about 20 minutes including time to debrief.

How should I debrief?
Start by asking students how many errors they found. If they are not close to the 15 errors, ask them to continue looking. If you have had them do it individually, have them get into groups to compare errors. Then ask the groups to report out. You could ask the groups to write a new cover letter for Marcus and have the groups report out on the new cover letter.

EXERCISE 13.4 CIRCLING THE RIGHT CAREER

Why do this activity?
Often, students do not understand the underlying motivators in selecting a career. This brainstorming activity will help students to think about service, money and power as career motivators. Also, money and power can have negative implications, but point out that this is not always true. For example, a college instructor could fit in the Service circle as well as the Power circle.

What are the challenges and what can you expect?
Some students may need a bit of time to brainstorm careers and then put them in one or more of the circles.

How much time will it take?
This activity should take about 20-30 minutes to complete and debrief.

How should I debrief?
Ask students to share their work with the class. Do the students agree or disagree with the placement of the career? Did students come up with any careers that could go in all three circles? Which of the careers are most fulfilling to them?

---

7. Which additional exercises might enrich students' learning?

Revisiting the Envelope
Writing/Reflection/Home work activity
Materials needed: The letter students wrote themselves from chapter 2
Time: 60 minutes
Goal: To have students review the letter they wrote earlier in the term (see Instructor's Manual, chapter 2) and see if their predictions came true.
In chapter 2, students wrote a letter to themselves answering some important questions. Now return the envelope to the student and the predictions they made at the start of the class can become the basis of their final class 2-3 page writing assignment.

Life in a Manila Envelope
Class activity
Materials needed: 4 manila envelopes containing: case study, help wanted ads, apartment/house listings, grocery advertisements, and a sealed Life Surprise envelope
Time: 50-60 minutes

Goal: To help students understand the need to develop solid budgeting and planning skills

Divide the class into four groups. Each group is given an envelope that contains a brief background on an individual, financial parameters, family size, etc. Each case should be different. A sample case is included on the next page. Each group should find their assigned person a job, a place to live, and plan a meal within the budget and family guidelines.

Some of your case studies should be easy; the others should be more challenging. Each manila envelope should contain a smaller, sealed envelope entitled Life Surprise. These surprises can be "You have inherited Aunt Sally's life savings of $1,000," "Your car needs repaired, pay $500," "You have just had another child." Only one of the Life Surprises should give them additional funds.

Debrief this exercise by asking the groups if they were able to meet their budgeting goals and if this was easy or more difficult then they thought it was going to be. This exercise should produce a good discussion on the need to develop good budgeting and life planning skills.

Sample Case Study:

Managing Career & Money

Directions: Using your folder of information, determine the salary from the job posting on the front of the folder. Make a monetary goal for your client that you would like him/her to save each month. Complete all blanks with the assistance of your group members. You may want to use a calculator.

Goal to save: $_____

Case 1: Gino Roberts

Background: Age 18, single with one child

Job Title:_____

Annual Salary:_____ (Annual Salary minus 23% for taxes)

Monthly Salary:_____ (Answer above /12)

Assigned Expenses

Rent: Name of Apartment Complex:_____ Monthly Rent:_____

Food: $300.00

> Plan for a three course nutritious meal that would feed two people for
> $10.00 or less (included in the above food budget):
> First course:_____ Cost:_____
>
> Second course:_____ Cost:_____
>
> Third course:_____ Cost:_____
>
> Total cost for meal:_____

Entertainment: $75.00

Telephone: $70.00

Utilities: $80.00

Gasoline/public transportation: $150.00

Clothing/personal items: $100.00

Medical Care/insurance: $25.00

Miscellaneous/unexpected/childcare: $400.00

Can you meet your original savings goal?
How much money will you save/or owe per month?
If you owe, how can you help to reduce your client's expenses?

8. What other activities can I incorporate to make the chapter my own?

The classroom dynamics and exactly what is discussed in this chapter may vary widely, depending on the age of your students and their comfort level with you and each other. Find ways to engage all of your students and make the class meaningful for them. Included here, all in one place, are Activity Options taken from the Annotated Instructor's Edition.

ACTIVITY OPTION (p. 322): Have students visit http://vocationvacation.com and read through the categories and select a career and write up what would be the possible vocation vacations. Reassure students that this opportunity may not be financially possible, but it is helpful to know what types of services are available.

ACTIVITY OPTION (p. 324): If your college has a formal process for a portfolio, begin gathering the necessary documents. If not, have the class decide what should be in a portfolio and begin gathering the documents.

ACTIVITY OPTION (p. 328): Design a résumé template. Pass out the template and have students fill in as much information as possible. Then divide students into groups to critique each other's résumés. Have students submit the résumé for your comments. As an assignment, have students type their résumé for a final grade.

ACTIVITY OPTION (p. 328): To help students begin feeling comfortable speaking up for themselves, divide the class into partners. Have each pair write a scenario script with a part for a supervisor and one for the intern. Have students role-play the script, with each person taking a turn being the supervisor and the intern. To extend this activity, have the pairs switch scripts with another pair.

ACTIVITY OPTION (p. 329): Have students divide into groups. Instruct them to read the letter in Exercise 13.3. Encourage each group to write down the mistakes in the letter and then rewrite it correctly. There should be at least 15 errors, such as (1) The year is missing in the date; (2) Marcus has not called to find out to whom the letter should be addressed; (3) "Concern" is spelled incorrectly; (4) The exact name of the position is not listed; (5) Punctuation is different for business letters; (6) Marcus doesn't list his availability for an interview or a follow-up conversation; (7) The letter should be typed for a more professional appearance; (8) Salary should not be mentioned up front; (9) He shouldn't call attention to his lack of experience; (10) He should capitalize on his qualifications (this would be a great place to discuss his freelance work); (11) The name of the company should be correct throughout the letter; (12) The full name of the college should be listed, not the initials; (13) The closing is overly personal; (14) The ending is very general; and (15) He should ask if he can set up a date for a follow-up call.

ACTIVITY OPTION (p. 330): Have students divide into teams of three. Give each team a list of common interviewing questions. Have each student select a role: interviewer, interviewee and observer. As the interview is taking place, have the observer record answers that could have been phrased differently to help the interviewee be more successful. Have the participants switch roles and try again.

ACTIVITY OPTION (p. 332): Have an advisor or academic counselor make a presentation about transferring policies, transfer agreements, and transfer adjustment.

ACTIVITY OPTION (p. 336): Write down the words Career, Speaking, Writing, and Listening on the board. Have students suggest a career and what type of activities they would need to do under each category.

ACTIVITY OPTION (p. 338): For the final activity in the chapter, ask students to design a five-slide PowerPoint presentation. Students must include in their ten-year plan the following five components: (1) where they are now, (2) where they will be and what they will do when they graduate, (3) where they will be and what they will be doing five years from now, (4) where they will be and what they will be doing ten years from now, and (5) how they will know if they have been successful.

9. What homework might I assign?

Assign all students in the class to develop a résumé and cover letter for either a job they are currently seeking or one to be used in the future. Students should come back to the next class prepared to discuss these and, working with other students, receive written feedback for improvement. The goal is to help students understand the importance of creating a quality cover letter and résumé.

Journal Entries
One: Have students write a one-page journal entry or send you an e-mail describing their reaction to reading *Curiosity: FOCUS Your I's!* on page 316. For each "I" ask students to write a paragraph on how they could improve in this area.

Two: Have students write a one-page journal entry or send you an e-mail reflecting on their learning from this course. How have students grown this term? What lessons are they taking with them after completing this course?

Three: Use the Insight → Action steps as journal or blog assignment.

10. What have I learned in teaching this chapter that I will incorporate next time?

_____

_____

_____

_____

_____

FOCUS ON COMMUNITY COLLEGE SUCCESS

TEST BANK

RIC UNDERHILE & JOHN COWLES

CHAPTER 1: GETTING THE RIGHT START

LEVEL ONE: REMEMBERING & UNDERSTANDING (Questions attempt to progress in their level of challenge based on Bloom's [revised] Taxonomy.)

1. According to *FOCUS*, people generally attend community college:
A. because it is easier
B. to improve their skills or gain new skills
C. to be with friends
D. when they don't know what they want to major in

2. What, in particular, makes the community college classroom a rich learning environment?
A. the instructors are well prepared to teach
B. the textbooks contain important information
C. smart students helping others who are not as smart
D. the diversity of the students gathered in one place to discuss the same ideas

3. Students seeking a degree at a community college generally have two choices:
A. one with a career focus and one with a transfer focus
B. one focusing on study skills and one focusing on careers
C. one without a career focus and one with a focus on skills
D. none of the above

4. Which of the following is not suggested in your journey to becoming a professional student?
A. complete your assignments
B. reserve class time as a top priority
C. come prepared
D. all of the above are suggested

5. Engaged students are most likely to:
A. skip classes when an emergency arises
B. complain to the Dean when there is a problem
C. be tuned in and soak up everything the class has to offer
D. be angry when things don't go their way

6. The purpose of core classes is to provide students with:
A. an understanding of their chosen profession
B. an understanding of themselves
C. elective courses
D. an opportunity to become a more knowledgeable person

LEVEL TWO: APPLYING & ANALYZING

7. When you leave a voicemail message for your advisor or instructor, which of the following should you do?
   A. Leave your full name, ID number, class enrolled, telephone number and state your brief question
   B. Leave your first name and state your question
   C. State your question and ask them to call or email you back
   D. Leave your full name, ID number, class enrolled and state your question

8. Which of the following are examples of planning ahead for meeting with an advisor?
   A. dropping in to see if your advisor can talk to you
   B. waiting until the term is over and it's time to choose new classes before seeing your advisor
   C. making an appointment and having a prepared list of questions
   D. asking other students for advice on classes

9. Before dropping a class, you should first speak with:
   A. the instructor
   B. the health education office
   C. a student in the class
   D. the Dean

10. When should you skip a prerequisite?
    A. if you feel you have a good understanding of the material
    B. never
    C. if it will delay graduation
    D. if other students have done it

11. Which of the following examples is a better way to choose a major?
    A. after talking with relatives and finding out more about the careers they have chosen
    B. after researching the career and the major requirements
    C. after watching your favorite CSI show
    D. after hearing what your parents or other family members tell you to do

12. The formula for calculating GPA is:
    A. GPA=Final Grade ÷ Total Number of Classes
    B. GPA=Total Number of Credits ÷ Total Number of Classes
    C. GPA=Grade Point Value ÷ Total Number of Credits
    D. none of the above

13. In one study cited in this chapter, _____% of community college students required one or more remedial courses:

A. 90
B. 85
C. 55
D. 35

14. The syllabus can be thought of as:

A. a preview of what to expect
B. a contract between you and your instructor
C. a summary of all the assignments
D. all of the above

LEVEL THREE: EVALUATING & CREATING

15. Which of the following are examples of avoiding the PCP Syndrome?

A. bunching your classes together so you can get them out of the way on as few days as possible
B. going to work right after class
C. going to the grocery store right after class
D. getting involved in Student Government on your campus

16. According to motivational author Robert Collier:

A. success is the sum of small efforts
B. success is about money
C. success happens suddenly
D. success begins when students graduate

17. Which of the following is not a benefit of going to college?

A. higher earning potential
B. wisdom
C. lifelong learning
D. higher likelihood of being unemployed

18. According to the text, success courses like this one help students to:

A. earn more money
B. have more friends
C. stay in school and be successful
D. avoid transferring to a university

19. Risk factors for college success are:

A. predictors not determiners
B. determiners not predictors
C. reality not fiction
D. outcomes not precursors

20. A community college classmate of yours failed his first math exam. Which of the following recommendations would help?
A. use the services available on your campus
B. ask you for advice since you're good at math
C. figure things out on his own; it will make him stronger
D. none of the above

Chapter 1 Answer Key

1. B
2. D
3. A
4. D
5. C
6. D
7. A
8. C
9. A
10. B
11. B
12. C
13. B
14. D
15. D
16. A
17. D
18. C
19. A
20. A

CHAPTER 2: BUILDING DREAMS, SETTING GOALS

LEVEL ONE: REMEMBERING & UNDERSTANDING (Questions attempt to progress in their level of challenge based on Bloom's [revised] Taxonomy.)

1. "The system" used in this book to structure productive learning is:
A. Challenge—Insight—Reaction
B. Insight—Reaction—Challenge
C. Challenge—Reaction—Insight—Action
D. Reaction—Insight—Challenge

2. According to the *FOCUS* system, for any goal to be effective it must be:
A. concrete
B. abstract
C. vague
D. flexible

3. According to the text, dreaming is the ___ step to creating the future you want.
A. last
B. first
C. second
D. third

4. Research shows that students learn better through:
A. examples
B. reading
C. critical thinking
D. analysis

5. According to Rick Snyder's research, students who scored higher on a measure of ____ got higher grades.
A. curiosity
B. hope
C. challenge
D. career outlook

6. Research shows that what you *believe* about your own intelligence can make a difference in how successful you'll be in college. There are two basic ways to define the views on intelligence. People are either:
A. performers or learners
B. achievers or losers
C. smart or stupid
D. positive or negative

LEVEL TWO: APPLYING & ANALYZING

7. Insights have no impact unless they lead to:
A. knowledge
B. curiosity
C. beliefs
D. action

8. People who are extrinsically motivated learn in order to:
A. get a grade
B. earn credits
C. complete a requirement
D. all of the given answers

9. People who are intrinsically motivated are motivated:
A. by good teachers
B. by money
C. from within
D. from without

10. Performers believe that intelligence is:
A. flexible
B. inborn
C. constructed
D. complex

11. Learners believe you can grow your intelligence if you capitalize on opportunities to:
A. grow
B. take tests
C. learn
D. read

12. When performers tackle problems that are too difficult, they often feel:
A. inspired
B. challenged
C. excited
D. helpless

13. Students who are performers are often:
A. confident when tasks are easy
B. more intelligent than learners
C. introverted and shy
D. less intelligent than learners

14. According to the text, the *FOCUS* system begins by making your goal fit your:
A. values
B. character
C. identity
D. all of the given answers

15. According to the *FOCUS* system, your goals must please:
A. your parents
B. your friends
C. your teachers
D. yourself

LEVEL THREE: EVALUATING & CREATING

16. Which of the following fuels your motivation level?
A. Your attitude
B. Your feelings
C. Your level of stimulation
D. All of the given answers

17. Of the following, which describes the best place to start when you're learning something new?
A. What you wish you knew
B. What you don't know
C. What you already know
D. What others know

18. Which of the following describes the phrase "Some situations cannot be changed, but attitude can"?
A. Math has always been difficult for you. You changed majors because your current major requires you to take two math classes.
B. Your teacher has an accent and it makes it hard for you to understand her. You make an appointment to see her to ask if you can get her notes.
C. Your college roommate is a neat freak. You have a talk with her and tell her to lighten up.
D. Your friend just bought an expensive Wii system. Inside you are jealous. He never has to work and you work every weekend.

19. This chapter stresses the importance of motivation. What do you think the following phrase means? "If you can and you don't, it means you won't."
A. If you try hard enough, you will succeed.
B. If you fail, try again.
C. If you have the ability and don't try, you won't succeed.
D. If you have the ability, you will succeed.

20. Which of the following statements accurately reflects the relationship of physical, mental and spiritual health to academic health?

A. Physical, mental and spiritual health are not related to academic health.

B. Without spiritual health, physical health will suffer.

C. It is important to keep physical, mental and spiritual health in balance so they can complement academic health.

D. None of the above statements are accurate.

Chapter 2 Answer Key

1. C
2. A
3. B
4. A
5. B
6. A
7. D
8. D
9. C
10. B
11. C
12. D
13. A
14. D
15. D
16. D
17. C
18. B
19. C
20. C

CHAPTER 3: LEARNING ABOUT LEARNING

LEVEL ONE: REMEMBERING & UNDERSTANDING
(Questions attempt to progress in their level of challenge based on Bloom's [revised] Taxonomy.)

1. According to researchers, when you are _____, you are in the best state for learning:
   A. extrinsically motivated
   B. totally motivated
   C. somewhat motivated
   D. intrinsically motivated

2. According to researchers, students learn best when they are:
   A. stressed
   B. relaxed
   C. relaxed and alert
   D. stressed and alert

3. When you become so absorbed in what you are doing that you lose track of everything else, you are in a state that researchers call:
   A. obsessed
   B. flow
   C. learning
   D. intelligent

4. According to the text, you can learn better if you use confusion as a:
   A. stressor
   B. motivator
   C. depressor
   D. all of the given answers

5. If you learn through symbolic representations, then your learning style is:
   A. visual
   B. aural
   C. read/write
   D. kinesthetic

6. If you learn through hearing, then your learning style is:
   A. visual
   B. aural
   C. read/write
   D. kinesthetic

7. If you decide to learn how to sew by buying a book, then your learning style is likely:
A. visual
B. aural
C. read/write
D. kinesthetic

8. If you decided to learn how to sew by getting out a needle and thread, then your learning style is likely:
A. visual
B. aural
C. read/write
D. kinesthetic

LEVEL TWO: APPLYING & ANALYZING

9. Of the choices below, which is a strategy for improving your linguistic intelligence?
A. illustrate your notes
B. rewrite your class notes
C. sing or hum as you work
D. study outside

10. VARK preferences are not necessarily:
A. weaknesses
B. modalities
C. multimodal
D. strengths

11. Ultimately, learning at your best is up to:
A. your parents
B. you
C. your teachers
D. your friends

12. The human brain consists of a complex web of connections between:
A. neurons
B. neutrons
C. electrons
D. all of the above

13. Which of the following describes the best kind of learning?
A. conscious
B. unconscious
C. conscious and unconscious
D. passive

14. According to Harvard psychologist Howard Gardner, people can be intelligent in at least how many ways?
A. 2
B. 4
C. 6
D. 8

15. Most college classes emphasize which VARK modality?
A. visual
B. aural
C. read/write
D. kinesthetic

LEVEL THREE: EVALUATING & CREATING

16. If a class is delivered through lectures and your preferred modality is visual, you should:
A. use your visual modality as a way to understand the lecture
B. ask the instructor to change delivery styles
C. ask your friends to take notes for you
D. transfer to another class

17. If Mary, a read/write learner, isn't sure which spelling is correct for a word, she will likely:
A. envision the word in her mind
B. think about how the word sounds
C. find it in the dictionary
D. write the word on paper

18. If Jack, an aural learner, has to give someone directions to find a certain office on campus, he will likely:
A. draw or give her a map
B. tell her the directions
C. write down the directions (without a map)
D. go with her

19. We acquire most of our information through:
A. emotions
B. thoughts
C. teachers
D. senses

20. According to researchers, the learning preference of most people is:
A. multimodal
B. visual
C. kinesthetic
D. read/write

1. D
2. C
3. B
4. B
5. A
6. B
7. C
8. D
9. B
10. D
11. B
12. A
13. C
14. D
15. C
16. A
17. C
18. B
19. D
20. A

CHAPTER 4: MANAGING YOUR TIME, ENERGY AND MONEY

LEVEL ONE: REMEMBERING & UNDERSTANDING
(Questions attempt to progress in their level of challenge based on Bloom's [revised] Taxonomy.)

1. Time management is not just about managing time, but also managing your:
A. skills
B. interests
C. attention
D. relationships

2. Succeeding in school, at work, and in life is about what you do and:
A. what you don't do
B. how much you make
C. what gets done
D. none of the above

3. You can't control time, but you can manage your:
A. sleep
B. homework
C. output
D. energy

4. According to your text, which of the following is <u>not</u> a dimension of energy?
A. physical
B. emotional
C. financial
D. spiritual

5. Physical energy is measured in terms of:
A. quality
B. input
C. quantity
D. exercise

6. Emotional energy is measured in terms of:
A. quality
B. input
C. quantity
D. exercise

7. Research shows that the average adult requires ___ hours of sleep each night.
A. 4-6 hours
B. 7-8 hours
C. 9-10 hours
D. 11-12 hours

8. According to Michael Fortino, the average American spends __ year(s) in meetings.
A. 1
B. 2
C. 3
D. 4

9. According to the text, ___ of college students admit to procrastinating.
A. 40%
B. 50%
C. 60%
D. 70%

LEVEL TWO: APPLYING & ANALYZING

10. You are least productive when you are operating with ___ energy:
A. high negative
B. high positive
C. low negative
D. low positive

11. One way to get physically energized is to:
A. go with the flow
B. communicate like it matters
C. choose how you renew
D. let others renew you

12. According to the text, in the A-B-C method, "A" tasks are:
A. the highest priority
B. unimportant
C. necessary
D. somewhat important

13. The two factors to consider when assigning a priority level to a to-do item are:
A. time and cost
B. time and effort
C. importance and urgency
D. ease and effort

Not For Sale

14. Which study habit is <u>not</u> linked to procrastination?
A. writing down your excuses
B. waiting for an adrenaline rush
C. fearing failure
D. perfectionism

15. Which of these is <u>not</u> an example of how students waste time?
A. e-mailing
B. saying no
C. social networking
D. unscheduled visiting

LEVEL THREE: EVALUATING & CREATING

16. Someone whose motto is "I want to have it all, but not all at once," is a(n):
A. alternator
B. outsourcer
C. bundler
D. techflexer

17. Someone whose motto is "I want to have it all, not do it all," is a(n):
A. alternator
B. outsourcer
C. bundler
D. techflexer

18. Someone whose motto is, "I want to get more mileage out of the things I do by combining activities," is a(n):
A. simplifier
B. outsourcer
C. bundler
D. techflexer

19. Someone whose motto is, "I want to use technology to accomplish more, not be a slave to it," is a(n):
A. alternator
B. simplifier
C. bundler
D. techflexer

20. Which of the following is a good tip for managing your time?
A. turn off your cell phone
B. learn to say no
C. keep track of what distracts or derails you
D. all of the given answers

Chapter 4 Answer Key

1. C
2. C
3. D
4. C
5. C
6. A
7. B
8. C
9. D
10. C
11. A
12. A
13. C
14. A
15. B
16. A
17. B
18. C
19. D
20. D

CHAPTER 5: THINKING CRITICALLY AND CREATIVELY

LEVEL ONE: REMEMBERING & UNDERSTANDING
(Questions attempt to progress in their level of challenge based on Bloom's [revised] Taxonomy.)

1. When your thinking produces ideas, you are engaging in:
A. critical thinking
B. creative thinking
C. active thinking
D. passive thinking

2. When you evaluate your ideas or the ideas of others, you are engaging in:
A. critical thinking
B. creative thinking
C. active thinking
D. passive thinking

3. When you are thinking critically, you are:
A. not finding faults
B. being distracted
C. being discerning
D. disregarding evidence

4. According to the Question Pyramid, questions that can be answered with a "yes" or "no" answer are:
A. Level I
B. Level II
C. Level III
D. Level IV

5. According to the Question Pyramid, "who and what questions" that can be answered by memorizing a section of text are:
A. Level I
B. Level II
C. Level III
D. Level IV

6. According to the Question Pyramid, "why and how questions" that require evidence to be answered are:
A. Level I
B. Level II
C. Level III
D. Level IV

7. An argument that moves from specific observations to general conclusions is:
A. inductive
B. deductive
C. selective
D. active

8. An argument that moves from broad generalizations to specific conclusions is:
A. inductive
B. deductive
C. selective
D. active

LEVEL TWO: APPLYING & ANALYZING

9. As speakers and writers, students use what type of critical thinking skills?
A. receptive
B. productive
C. potential
D. constructive

10. As readers and listeners, students use what type of critical thinking skills?
A. receptive
B. productive
C. potential
D. constructive

11. If you react to a challenge by criticizing the challenger, you are slipping into the logical fallacy of:
A. false cause and effect
B. unwarranted assumption
C. personal attack
D. emotional appeal

12. If you appeal to someone's feelings to gain acceptance of an argument, you are slipping into the logical fallacy of:
A. false cause and effect
B. unwarranted assumption
C. personal attack
D. emotional appeal

13. When you have to solve a problem, begin by:
A. defining it
B. brainstorming
C. evaluating your options
D. choosing a solution

14. People who prefer structure and use practical data to make decisions are:
A. directives
B. analyticals
C. conceptuals
D. behaviorals

15. People who search carefully for the best decision are often described as:
A. directives
B. analyticals
C. conceptuals
D. behaviorals

16. People who emphasize the big picture in their decision-making process are:
A. directives
B. analyticals
C. conceptuals
D. behaviorals

17. People who use their feelings to assess situations in their decision-making process are:
A. directives
B. analyticals
C. conceptuals
D. behaviorals

LEVEL THREE: EVALUATING & CREATING

18. Of the choices below, which one way is a strategy to improve your critical thinking skills?
A. ignore the opposition
B. trust completely
C. admit what you don't know
D. ignore your emotions

19. The creative style that best describes people who are systematic, concentrate on problem-solving, and rely on data is:
A. intuitive
B. innovative
C. imaginative
D. inspirational

20. Which of the following is <u>not</u> a technique to use in becoming a more creative thinker?
A. The Pillow Method
B. Focus your senses and emotions
C. Accept your creativity
D. Generate only one idea

Chapter 5 Answer Key

1. B
2. A
3. C
4. A
5. B
6. C
7. A
8. B
9. B
10. A
11. C
12. D
13. A
14. A
15. B
16. C
17. D
18. C
19. B
20. D

CHAPTER 6: DEVELOPING TECHNOLOGY, RESEARCH, AND INFORMATION LITERACY SKILLS

LEVEL ONE: REMEMBERING & UNDERSTANDING
(Questions attempt to progress in their level of challenge based on Bloom's [revised] Taxonomy.)

1. One benefit of the Internet is the ability to keep information updated. This is called:
A. interactivity
B. scope
C. availability
D. currency

2. A danger of the Internet is that not everything online is true or correct. This is called:
A. overdependence
B. addiction
C. inaccuracy
D. laziness

3. In a major study discussed in this chapter, students noted which of the following academic benefits of technology?
A. Manage their courses
B. Manage their social network
C. Manage their finances
D. Communicate with family and friends

4. Which of the following is a violation of netiquette?
A. Waiting to hit the send key until you've cooled off
B. Forgetting to fill in the subject line
C. Deleting a chain e-mail
D. All of the above are violations

5. A benefit of e-learning is:
A. you control when you learn
B. you control what you learn
C. courses are easier online
D. courses are less expensive online

6. The key to making the most of databases in research is:
A. asking a librarian to do it for you
B. finding the right search words
C. walking around the stacks
D. understanding the Library of Congress classification system

7. Structured learning that takes place without a teacher at the front of a classroom is called _____?
A. C-learning
B. Group Work
C. E-learning
D. Note-taking

8. Spell-check can let you down when:
A. you are not exactly sure what the word means
B. you use the same word multiple times
C. you use an actual word but not the right one
D. you don't exactly know how to spell the word

9. John is researching teaching and learning techniques for a paper he is writing. Which database would he use?
A. ERIC
B. Business Source Premier
C. PsychInfo
D. None of the above

10. Which of the following is an example of the *Locate* step in the Six Steps to Information Literacy model?
A. Bookmarking electronic resources
B. Physically finding print resources
C. Requesting interlibrary loan for materials not held by your library
D. All of the above

11. Hector's assignment ask him to read two Shakespeare plays: *Othello* and *King Lear*. The assignment is probably going to require using a:
A. problem-solution format
B. cause and effect format
C. compare and contrast format
D. I search format

12. When reviewing a website to determine if it just presents one side of an issue or a very small piece of a larger picture, you are evaluating it for:
A. authority
B. currency
C. availability
D. coverage

13. The last of the *Six Steps to Information Literacy* asks you to think about what you have accomplished, what have you learned, and what you will do differently next time. This step is called:
A. interactivity
B. reflect
C. review
D. rewrite

14. When Dario cut and pasted information from the Internet to complete his paper, he committed:
A. information literacy
B. plagiarism
C. location errors
D. unintentional fraud

LEVEL THREE: EVALUATING & CREATING

15. Which of the following students might most benefit from e-learning?
A. Bob: a first semester community college student who has never used the Internet
B. Javier: a second year student who is an independent, self-motivated learner
C. Janine: an extravert who enjoys having discussions with students in class
D. None of the above would benefit from e-learning

16. The Internet may be best summarized by which of the following statements?
A. The Internet is neutral and can be used constructively or destructively
B. The Internet has very little academic use
C. The Internet creates dependency and should be regulated
D. The Internet has a mostly negative impact on college students' academic experiences

17. Which of the following is most true about research?
A. Research is a search and employ mission.
B. Research begins with going through the library to see what you can find.
C. Research is doing a quick Internet search.
D. Research often involves combining several small questions into a more meaningful question.

18. Which of the following is an example of rewriting?:
A. correcting grammar and spelling
B. making major overhauls if necessary
C. proofreading
D. all of the above

19. Which of the following would **not** be examples of Internet addiction?
A. Obsessing about your online life
B. Spending more time with online friends than your real friends
C. Not going online during a family vacation
D. Using IM to communicate instead of e-mail

20. Which of the following is an example of unintentional plagiarism?
A. Forgetting which book you used and not citing it
B. Cutting and pasting from the Internet
C. Changing every fifth word to something else
D. Buying and downloading a paper from the Internet

Chapter 6 Answer Key

1. D
2. C
3. A
4. B
5. A
6. B
7. C
8. C
9. A
10. D
11. C
12. D
13. B
14. B
15. B
16. A
17. D
18. D
19. C
20. A

CHAPTER 7: ENGAGING, LISTENING, AND NOTE-TAKING IN CLASS

LEVEL ONE: REMEMBERING & UNDERSTANDING
(Questions attempt to progress in their level of challenge based on Bloom's [revised] Taxonomy.)

1. If you are engaged in your classes, you are:
A. reading
B. listening
C. taking good notes
D. all of the given answers

2. Which of the following is <u>not</u> a recommended way of preparing for class?
A. reviewing the syllabus
B. sitting next to your best friend
C. sitting up straight
D. pretending to be a reporter

3. Which of the following is **not** a "Rule of Engagement" in the classroom?
A. talking in class
B. turning off your cell phone
C. eating before class
D. arriving on time

4. Experts estimate that students spend ___ percent of their time listening to lectures:
A. 20
B. 40
C. 60
D. 80

5. According to the text, gestures that indicate importance during a lecture are:
A. a raised index finger
B. leaning forward
C. walking up the aisle
D. all of the given answers

6. According to the text, the four stages of focused listening are:
A. sensing—evaluating—responding—interpreting
B. evaluating—sensing—responding—interpreting
C. responding—evaluating—sending—interpreting
D. sensing—interpreting—evaluating—responding

LEVEL TWO: APPLYING & ANALYZING

7. When you are listening to chit-chat and emotionally charged situations, you are most likely engaged in:
   A. soft listening
   B. hard listening
   C. discerning listening
   D. decisive listening

8. When you are listening to new information or to someone trying to persuade you of something, you are most likely engaged in:
   A. soft listening
   B. hard listening
   C. discerning listening
   D. decisive listening

9. When your instructor helps you discover new information on your own, the instructor is acting as a(n):
   A. facilitator
   B. orator
   C. deliverer
   D. inquisitor

10. The lecturer who uses extensive discipline-specific jargon is the:
    A. Rapid-Fire Lecturer
    B. Slow-Go Lecturer
    C. Content-Intensive Lecturer
    D. Active-Learning Lecturer

11. According to the text, what percentage of students edit their notes after class?
    A. 47%
    B. 29%
    C. 12%
    D. 0%

12. The Cornell system of note-taking encourages you to write key words and questions on the ___ of the page.
    A. right side
    B. left side
    C. bottom
    D. top

13. What type of learner is most likely to benefit from using mind maps as a note-taking method?
A. visual
B. aural
C. read/write
D. kinesthetic

LEVEL THREE: EVALUATING & CREATING

14. If you miss class and your instructor provides e-support for the in-class slides, which of the following study strategies might you use to take notes?
A. Cornell
B. Mind map
C. PowerPoint miniatures
D. Parallel

15. The process of typing your notes out later is best defined as:
A. manipulating
B. paraphrasing
C. summarizing
D. mapping

16. Which of the following would be the least effective way for students to learn from their class notes?
A. Make flash cards from the notes they take after organizing them.
B. Make a matrix of the important points and a brief summary of the points.
C. Compare the notes with classmates and reorganize them based on both sets of information.
D. Purchase Cliff Notes or a similar commercial product to see if they have covered everything about the subject.

17. If you write a brief overview of your notes from one lecture, you are:
A. manipulating
B. paraphrasing
C. summarizing
D. mapping

18. For effective learning, which is the best place to sit in class?
A. front and center
B. middle of the room
C. back of the room
D. doesn't matter

19. Interspersing short lectures with activities and small-group discussions is common among what type of teachers?
A. Rapid-Fire Lecturer
B. Slow-Go Lecturer
C. Active-Learning Lecturer
D. Content-Intensive Lecturer

20. Creative note-taking allows you to use which of the VARK modalities?
A. visual
B. read-write
C. kinesthetic
D. all of the given answers

Chapter 7 Answer Key

1. D
2. B
3. A
4. D
5. D
6. D
7. A
8. B
9. A
10. C
11. B
12. B
13. A
14. C
15. A
16. D
17. C
18. A
19. C
20. D

CHAPTER 8: DEVELOPING YOUR MEMORY

LEVEL ONE: REMEMBERING & UNDERSTANDING
(Questions attempt to progress in their level of challenge based on Bloom's [revised] Taxonomy.)

1. If you memorize information, you are learning to:
A. recall
B. recognize
C. think critically
D. analyze

2. The three R's of remembering are:
A. realize, recognize, retain
B. realize, retain, retrieve
C. record, retain, retrieve
D. recognize, retain, retrieve

3. When you consolidate memories in your brain, you are:
A. recording
B. retaining
C. retrieving
D. realizing

4. You use your working memory when you:
A. store knowledge
B. remember a phone number long enough to dial it
C. retrieve information
D. none of the given answers

5. What type of rehearsal helps you keep something in your working memory for a short time?
A. Elaborative
B. Maintenance
C. Complex
D. Repetitive

6. Verbal or visual memory aids are called:
A. sound devices
B. visual devices
C. mnemonic devices
D. kinesthetic devices

7. According to your text, memory is defined as a:
A. knack
B. process
C. gift
D. sign of intelligence

LEVEL TWO: APPLYING & ANALYZING

8. What is the primary benefit of the loci mnemonic system?
A. it uses cues
B. it incorporates associations
C. it orders information into a sequence
D. all of the given answers are benefits

9. Which of the following is a common problem among students when trying to memorize course topics that overlap?
A. Over-learning
B. Minding the middle
C. Interference
D. Rehearsing

10. Which of the following does not enhance memory and recall?
A. emotions
B. connections
C. personalization
D. distractions

11. Which of the following does the Peg system of memorization most commonly use?
A. Rhymes
B. Stories
C. Numbers
D. Sentences

12. According to researchers, our working memory can typically recall how many pieces of information at a time?
A. 5, plus or minus 2
B. 7, plus or minus 2
C. 9, plus or minus 2
D. 11, plus or minus 2

13. The concept of finding ways you can relate what you're memorizing to your own life is called:
A. feel
B. connect
C. personalize
D. rehearse

14. The most effective learners use what kind of processing?
A. surface-level
B. deep-level
C. focused-level
D. attentive-level

LEVEL THREE: EVALUATING & CREATING

15. Which of the following best defines what is included in your sensory memory?
A. touch (haptic memory)
B. sound (echoic memory)
C. sight (iconic memory)
D. all the given answers

16. If you are an *active* reader, you might:
A. read the book three times
B. highlight while you read
C. think about the reading
D. none of the given answers

17. What advice is **least** helpful to increase your attention when it wanders?
A. Ignore the distraction.
B. Turn off the TV.
C. Turn down the music.
D. Close the extra windows on your browser.

18. Which of the following is a memory principle that could help an actor memorize lines?
A. checking
B. choosing
C. chunking
D. chopping

19. A useful way to remember what you read is to:
A. read extra slowly
B. skim quickly
C. take notes in your own words
D. all the given answers

20. Nate finds it difficult to forget something that he would like to forget. Nate is experiencing which of the following?
A. bias
B. inventing
C. persistence
D. fading

Chapter 8 Answer Key

1. A
2. C
3. A
4. B
5. B
6. C
7. B
8. D
9. C
10. D
11. A
12. B
13. C
14. B
15. D
16. B
17. A
18. C
19. C
20. C

CHAPTER 9: READING AND STUDYING

LEVEL ONE: REMEMBERING & UNDERSTANDING (Questions attempt to progress in their level of challenge based on Bloom's [revised] Taxonomy.)

1. Good readers read:
A. quickly
B. slowly
C. for understanding
D. by skimming

2. Reading challenges can be caused by:
A. physical factors
B. psychological factors
C. physical and psychological factors
D. none of the given answers

3. First-year students often need to read and understand:
A. 50-75 pages per week
B. 75-100 pages per week
C. 100-150 pages per week
D. 150-200 pages per week

4. When you read a textbook or a novel, you should treat it like a _____ experience.
A. fine dining
B. fast food
C. boring
D. tiresome

5. In every book you read, the author is trying to:
A. convince you
B. entertain you
C. consider you
D. train you

6. One way to determine what is and what is not important in a reading is to:
A. guess
B. read everything
C. ask your instructor
D. none of the given answers

7. One way to master a challenging reading assignment is to:
A. take notes
B. skim
C. doodle
D. memorize

8. Which of the following describes core knowledge that puts things into context and gives them meaning?
A. computer literacy
B. cultural literacy
C. economic literacy
D. social literacy

9. According to the textbook, which one of the following is <u>not</u> one of the six "Rs" of reading?
A. Read
B. Recite
C. Reflect
D. Revise

10. When you evaluate whether or not you understand an article on your own, you are:
A. rehashing
B. reciting
C. rethinking
D. remembering

11. The first step in making a master study plan is to:
A. understand your assignments
B. make a schedule
C. take a break
D. review

12. Making a master plan requires you to think about:
A. the past
B. the present
C. the future
D. all of the given answers

13. According to the text, it is more effective to study:
A. during the day
B. at night
C. after midnight
D. none of the given answers

14. Which of the following is a method of "conversing" with an author of a textbook:
A. highlight everything
B. write comments in the margins
C. memorize the important points
D. all of the given answers

LEVEL THREE: EVALUATING & CREATING

15. If reading your assignments aloud helps you retain information, you are likely a(n) _____ learner.
    A. visual
    B. aural/auditory
    C. read/write
    D. kinesthetic

16. If cutting up your instructor's notes and reassembling them helps you retain information, you are likely a(n) _____ learner.
    A. visual
    B. aural/auditory
    C. read/write
    D. kinesthetic

17. According to the text, metacognition is defined as:
    A. thinking about the thought process
    B. considering schedule planning
    C. reading with attention
    D. memorizing through mnemonics

18. Talking to yourself while you're studying:
    A. suggests you need counseling
    B. shows you're overtired
    C. helps you figure things out
    D. all of the given answers

19. Which of the following is not a helpful study strategy?
    A. taking appropriate study breaks
    B. adding variety by switching from one subject to another
    C. pulling an all-nighter/study non-stop
    D. paying attention to details/aiming for accuracy

20. According to your text, shortcuts in studying:
    A. are rarely acceptable
    B. are rarely necessary
    C. should be followed frequently
    D. can function as "triage" in an academic emergency

Chapter 9 Answer Key

1. C
2. C
3. D
4. A
5. A
6. C
7. A
8. B
9. D
10. C
11. A
12. D
13. A
14. B
15. B
16. D
17. A
18. C
19. C
20. D

CHAPTER 10: TAKING TESTS

LEVEL ONE: REMEMBERING & UNDERSTANDING
(Questions attempt to progress in their level of challenge based on Bloom's [revised] Taxonomy.)

1. Test anxiety has ____ different components.
   A. 1
   B. 2
   C. 3
   D. 4

2. Which aspect of test anxiety leads to nonproductive thoughts that run through your mind?
   A. cognitive
   B. emotional
   C. behavioral
   D. physiological

3. The ____ aspect of test anxiety leads to negative feelings that you experience related to the exam.
   A. cognitive
   B. emotional
   C. behavioral
   D. physiological

4. The ____ aspect of test anxiety leads to observable indications of stress.
   A. cognitive
   B. emotional
   C. behavioral
   D. physiological

5. If you experience butterflies in your stomach you are experiencing a/an ____ aspect of test anxiety.
   A. cognitive
   B. emotional
   C. behavioral
   D. physiological

6. One way to address the ____ aspect of test anxiety is to stop nonproductive self-talk.
   A. cognitive
   B. emotional
   C. behavioral
   D. physiological

7. Eating well and getting plenty of sleep are examples what aspect of test anxiety?
A. cognitive
B. emotional
C. behavioral
D. physiological

8. One way to address the _____ aspect of test anxiety is to take a walk.
A. cognitive
B. emotional
C. behavioral
D. physiological

9. Speaking with a counselor or going to a relaxation training are examples of reducing what type of test anxiety?
A. cognitive
B. emotional
C. behavioral
D. physiological

10. Tests that ask you to recognize the correct answer from several alternatives are:
A. subjective
B. objective
C. relative
D. difficult

11. A multiple-choice test is:
A. subjective
B. objective
C. relative
D. difficult

12. An essay test is:
A. subjective
B. objective
C. relative
D. critical

13. For a statement to be true, _____ of the statements must be true.
A. some
B. all
C. part
D. none

14. Statistically, exams usually contain ___ true answers.
A. fewer
B. more
C. half
D. 70 percent

LEVEL THREE: EVALUATING & CREATING

15. Words like *sometimes, often*, and *ordinarily* often make a statement on an exam:
A. true
B. false
C. wrong
D. right

16. An essay question that asks you to examine two or more things to find similarities will often use the verb:
A. compare
B. contrast
C. define
D. discuss

17. An essay question that asks you to provide a detailed account will often use the verb:
A. contrast
B. describe
C. prove
D. interpret

18. An essay question that asks you to give concrete examples to demonstrate something will often use the verb:
A. define
B. relate
C. illustrate
D. prove

19. An essay question that asks you to make a judgment or describe the pros and cons of something often use the verb:
A. define
B. evaluate
C. illustrate
D. prove

20. Storing math formulas on your cell phone for a test is considered cheating. Which term or concept below is related to this example?
A. creating a study sheet
B. rifling your answer
C. generalizations
D. ethical standards

Chapter 10 Answer Key

1. D
2. A
3. B
4. C
5. D
6. A
7. B
8. C
9. D
10. B
11. B
12. A
13. B
14. B
15. A
16. A
17. B
18. C
19. B
20. D

CHAPTER 11: BUILDING RELATIONSHIPS, VALUING DIVERSITY

LEVEL ONE: REMEMBERING & UNDERSTANDING
(Questions attempt to progress in their level of challenge based on Bloom's [revised] Taxonomy.)

1. A set of skills that determines how well you cope with the demands and pressures you face every day is called:
   A. linguistic intelligence
   B. mathematical intelligence
   C. emotional intelligence
   D. kinesthetic intelligence

2. The ability to relate to others is an indication of what kind of skills?
   A. interpersonal
   B. stress management
   C. adaptability
   D. general mood

3. The ability to manage your emotions so that they work for you and not against you indicates that you have strong _____ skills.
   A. interpersonal
   B. stress management
   C. adaptability
   D. general mood

4. If you cope well when things don't go according to plan you have strong _____ skills.
   A. interpersonal
   B. stress management
   C. adaptability
   D. general mood

5. If you are generally optimistic and content, you have strong _____ skills.
   A. interpersonal
   B. stress management
   C. adaptability
   D. general mood

6. A person who requests a desired behavior from a partner and then attacks the partner for complying is a _____.
   A. trapper
   B. blamer
   C. mindreader
   D. gunnysacker

LEVEL TWO: APPLYING & ANALYZING

7. A person who tries to solve problems by telling a partner what the partner is really thinking is a _____.
A. blamer
B. mindreader
C. gunnysacker
D. "Benedict Arnold"

8. According to the text, what percent of today's college students are "traditional"?
A. 17%
B. 27%
C. 37%
D. 47%

9. How many more minority students are enrolled in college today than 20 years ago?
A. twice as many
B. three times as many
C. four times as many
D. five times as many

10. According to the text, in 2005 what was the dollar value of community service performed by college students?
A. $1.45 billion
B. $2.45 billion
C. $3.45 billion
D. $6.50 billion

11. Which of the following is **not** true about emotional intelligence?
A. Emotional intelligence is important to college success.
B. Emotional intelligence can be learned.
C. Emotional intelligence is fixed.
D. Genes play a role in emotional intelligence.

12. The ability to understand yourself well indicates that you have good_____ skills.
A. intrapersonal
B. interpersonal
C. adaptability
D. stress management

13. In *Why We Love*, anthropologist Helen Fisher defined love as consisting of psychological and _____ characteristics.
A. emotional
B. physiological
C. mental
D. spiritual

LEVEL THREE: EVALUATING & CREATING

14. Anthropologist Helen Fisher found that people in love have all the following symptoms **except**:
A. mood swings
B. low energy
C. interfering thoughts
D. hypersensitivity

15. When you're newly infatuated with someone, the following levels of dopamine, norepinephrine, and serotonin are in your brain:
A. elevated dopamine and norepinephrine, but lower serotonin
B. elevated dopamine, norepinephrine, and serotonin
C. lowered dopamine and norepinephrine, and serotonin
D. none of the given answers

16. According to your text, which of these statements **best** defines love?
A. Love is an emotion.
B. Love is a decision.
C. Love requires commitment.
D. All of the given answers.

17. According to your text, what is at the heart of every quality relationship?
A. love
B. sex
C. communication
D. money

18. Unproductive communication patterns are a sign of low _____ skills.
A. intrapersonal
B. interpersonal
C. stress management
D. adaptability

19. According to the authors of *How Full Is Your Bucket?* giving small, unexpected gifts to fill someone else's bucket is an example of which of their recommendations?
   A. Dip less
   B. Make more than one best friend
   C. Fill a drop at a time
   D. The Golden Rule

20. According to research, which of the following is **not** a characteristic of couples in a healthy relationship?
   A. They are good listeners.
   B. They can share feelings and ideas.
   C. They find it easy to think of things to do together.
   D. They spend all their time together.

1. C
2. A
3. B
4. C
5. D
6. A
7. B
8. B
9. A
10. D
11. C
12. A
13. B
14. B
15. A
16. D
17. C
18. B
19. C
20. D

CHAPTER 12: CHOOSING A COLLEGE MAJOR AND A CAREER

LEVEL ONE: REMEMBERING & UNDERSTANDING
(Questions attempt to progress in their level of challenge based on Bloom's [revised] Taxonomy.)

1. ____ are traits that capitalize on qualities you can develop.
A. Strengths
B. Weaknesses
C. Opportunities
D. Threats

2. ____ are conditions that could have bad effects.
A. Strengths
B. Weaknesses
C. Opportunities
D. Threats

3. ____ forces include motivation and skill.
A. Internal
B. External
C. Positive
D. Negative

4. The job market is an example of a(n) ____ force.
A. internal
B. external
C. positive
D. negative

5. Reviewing information on majors such as what are its introductory courses, which courses are required, and where the office for the major is located is described as:
A. Follow your bliss
B. Take a good look at yourself
C. Conduct preliminary research
D. All of the above

6. Colleges and universities help societies to:
A. preserve the past
B. create the future
C. preserve the past and create the future
D. none of the above answers

7. Which is an example of the interconnectedness of knowledge that is described in the text?
A. Comparison and contrast exercise
B. College in a Box
C. Pie chart activity
D. Circle of Learning

LEVEL TWO: APPLYING & ANALYZING

8. According to the text, when you are considering career options, all of the following are useful questions to ask **except**:
A. What will I enjoy doing the most?
B. How much money can I make?
C. What am I capable of doing?
D. Am I willing to invest what it takes to reach my career goal?

9. The "I's" of career-life readiness include all of the following qualities **except**:
A. inner direction
B. interaction
C. instrumentation
D. incubation

10. Searching for a career is achieved through a combination of:
A. idealism and optimism
B. idealism and realism
C. optimism and realism
D. optimism and pessimism

11. People and relationships are part of every profession. This is called:
A. Inner Direction
B. Interpretation
C. Instrumentation
D. Interaction

12. Conditions or circumstances that work in your favor are called:
A. negative
B. opportunities
C. challenges
D. positive

LEVEL THREE: EVALUATING & CREATING

13. An example of the interconnectedness of courses is the close connection between:
    A. literature and history
    B. literature and math
    C. literature and biology
    D. literature and physics

14. In a fact-finding mission about a major, which of the following is the **least** valuable question to ask someone you are interviewing?
    A. What are the department's requirements for this major?
    B. What is the reputation of this department on campus?
    C. How easy is the major in this discipline?
    D. Why should a student major in this discipline?

15. If making others happy makes you happy, your "Academic Anatomy" preference is likely to be working with your:
    A. head
    B. heart
    C. hands
    D. whole body

16. If you like building things, your "Academic Anatomy" preference is likely to be working with your:
    A. head
    B. heart
    C. hands
    D. whole body

17. If you like solving problems, your "Academic Anatomy" preference is likely to be working with your:
    A. head
    B. heart
    C. hands
    D. whole body

18. If you are athletic, your "Academic Anatomy" preference is likely to be working with your:
    A. head
    B. heart
    C. hands
    D. whole body

19. Which of the following is an example of *Instrumentation*?
A. Engaging in high-level thinking, brainstorming and problem solving
B. Knowing yourself and your direction
C. Interpreting and applying information
D. Having the inner direction you need

20. If you chose a major based on your passions, you would be:
A. following your bliss
B. considering your career, not your major
C. exploring threats
D. none of the above

Chapter 12 Answer Key

1. A
2. D
3. A
4. B
5. C
6. C
7. D
8. B
9. D
10. B
11. D
12. B
13. A
14. C
15. B
16. C
17. A
18. D
19. A
20. A

CHAPTER 13: CREATING YOUR FUTURE

LEVEL ONE: REMEMBERING & UNDERSTANDING
(Questions attempt to progress in their level of challenge based on Bloom's [revised] Taxonomy.)

1. How is a career different from a job?
A. A career is temporary, while a job is permanent.
B. A career is permanent, while a job is temporary.
C. A career is a profession you've chosen and prepared for.
D. All of the given answers are true.

2. What is a portfolio?
A. A record of what you accomplished in each class.
B. A collection of drawings you have accumulated.
C. Work that you must resubmit to your instructor for grading.
D. Examples of your work that must be improved.

3. ____ is the process of building professional contacts and staying informed about your chosen career field.
A. Friend-making
B. Spying
C. Networking
D. Portfolio building

4. A job interview is like:
A. a first date.
B. a life-long partner.
C. a bad relationship.
D. an outing with an old friend.

5. Asking an interviewer "What's a typical day like for you?" is an example of:
A. left-field questions.
B. giving and getting answers.
C. staying focused.
D. all of the above

6. Your credit history is based on:
A. how many credit cards you owe money on
B. how much money you owe
C. how many late payments you make
D. all of the above answers

7. Which is an example of interviewing at your best?
A. Write a good résumé
B. Stay focused
C. Answer quickly
D. Don't over prepare

LEVEL TWO: APPLYING & ANALYZING

8. This chapter discussed three ways to "*try a job on for size.*" What were they?
A. Part-time work, service learning and full-time work.
B. Co-op programs, part-time work, and full-time work.
C. Networking, part-time work, and full-time work.
D. Internships, co-op programs, and service learning.

9. A résumé that details job by job arranged in time order is an example of a _____ approach.
A. skills
B. thematic
C. chronological
D. networking

10. Which of the following does the author suggest for interviewing at your best?
A. Ask the salary question first.
B. Be up front about all your faults.
C. Stay focused.
D. Don't over research the company.

11. As the level of education increases, unemployment goes _____ and earnings go_____.
A. up, up
B. down, up
C. up, down
D. down, down

12. Being tuned in and understanding the culture of the organization you work for is an example of:
A. learning the rules of the game.
B. detecting opportunities.
C. going for extra credit.
D. speaking and writing well.

13. Which of the following best describes a quarterlife crisis:
A. Jane is feeling overwhelmed with the decisions that must be made. She has graduated with her nursing degree and is about to start working full-time as a Registered Nurse.
B. Tore is unsure of which major he wants to pursue after graduating with his associate's degree.
C. Marcus has just turned 50 and is rethinking the direction of his life.
D. Sophia is trying to decide between buying a compact hybrid car and a scooter.

14. All of the following are examples of networking, **except**:
A. Having coffee with someone who works in the field you are pursuing.
B. Connecting to other professionals on LinkedIn.
C. Researching your career choice in the Occupational Outlook Handbook.
D. Attending a job fair and meeting others who work in your field.

15. Rhea has little work experience in her chosen field, but has had solid courses and a well-developed portfolio showcasing examples of her skills. Which approach to her résumé should she use?
A. skills
B. reverse chronological
C. reflective
D. active portfolio

16. Telling the interviewer you can get by on $25,000 a year when she was prepared to offer you $50,000 is **not** an example of:
A. staying focused.
B. giving and getting answers.
C. playing up the positive.
D. negotiating wisely.

17. Which of the following is an example of exhibiting a work ethic:
A. Jim is an expert PowerPoint user and creates interesting presentations for his boss.
B. Stephanie stayed at work until 1 a.m. to finish a report that was due to her director the next day.
C. Jose, a financial manager, came up with a budget savings technique for buying office supplies.
D. Leslie, an office assistant, found a file that had been misplaced a month ago.

18. This type of learning is connected with your class and emphasizes hands-on learning:
A. service learning
B. internship
C. VARK learning
D. cooperative learning

19. Jin is completing his associate's degree in criminal justice. His major requires students to work alongside a professional in criminal justice during their last term. This is called:
A. service learning
B. cooperative learning
C. internship
D. none of the above

20. If Arthur decides that he cannot continue in college now, he should:
A. take time off and regroup.
B. never consider coming back to college.
C. keep going regardless of what has happened in his life.
D. just stop coming to classes.

Chapter 13 Answer Key

1. C
2. A
3. C
4. A
5. B
6. D
7. B
8. D
9. C
10. C
11. B
12. A
13. A
14. C
15. A
16. D
17. B
18. A
19. C
20. A

ADDITIONAL RESOURCES

By Constance Staley

AUTHOR RECOMMENDED ADDITIONAL ACTIVITIES

Passport to Learning

By Constance Staley. Based on Jaques, D. (2000). *Learning in groups* (3rd ed.). London: Kogan Page, p. 206. Used with permission.

Recommended for pre-course planning as a possible course requirement

Group Size: Any size group
Time Required: Five minutes to collect cards at the beginning of class
Materials: Index cards, provided by students
Physical Setting: Home or residence hall
Goals: To improve attendance and encourage reading in first-year (or any) courses

In order to improve attendance, announce the first day of class that the course will use a "passport" system. If you wish, insist that no student will be admitted to each class without a "passport." At the beginning of class (and only then), students submit an index card (passport), covered front and back with notes from the day's reading assignment. Tell students that missing cards may <u>not</u> be replaced at any time during the term, that no one else may submit a card on their behalf, and that you will keep these cards (organized by student) until the final exam, when each student's stack will be returned to him or her. Students are welcome to use the entire stack during the test to maximize their performance.

Find an Expert

By Constance Staley
Recommended for Chapter 2 Building Dreams, Setting Goals as an icebreaker

Group Size: Any size group
Time Required: 15-20 minutes, followed by in-class processing and student introductions
Materials: Interview questions on following to photocopy and handout to students
Physical Setting: Classroom
Goals: To reassure beginning students that they are experts in particular areas (in fact, areas that instructors and classmates may not know much about)
Hand out the "Find an Expert" sheet following this page, one to each student, and read the instructions. Ask students to circulate to meet one another and discover what types of expertise students have cultivated before coming to college.

Variation: Add your own expertise categories, based on your particular students, institution, or location.

Find an Expert

Find someone in our group with expertise in each of the areas described. As you circulate around the room, introduce yourself, fill in your interviewee's first name below, describing your own experience as it relates and something in particular your interviewee knows about the subject that you don't. Find someone…

1. Who knows a lot about **cars**. Name:_____
_____

2. Who has had a piece of **writing published**. Name:_____
_____

3. Who is a **fast food** junkie. Name:_____
_____
_____

4. Who knows how **families** work as a result of having five or more siblings. Name:____
_____

5. Who knows the campus because a **friend or sibling previously attended**. Name: ____
_____

6. Who's had a stellar career in **high school athletics**. Name: _____
_____

7. Who's never gotten anything but **A's in math**. Name: _____
_____

8. Who studied **art or dance** growing up. Name: _____
_____

9. Who knows the food service industry well from working as a **server**. Name:
_____

10. Who is a relationship expert as a result of a **long-lasting romance**. Name:
_____
_____

Finally, what kind of expertise do you hope to develop during your first term in college?
_____
_____

Giving Something Up To Give It All You've Got

By Constance Staley
Recommended for Chapter 2 Building Dreams, Setting Goals

Group Size: Any size group
Time Required: Approximately 20 minutes to discuss, depending on the size of the group
Materials: One index card per student
Physical Setting: Classroom (or completed as a homework assignment and brought to class)
Goals: To help students realize that achieving excellence may require making sacrifices

To emphasize managing one's time *and* achieving excellence, after describing the major assignment in your course, ask students how many of them would like to excel and achieve the best results possible. Most students will probably raise their hands. Then distribute index cards and ask students to identify what they are willing to give up in order to accomplish this goal. Continuing to "pile on," adding more and more to their already full lives, is not necessarily realistic. Getting the best results often requires eliminating something, clearing time to invest elsewhere. Are they willing to give up a hobby, pastime, leisure activity, extra hours at work, etc. in order to excel on the assignment? Students should identify their "sacrifice," write it on an index card, and submit it—not only to symbolize and publicize their personal commitment, but for discussion purposes as a group. If individuals are not willing to sacrifice anything, that response may be discussed, too.

What Rules Your Life?

By Constance Staley
Recommended for Chapter 2 Building Dreams, Setting Goals

Group Size: Any size class
Time Required: May vary, depending on the amount of discussion generated
Materials: Inexpensive wooden rulers, bought in bulk, and neon sticky dots (or any color scheme) in sheets of 35 (red, orange, yellow, green, and an additional row of red on the bottom), cut into strips to give each student five different colored dots
Physical Setting: Normal classroom
Goal: To help students explore their priorities as each one relates to college success
As a class, decide what each color dot will represent, using red as the top priority in life. (Having two red dots helps students not feel guilty about putting something important in second place.) Priorities may include such things as a college education, family, spouse, children, parents, siblings, pet, job, religion, romantic partner, scholarship, athletics, and so forth. Students should place the highest priority item in their lives at the top of the ruler while holding it vertically, closest to the 12" mark, and then move down the ruler with other colored dots. Ask students to justify their rankings, if they're willing. How do they know a dot belongs where they've placed it? Listen to students as they discuss these items. Do their priorities shift and change? Should they? If so, in what types of circumstances? A student who is attending college to avoid a dead-end job later on in life, ironically, may be working so many hours at a dead-end job now to finance a college education (and possibly support an expensive lifestyle), that the student is putting academic success too far down the ruler (priority list), and earning a degree will be jeopardized. For many students, if they're honest, school is a lower priority than it should be. Stress the importance of prioritizing intentionally, based on long-term, rather than short-term goals.

Variation: Base the activity on prioritizing a day's schedule with colored dots representing the most important activities to complete.

Syllabus or Syllabox?

By Constance Staley (with thanks to Professor Mike Larkin, Department of Geography
and Environmental Studies, UCCS)
Recommended for Chapter 3 Learning about Learning

Group Size: small class size because of the time investment
Time Required: may vary
**Materials: small cardboard boxes, large enough to hold a CD and useful materials
to introduce or demonstrate the content of a new course**
Physical Setting: normal classroom
**Goal: to demonstrate to students a willingness to address all learning modalities:
visual, aural, read/write, kinesthetic and multimodal**

Syl-la-bus [silləbəss] (plural syl-la-bi)
Definition: 1. a summary of the main topics of a course of study

Instead of the standard Read/Write syllabus students are used to, create something
different. For example, for a course in cultural geography, include a CD of ethnic music
you've downloaded (but be careful of downloading and music sharing rules), origami, the
course schedule (as a puzzle to be fitted together), etc.

Variation: Present a very basic, "plain vanilla" Read/Write syllabus, ask students to take
the VARK and discuss their results, and then ask students to create a multimodal syllabus
of their own to bring and demonstrate to the class. Tell them they must justify each item
they choose to include. You may be surprised to see just how creative they are and get
valuable ideas for the next time you teach the course!

What's Your Choiceprint?

By Constance Staley

Recommended for Chapter 4 Managing Your Time and Energy (particularly in conjunction with the "CONTROL: Choose to Choose" feature on p. 81)

Going to college is about a becoming part of a *community* of learners. However, with so many choices about where to live and work, which classes to take, and what activities to participate in, developing and finding *community* can be a challenge. Think about all the choices you've made in coming to college. When you total them up, your individual choices give you your own unique "choiceprint" that may not be identical to any other student's. After you fill out Part I, circulate and find the person in class whose "choiceprint" is most similar to yours. What else do you have in common? After you fill out Part II, discuss your responses as a group.

PART I

1. Where did you choose to live this term? _____

2. Which classes did you choose to take? _____

3. Who are the people you've chosen to be part of your small circle of friends? _____
_____

4. Which student organizations have you chosen to join? _____

5. Which campus activities will you choose to participate in this week?
_____

6. Which off-campus, close-by restaurants do you choose to frequent most often? _____
_____

7. Which of the available campus college success resources will you choose to use? ____
_____

8. What would you choose to do with an extra $500 if it appeared magically? _____

9. Which class would you choose *never* to miss this term? _____

10. Which of your professors will you choose to visit first during office hours? _____

PART II

Identify three choices you've made <u>today</u>, ones that you did a fair amount of thinking about. Why did you make the specific choice you made?

1. _____
   _____
   _____
   _____
   _____

2. _____
   _____
   _____
   _____
   _____

3. _____
   _____
   _____
   _____
   _____

Life is about making choices. Psychologist and professor Barry Schwartz in his book, *The Paradox of Choice: Why Less is More*, explains that in today's complex world we are continuously bombarded with choices. He describes the difference between "maximizers" and "satisficers." Maximizers don't rest until they find the best. They spend inordinate amounts of time searching for some ideal, making certain they've made the very best choice, and when they finally settle on something, they may even regret choices they passed up. "Satisficers," on the other hand, are satisfied with what's good enough, based on their most important criteria. Of course, we all do some "maximizing" and some "satisficing," but generally, which are you? For each decision you made, did you "maximize" or "satisfice" appropriately? Why or why not?

Get a Life!

By Constance Staley

Recommended for Chapter 12 Choosing a College Major and Career

Group Size: Any size group
Time Required: Out-of-class assignment in teams, followed by in-class processing
Materials: List of "Get a Life!" questions and Internet access
Physical Setting: Classroom or computer lab activity
Goals: To help students think about their own futures and realize the investment required to achieve and sustain "their dreams"

Hand out the "Get a Life!" assignment on the following page and ask students to work in pairs or trios to research the answers. They may present their profiles in class orally, in written form, or as PowerPoint presentations. Stress accuracy, thoroughness, and creativity.

Variation: Add questions/characteristics, and be as creative as you like to help engage students in the activity.

Get a Life!

The point of this exercise is to try on someone else's life. Work with two or three classmates to create a fictitious person. Search the Internet for answers to the following questions. Be as creative (but realistic) as you like, compile information to develop the person's personal financial profile, and present your findings to the class. Put all of your financial answers into a *monthly* average.

1. What is this person's name?
2. How old is this person?
3. Is this person male or female?
4. What is the person's marital status?
5. Does the person support others financially?
6. In which city and state does the person live? Select a place you might like to live someday.
7. If this person supports others, how much does it cost to raise one child (or more), for example, in this part of the country?
8. Where does the person live—in a house or apartment, for example? What is the average price of a house or apartment in this city?
9. If the person owns a home, what were the mortgage rates at the time? What is his or her monthly payment, including taxes and insurance?
10. What other home expenses does this person have each month? (fee for parking garage, homeowner's dues for condo, etc.)
11. What kind of car does this person drive? What year?
12. What is the average price of this car?
13. What is his or her monthly car payment?
14. What does this person spend for food each week? (self or family)
15. What are this person's average monthly utility costs (garbage removal, water, heat, etc.)?
16. If the person doesn't own a car, what are his or her transportation costs (subway, train, etc.) per month?
17. How much money does this person spend on entertainment each month? (movies, sports tickets, CDs, etc.)
18. What other monthly costs should be added in?
19. What are this person's average monthly credit card bills?
20. Is this person repaying college loans? If so, how much are those payments? Figure four or five years of college at your institution's tuition rates.
21. What is the person's occupation? Select a career you might be interested in.
22. How much education is required for this career field?
23. What is this person's monthly salary, based on average salary for this profession at this point in someone's career?
24. How much does the person invest or save each month?
25. Does this person earn enough monthly income to support his or her lifestyle? Which items in your profile may need to be adjusted?

What did you learn in researching your fictitious person? What surprised you? Did this activity change your thinking at all? Is this a career you might really be interested in? Is this a life you'd want?

A Quote for All Reasons

From Staley, C. (2003). *50 Ways to Leave Your Lectern*. Belmont, CA: Wadsworth, pp. 120-121.

Recommended for Chapter 4 Managing Your Time and Energy

Group size: Any size class
Time required: Any portion of normal class time
Materials: Paper and writing utensil
Physical setting: Any classroom setting; however, a U-shape or circle works well
Goals: To help students organize their thoughts, present their ideas clearly, and generally hone their oral communication skills
Cut the quotations on the following pages into strips so that each student can draw one and place it face down in front of him or herself (or create your own list of quotes). Choose a student volunteer to begin the exercise. He or she should turn over the slip, read the quotation, and offer a one-minute response by first agreeing or disagreeing with the quote and then identifying two pieces of support from personal experience, course material, or other relevant information sources. When one student begins to speak, the next student to speak may turn over his or her slip and begin formulating a response. If students seem anxious about speaking in front of classmates, reassure them that everyone will start on "equal footing" and reassert the value of learning to "speak on your feet."

Variation: Identify similar individual "quotations" from your lecture, or particular important points you plan to make, and hand them out on slips before you begin. Ask students to listen for their point, and after you conclude the lecture, to agree, disagree, or comment on the point they have been dealt. If the group is large, give slips to several volunteers or "Quotefinder" designees for the class session, instead of everyone.

Time Management Quotes for "A Quote for All Reasons" Activity

Cut out the following quotes into strips to hand out to your students.

- -

"This constant, unproductive preoccupation with all the things we have to do is the single largest consumer of time and energy." *~Kerry Gleeson*

- -

"Life is denied by lack of attention, whether it is to cleaning windows or trying to write a masterpiece." *~Nadia Boulanger*

- -

"Blessed are the flexible, for they shall not be bent out of shape." *~Michael McGriffy, M. D.*

- -

"The art of resting the mind and the power of dismissing from it all care and worry is probably one of the secrets of our great men [and women]." *~Captain J. A. Hatfield*

- -

"Time is the quality of nature that keeps events from happening all at once. Lately it doesn't seem to be working." *~Anonymous*

- -

"Almost every project could be done better, and an infinite quantity of information is now available that could make that happen." *~David Allen*

- -

"Rule your mind or it will rule you." *~Horace*

- -

"Now, for many of us, there are no edges to most of our projects. Most people I know have at least half a dozen things they're trying to achieve right now, and even if they had the rest of their lives to try, they wouldn't be able to finish these to perfection." *~David Allen*

- -

"There is one thing we can do, and the happiest people are those who can do it to the limit of their ability. We can be completely present. We can be all here. We can… give all our attention to the opportunity before us." ~*Mark Van Doren*

"There is usually an inverse proportion between how much something is on your mind and how much it's getting done." ~*David Allen*

"Vision is not enough; it must be combined with venture. It is not enough to stare up the steps; we must step up the stairs." ~*Vaclav Havel*

"A paradox has emerged in this new millennium: people have enhanced quality of life, but at the same time they are adding to their stress levels by taking on more than they have resources to handle. It's as though their eyes were bigger than their stomachs. And most people are to some degree frustrated and perplexed about how to improve the situation." ~*David Allen*

"I am rather like a mosquito in a nudist camp; I know what I want to do, but I don't know where to begin." ~*Stephen Bayne*

"Let our advance worrying become advance thinking and planning." ~*Winston Churchill*

"The middle of every successful project looks like a disaster." ~*Rosabeth Moss Cantor*

"The best place to succeed is where you are with what you have." ~*Charles Schwab*

Press Conference

By Constance Staley
Recommended for Chapter 9 Reading and Studying

Group size: Any size class
Time required: Variable
Materials: None required or index cards for students to write out questions
Physical setting: Any classroom setting
Goals: To engage students in questioning techniques as a form of classroom engagement, and to focus on speaking skills

Before beginning class (or the previous week), announce that you will hold a press conference at the end of class. The group will play the role of reporters from print media outlets of their own choosing or as assigned. (See the accompanying list on the next page.) If you wish, discuss the press conference as a communication tool, the importance of speaking skills in political or media careers, and the interests of particular outlets, based on their reading audience. You may also wish to discuss challenging situations in which public figures must communicate with care and sensitivity as they react to volatile issues. If you wish, ask students to view an upcoming press conference or show a videotaped one in class. Or use a recent, perhaps controversial, campus-related incident as a springboard. Try to make the experience as realistic as possible, using course content as the material to be covered during the press conference. Explore with students the value of asking questions in their classes and how to do so effectively.

Variation: Select a panel of student volunteers to answer questions at the press conference, or have students work in groups to generate high-quality questions.

Major Media Outlets to Accompany Press Conference Activity

Washington Post

Self Magazine

Los Angeles Times

New York Times

Miami Herald

USA Today

New York Post

New York News

Atlanta Journal-Constitution

Dallas Morning News

Washington Times

Denver Post

Philadelphia Inquirer

Boston Globe

Chicago Tribune

Detroit Free Press

Phoenix Arizona Republic

San Francisco Chronicle

Tampa Tribune

Orlando Sentinel

Baltimore Sun

Charlotte Observer

Popular Science

Chicago Sun-Times

O, the Oprah Magazine

Cleveland Plain Dealer

St. Louis Post-Dispatch

Indianapolis Star

Fort Lauderdale Sun-Sentinel

Wall Street Journal

Financial Times

New York Village Voice

Army Times

Byte

Multimedia World

Fortune

Forbes

Money

People

Life

Entertainment Weekly

Rolling Stone

Vogue

Mademoiselle

Glamour

Chronicle of Higher Education

Who's To Blame?

By Constance Staley. This activity is a modern-day version of the "Drawbridge Exercise."
Recommended for Chapter 11 Building Relationships, Valuing Diversity

Jason, a rising young executive, and Jennifer, who was finishing her master's degree in social work, had been married for a year. Although Jason had once had a serious drug problem that had gotten him in trouble with the law, he'd gotten his life back together and managed to get a good job.

One morning, Jason announced, "My company is sending me to China for six months on business. I leave on Monday. I'll be at remote sites in the countryside. I doubt I'll have cell phone coverage. But I'll send you some e-mails." He continued, "While I'm away, don't spend any time on the Internet. Plenty of marriages break up when people meet someone else online. If you do that, believe me, you're going to regret it!"

But toward the end of the six months, Jennifer began thinking about Jeff, her old college boyfriend. She went online and found his e-mail address. "Hey, great to hear from you!" Jeff replied. "I've been thinking a lot about you too lately. I just bought a new time-share condo in Las Vegas. How about coming for a visit? It'd be great to see you again!"

What a tempting invitation, Jennifer thought. Before she knew it, she had e-mailed Jeff back and bought a special $79 one-way airline ticket. *Great price: I can't pass that up!* she thought. *I'll have a really good time in Las Vegas with an old friend, be back in plenty of time, and Jason will never even find out.*

The week with Jeff was glorious. They saw some great shows, ate some fabulous meals, spent lots of time (and money) in the casinos, and one thing led to another. They rekindled their old romance.

But when Jennifer tried to buy a return plane ticket back home, she found that all her credit cards were maxed out. She'd gone to the ATM over and over while she was on a winning streak, and then lost it all. What was she going to do?

When Jennifer consulted Jeff, she was shocked at his reply, "Hey, you're married. This was purely physical. I'm not going to invest money in someone else's wife."

Jennifer called the airline and tried to explain things as sensitively as she could. "Look, lady, I'm sorry things didn't work out," said Jan, the person on the other end of the line. "But I can't give you a free ticket. That's all there is to it!"

In desperation, Jennifer called her best friend back home, Jessica, to ask her to wire money. Shocked, Jessica said, "You did what? You know Jason's very possessive. He's going to kill you! I don't want any part of this!" and she hung up.

Finally with time running out and her anxiety mounting, Jennifer decided to hitchhike. The trip home would be a long one. She left the hotel late that night since time was important. It was dark, and she knew it was risky, but she couldn't think of any other option.

Unfortunately, someone who called himself Jack, the sweatshirt-hooded driver of the car that picked her up, was an escaped felon who'd done hard time at a federal penitentiary. Her body was never found.

Think through all the options, and rank the following individual's responsibility from 1 (most responsible) to 6 (least responsible) for Jennifer's fate. After all class members have completed their individual rankings, discuss the exercise in groups of five students. Your group must reach a consensus, and be ready to provide a rationale for each ranking when the entire class reconvenes.

INDIVIDUAL RANKING

Jason, the husband _____
Jennifer, the wife _____
Jeff, the lover _____
Jan, the airline employee _____
Jessica, the friend _____
Jack, the escaped felon _____

GROUP RANKING

Jason, the husband _____
Jennifer, the wife _____
Jeff, the lover _____
Jan, the airline employee _____
Jessica, the friend _____
Jack, the escaped felon _____

Is this a healthy relationship? Why or why not? What information from the story would you use to back up your answer? As a class, discuss the themes that emerge in this story that are vital to positive, fulfilling romantic relationships and themes that identify troubled relationships.

FOCUS Roadmap to College Success

"Success is a journey, not a destination." Ben Sweetland

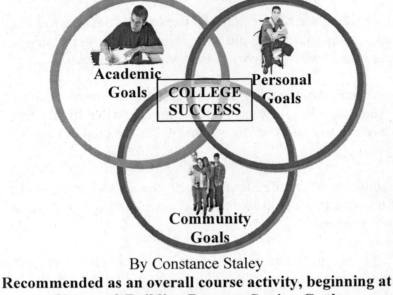

Academic Goals

COLLEGE SUCCESS

Personal Goals

Community Goals

By Constance Staley
**Recommended as an overall course activity, beginning at
Chapter 2 Building Dreams, Setting Goals**

You can't get anywhere if you don't know where you're going, right? You've begun a journey that is an investment in yourself and your own future. Your college success will be determined by the intersection of three types of goals: academic, personal, and community goals. Your teachers will identify some of these goals for you, but, you must discover and work toward these goals yourself. It's not enough to just point yourself toward your diploma four or five years from now. You must make continual progress and monitor your efforts along the way.

When you're on your way somewhere you have to pay attention: Did I make a left turn when I should have made a right one? Did I miss a piece of information on that last road sign? Is this the right exit? Which milepost am I watching for? You don't just head for a new destination and hope for the best.

In the same way, as you make your way through college, you should be asking yourself similar questions: Am I putting forth my best effort? Is this major right for me? Is the career I'm focusing on one I'm well suited for? Do I have access to friends and professors that care about my progress? Do I feel a part of my campus community?

This four-part activity will serve as your Roadmap to College Success and ask you to monitor your progress while communicating with your first-year seminar instructor all along the way. The Roadmap will ask you to complete four milepost activities. You will be asked to respond to an initial *challenge*, a few weeks later after your have your "bearings," to provide your *reaction* to that initial challenge, to identify the *insight* you've gained about yourself and your progress a few weeks after that, and finally, at the end of the course (or at the end of your first year of college if your instructor wishes), to list every *action* you've taken to help you succeed. Are you ready? Okay, let's go.

Milepost 1: CHALLENGE

Here's a challenge: What are your academic, personal, and community goals? Identify them now and be as specific as possible. For example, getting good grades would be a very general academic goal. Figuring out who I am would be a general personal goal, and making lots of friends would be a general community goal. General goals aren't always particularly helpful.

Examples of specific goals would be getting extra tutoring for my calculus class (academic), making an appointment to visit the Counseling Center to learn more about myself (personal), or attending three events next month to get involved on campus (community). List your goals in these three areas below, and then give/send this completed page to your first-year seminar instructor.

ACADEMIC	PERSONAL	COMMUNITY

Milepost 2: REACTION

Now that several weeks of class have gone by, it's time to react to your original goals. Were they realistic? Have you discovered some new ones? For example, perhaps you know now that tutoring is not all you'll need to be successful in your calculus class. You may need to make an appointment with your instructor to get some additional direction from him or her (academic). Perhaps when you visited the Counseling Center, you learned that you have a relationship that's getting in the way of your success to repair (personal). Perhaps you've decided that in order to pay your bills, you'll have to take on an extra job, and that attending three campus events in one month will be very difficult (community). You need to revise your goal to attending two campus events. Take a look now and provide a reaction to what you initially wrote in response to the challenge presented in Milepost 1. Revise your goals, if you need to, now that reality has set in, and send this completed page to your first-year seminar instructor.

ACADEMIC	PERSONAL	COMMUNITY

Milepost 3: INSIGHT

Now that you've handed in several papers in your classes, you've gotten your midterm exam grades back, perhaps you're beginning to feel the tug of a particular major, and you've forged some new relationships on campus, it's time for Milepost 3. Think about the insight you've gained about yourself, and list specific insights in the three areas below. Send this completed page to your first-year seminar instructor.

ACADEMIC	PERSONAL	COMMUNITY

Milepost 4: ACTION

It's now the end of your first-year seminar course (or the end of your first year of college). You've accomplished a great deal in these three areas. You're well on your way to your destination. Make a list of the ACTION you've taken that has contributed to your success, or list things you now wish you had done that would have made you more successful. Vow to do these things during your next term. Send this completed page to your first-year seminar instructor.

ACADEMIC	**PERSONAL**	**COMMUNITY**

Synthesis: Finally, react to this activity. Send your first-year seminar instructor an e-mail, or if assigned, write a synthesis paper about this assignment. Did it help you think about college as a journey? Did it help you monitor your progress? Did it help you focus and stay on course?

Wellness Bingo

By Stephanie Hanenberg, University of Colorado at Colorado Springs (used with permission)

Goal: to help students discover content about wellness via a non-lecture format
Group Size: any size class
Time Required: may vary, depending on the amount of follow-up discussion that ensues
Materials: Wellness Bingo sheets (following); key provided for instructors
Physical Setting: classroom
Process: Hand out the Wellness Bingo sheets (with content front and back). Allow students fifteen minutes to circulate around the room and find the answers to the questions from classmates. They may only get two answers from one student, and then they must move on. At the end of the fifteen minutes, debrief the answers, elaborate where necessary, and correct any misperceptions about the health issues listed. Students will most likely not know all the answers. Make the point that many students obtain all their health information from friends (and the Internet), when, in fact, medical professionals are the best source of accurate information.

Variation: This game format may be used with virtually any topic in the course.

Wellness Bingo

By Stephanie Hanenberg, University of Colorado, Colorado Springs

What game that college students play does the Centers for Disease Control and Prevention think contributed to a 230% increase in oral herpes in 2007?	When should a woman have her first well woman exam/pap and how often should she have them after this?	Name three types of foods that are a good source of protein.	Can antidepressants also be used to treat anxiety?	Is it common for men to get urinary tract infections?
Name four things you can do on a regular basis to stay healthy.	What is the difference between a doctor who is a M.D. versus a doctor who is a D.O.?	What is Gardasil?	What type of candy is heart healthy?	Why shouldn't someone take antibiotics when they have a common cold?
Name three over-the-counter products that are a good source of Vitamin C (not foods).	What is a colposcopy?	Can you get the flu from the flu shot?	What is the most common cancer found in males aged 15-35?	Can men be tested for Human Papilloma Virus?

What vitamin deficiency can lead to anemia?	What state has been voted as the fittest in the nation more than once?	Name the only birth control method that is 100% effective against the transmission of STI's.	What is the American Heart Association's recommendation for the amount of exercise a person should engage in per week?	Is alcohol a good remedy when you're cold?
What causes heartburn?	What is the difference between a bacterial sexually transmitted disease versus a viral one?	What vitamin complex is the most important for women to consume during pregnancy?	Can taking too much Ibuprofen cause someone to have more headaches?	What are hookahs and are they harmful?
Name three things you can do for a headache besides taking medicine.	Bacterial meningitis can cause hearing loss, paralysis, loss of limbs, and even death. True of False	What is the difference between a nurse practitioner and a physician's assistant?	What is the recommended daily amount of water intake?	Which of the following foods has the least amount of calories? a) McDonald's double cheeseburger b) Subway's 6" meatball sub c) Panera Bread tuna salad sandwich on whole wheat d) Ruby Tuesday's Cajun chicken salad with ranch

WELLNESS BINGO (KEY)

By Stephanie Hanenberg, University of Colorado, Colorado Springs

What game that college students play does the Centers for Disease Control and Prevention think contributed to a 230% increase in oral herpes in 2007? *Beer pong*	When should a woman have her first well woman exam/pap and how often should she have them after this? *At age 21 or within 3 years of becoming sexually active.*	Name three types of foods that are a good source of protein. *Chicken Beans Beef Nuts Eggs Seeds Dairy*	Can antidepressants also be used to treat anxiety? *Yes, some SSRI's.*	Is it common for men to get urinary tract infections? *No. Most men that think they have UTI's actually have STD's. If men get more than one UTI, they should see a specialist. (Men have longer urethras than women which is why.)*
Name four things you can do on a regular basis to stay healthy. *Sleep at least 8 hours a night. Eat a healthy diet. Drink at least 8 glasses of water/day. Exercise regularly.*	What is the difference between a doctor who is an M.D. versus a doctor who is a D.O.? *Medical doctors use more medications, etc. Doctors of osteopathic medicine use more alternative treatments, herbal remedies, adjustments, etc., and are more oriented toward wellness.*	What is Gardasil? *The vaccine for females between the ages of 9-26 to build immunity to four strains of the human papillomavirus.*	What type of candy is heart healthy? *Dark chocolate.*	Why shouldn't someone take antibiotics when they have a common cold? *A cold is a virus which can't be cured with antibiotics. It also builds up antibiotic resistance which can be very harmful.*
Name three over-the-counter products that are a good	What is a colposcopy? *An examination that may be needed when a*	Can you get the flu from the flu shot? *No, it is not a live virus.*	What is the most common cancer found in males aged 15-35? *Testicular.*	Can men be tested for Human Papilloma Virus?

source of Vitamin C (not foods). *Airborne, EmergenC, Vitamin C tablets Vitamin C drops*	*female has an abnormal pap. A biopsy of the cervix can be taken during this procedure.*			*No, unless you can visibly see genital warts, there is no test that can diagnose HPV.*
What vitamin deficiency can lead to anemia? *Iron*	What state has been voted as the fittest in the nation more than once? *Colorado*	Name the only birth control method that is 100% effective against the transmission of STD's. *Abstinence*	What is the American Heart Association's recommendation for the amount of exercise a person should engage in per week? *30 minutes 5 days a week of moderate activities or 20 minutes 3 days a week of vigorous exercise*	Is alcohol a good remedy when you're cold? *No, alcohol may make you feel warm, but it does not actually raise your body temperature.*
What causes heartburn? *Increased stomach acid. Reflux of acid into the esophagus.*	What is the difference between a bacterial sexually transmitted disease versus a viral one? *Bacterial (gonorrhea, Chlamydia, Trichomoniasis, syphilis) can be cured with antibiotics and viral (HIV, herpes, HPV, and Hepatitis B) cannot.*	What vitamin complex is the most important for women to consume during pregnancy? *Vitamin B*	Can taking too much Ibuprofen cause someone to have more headaches? *Yes, they are called rebound headaches.*	What are hookahs and are they harmful? *Flavored tobacco.* *Still contain carcinogens, and people use the same tubing and sometimes mouth piece so they share germs and can acquire illnesses, herpes, etc.*

Name three things you can do for a headache besides taking medicine.	Bacterial meningitis can cause hearing loss, paralysis, loss of limbs, and even death.	What is the difference between a nurse practitioner and a physician's assistant?	What is the recommended daily amount of water intake?	Which of the following foods has the **least** amount of calories?
Sleep. Drink plenty of water. Get a massage. Decrease stress.	True of False *True.* *Get vaccinated; it's very important!*	*Nurse practitioners have to have a master's degree to write prescriptions, practice on their own license, and tend to allow more time for appointments to see the "entire picture" and not just the chief complaint.*	*64 ounces*	a) McDonald's double Cheeseburger- *490 calories* b) Subway's 6" meatball sub- *540 calories* c) Panera Bread tuna salad sandwich on whole wheat- *720 calories* d) Ruby Tuesday's Cajun chicken salad with ranch- *903 calories*

"Uniformly Successful"

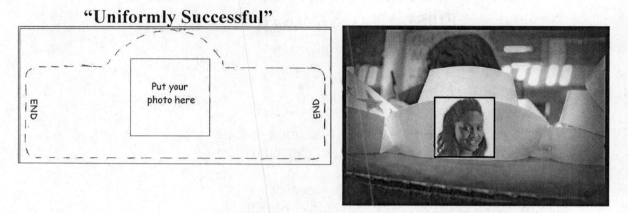

Courtesy of Judith Cartee-Bryant, Central Texas College

Goals: to help students envision themselves working toward and completing a career goal

Group size: any size class

Time required: could be done in class, but this task would make a good homework assignment

Materials: paper, pattern, glue, headshot of each student

Physical setting: any classroom (or home) setting

Process: On the first day of class, ask students to make themselves a nurse's hat and paste on their own photo. They should keep this as a "marker" of the beginning of their profession as a nurse and look at it for inspiration whenever they become overwhelmed with challenging coursework.

Variation: Change the "uniform" to fit other occupational goals.

SELECTED ONLINE RESOURCES ON COLLEGE AND FIRST-YEAR SEMINAR TEACHING

Derek Bok Center for Teaching and Learning
http://bokcenter.harvard.edu/icb/icb.do

Idea Center (Individual Development & Education Assessment)
http://www.idea.ksu.edu/resources/index.html

Online Resources: Faculty Development Associates
http://www.developfaculty.com/online/index.html

Teacher Videos
http://www.teachertube.com

Classroom Management
http://www.mccfl.edu/pages/1389.asp

Constructivism
http://www.2learn.ca/profgrowth/PDconstruct.asp

How People Learn
http://www.nap.edu/html/howpeople1/index.html

Top 10 Icebreakers of 2009
http://adulted.about.com/od/icebreakers/tp/topten2009.htm

Learning Style Models
- Dunn and Dunn- www.learningstyles.net
- Fender- www.ncsu.edu/effective_teaching/Learning_Styles.html
- Gregorc- www.gregorc.com
- Kolb- www.infed.org/biblio/b-explrn.htm#learning%20style
- VARK- http://www.vark-learn.com/english/index.asp

Lecturing Skills
http://www.ferris.edu/htmls/academics/center/Teaching_and_Learning_Tips/Developing%20Effective%20Lectures/8stepstoactive.htm

Motivating Students' Best Work
http://teaching.berkeley.edu/compendium/sectionlists/sect20.html

Teaching & Learning Centers (Global)
http://www.ku.edu/~cte/resources/websites.html

Faculty Development, Honolulu Community College
http://honolulu.hawaii.edu/intranet/committees/FacDevCom/guidebk/teachtip/teachtip.htm

Good Teaching Practices: Barbara Gross Davis (*Tools for Teaching*)
http://teaching.berkeley.edu/bgd/teaching.html

National Resource Center on the Firsts-Year Experience and Students in Transition
http://www.sc.edu/fye/

Office of Educational Development, University of California, Berkeley
http://teaching.berkeley.edu/teaching.html

Teambuildinginc.com
http://www.teambuildinginc.com/

Qualitycoach.net
http://www.qualitycoach.net/shop/shopexd.asp?id=6711

Teamwork and Teamplay
http://www.thiagi.com/book-teamwork-and-teamplay.html

RECOMMENDED READINGS: A SHORT LIST

Angelo, T. K., & Cross, K. P. (1993). *Classroom assessment techniques: A handbook for college teachers*. San Francisco: Jossey-Bass.

Bain, K. (2004). *What the best college teachers do*. Cambridge, MA: Harvard University Press.

Bean, J. (1996). *Engaging Ideas: The Professor's Guide to Integrating Writing, Critical Thinking, and Active Learning in the Classroo*m. San Francisco: Jossey-Bass.

Brandt, R. (1998). *Powerful learning*. Alexandria, VA: Association of Supervision and Curriculum Development.

Bransford, J. (2002). *How people learn*. Washington D. C., National Academic Press.

Brookfield, S. D. (1995). *Becoming a critically reflective teacher*. San Francisco: Jossey-Bass.

Davis, B. G. (2009). *Tools for Teaching, 2nd edition*. San Francisco: Jossey-Bass.

Erickson, B., Peters, C. B., & Strommer, D. W. (2006). *Teaching first-year college students*. San Francisco: Jossey-Bass.

Fink, D. (2003). *Creating significant learning experiences*: An integrated approach to designing college courses. San Francisco: Jossey-Bass.

Fleming, N. D. (2005). *Teaching and learning styles: VARK strategies*. Christchurch, NZ: Microfilm Limited.

Leamnson, R. (1999). *Thinking about teaching and learning: Developing habits of learning with first year college and university students*. Sterling, VA: Stylus.

Levine, M. (2005). *Ready or not, here life comes*. New York: Simon & Schuster.

McKeachie, W., & Svinicki, M. (2005). *McKeachie's teaching tips: Strategies, research, and theory for college and university teachers*. Boston: Houghton Mifflin.

Nathan, Rebecca. (2005). *My freshman year*. Ithaca, NY: Cornell University Press.

Nilson, L. B. (2007). *Teaching at its best: A research-based resource for college instructors*. San Francisco: Jossey-Bass.

Palmer, P. (1997). *The courage to teach: Exploring the inner landscape of a teacher's life*. San Francisco: Jossey-Bass.

Richlin, L., & Ronkowski, S. (2006). *Blueprint for learning: Creating college courses to facilitate, assess, and document learning*. Sterling, VA: Stylus.

Staley, C. (1999). *Teaching college success: The complete resource guide*. Belmont, CA: Wadsworth Publishing Company.

Staley, C. (2003). *50 ways to leave your lectern*. Belmont, CA: Wadsworth Publishing Company.

Sutherland, T., & Bonwell, C. C. (1996). *Using active learning in college classes: A range of options for faculty*. San Francisco: Jossey-Bass.

Svinicki, M. D. (2004). *Learning and motivation in the postsecondary classroom*. Bolton, MA: Anker Publishing Company.

Swing, R. (2001 & 2003). *Proving and Improving: Strategies for Assessing the First College Year*, Vols. 1 and 2. Columbia, SC: National Resource Center for theFirst-Year Experience and Students in Transition.

Weimer, M. (2002). *Learner-centered teaching*. San Francisco: Jossey-Bass.

Wiggins, G., & McTighe, J. (2005). *Understanding by design*. Boston: Prentice-Hall.

CPSIA information can be obtained
at www.ICGtesting.com
Printed in the USA
FFOW05n1638110713
1390FF